SYLVIA PORTER

Generously supported by

The Director's Circle

&

A gift in loving memory of Lucy Randel

Director's Choice

Our Director's Choice program is an opportunity to highlight a book from our list that deserves special attention. This selection came naturally to me, as a New York City native with a background in business, and I proudly support its publication.

Alice R. Pfeiffer

Alice Randel Pfeiffer
Director, Syracuse University Press

SYLVIA
AMERICA'S ORIGINAL PERSONAL FINANCE COLUMNIST
PORTER

TRACY LUCHT

Syracuse University Press

Copyright © 2013 by Syracuse University Press
Syracuse, New York 13244-5290

All Rights Reserved

First Edition 2013
13 14 15 16 17 18   6 5 4 3 2 1

Quotations from the following are reprinted with permission from the National Women and Media Collection/Western Historical Manuscript Collection, State Historical Society of Missouri: Sylvia Porter Papers; Russell Freeburg's Nov. 23, 1974, letter to Sylvia Porter; Donna Lee Goldberg's Apr. 29, 1974, academic paper; Donna Martin's Aug. 18, 1982, letter to Hal Meyerson; and John McMeel's Feb. 9, 1984, letter to Sylvia Porter. Quotations from Dorothy Schiff's memo and letters are reprinted with permission from Dorothy Schiff Papers, Manuscripts and Archives Division, The New York Public Library, Astor, Lenox, and Tilden Foundations.

∞ The paper used in this publication meets the minimum requirements of the American National Standard for Information Sciences—Permanence of Paper for Printed Library Materials, ANSI Z39.48-1992.

For a listing of books published and distributed by Syracuse University Press, visit our website at SyracuseUniversityPress.syr.edu.

ISBN: 978-0-8156-1029-8 (cloth)   978-0-8156-5249-6 (e-book)

Library of Congress Cataloging-in-Publication Data
Lucht, Tracy.
    Sylvia Porter : America's original personal finance columnist / Tracy Lucht. — First edition.
        pages cm
    Includes bibliographical references and index.
    ISBN 978-0-8156-1029-8 (pbk. : alk. paper) 1. Porter, Sylvia Field, 1913–   2. Finance, Personal.   3. Journalists—United States—Biography.   I. Title.
    HG179.L824 2013
    070.4'493320240092—dc23
    [B]   2013029837

Manufactured in the United States of America

For Paul

Tracy Lucht is assistant professor in the Greenlee School of Journalism and Communication at Iowa State University. She holds a Ph.D. from the University of Maryland and has worked at *USA Today*, the *Washington Post*, and the *Des Moines Register*.

Contents

Illustrations

Acknowledgments

Success is fulfillment, something you feel within yourself. I see someone on the street. Is she successful? How do I know? She may be bleeding her heart out. I see another woman. She may look a mess, but she is gloriously happy because she has just finished a book.

—Sylvia Porter, quoted in *The Self-Chosen*

THIS PROJECT HAS BENEFITED from the perspectives of many scholars and reviewers over the years. I am deeply indebted to Maurine Beasley at the University of Maryland, the leading historian of women and journalism. Maurine blazed a trail many would follow, and I feel incredibly fortunate to have had the opportunity to learn from her. As my dissertation adviser and academic mentor, Maurine nurtured this study in its fledgling stages and endured my fits of growing pains with forbearance and wisdom. Her belief in this project—and in me—never wavered. Personally and professionally, I offer my heartfelt thanks to Maurine for all she has done for multitudes of students and for the study of women's history. I am similarly grateful to Carol Rogers and Robyn Muncy, two other kind and remarkable scholars at the University of Maryland, who graciously took me under their wings and taught me about life, history, and feminism. This triad of brilliant women—Maurine, Carol, and Robyn—continues to influence my teaching and scholarship more than any of them probably realizes.

I have a long list of people to thank for their assistance with this project. Archivist Tom Miller at the State Historical Society of Missouri, which houses the National Women and Media Collection, generously lent me his

xi

time and expertise. Research specialists at the New York Public Library, Library of Congress, Museum of Television and Radio, and Schlesinger Library provided excellent and efficient assistance. Warren Boroson, the late Lee Cohn, Beth Kobliner, Lydia Ratcliff, and the late Brooke Shearer— all top writers in their fields—provided valuable insight and personal memories of Sylvia Porter. Adele Hall Sweet, daughter of *New York Post* publisher Dorothy Schiff, graciously permitted me to quote from her mother's unpublished manuscripts. Greg Daugherty, Russ Freeburg, Donna Goldberg, John McMeel, and Donna Martin also were kind enough to respond to my queries and grant me permission to quote from their own correspondence. Tom Kunkel, the late Michael Gurevitch, and James Gilbert provided excellent feedback and guidance during my doctoral research that helped shape the arc of my investigation. Deanna McCay at Syracuse University Press, my primary editor, guided me through the publication process with expertise, professionalism, and sensitivity. I am immensely grateful to her. Finally, Kay Kodner gave the finished manuscript a careful, thorough edit. Thank you to all.

I consider myself lucky to work with scholars who understand and support historical research, including Eric Abbott, Michael Bugeja, Raluca Cozma, Daniela Dimitrova, Joel Geske, Jane Peterson, and Lulu Rodriguez. These wonderful colleagues make my academic home at Iowa State University's Greenlee School of Journalism and Communication a very happy one. In addition, the Iowa State University Publication Endowment Fund provided me with financial assistance as the project moved toward completion, and Chenyan Shan, my talented research assistant, kept me from drowning in a sea of sources. I am grateful to everyone who read a draft of this manuscript, including Frank Colella, Marilyn Greenwald, Jane Marcellus, Brian Steffen, and several anonymous reviewers. Your thoughts and suggestions improved the final product immeasurably.

Most important, I must thank my family, who make my daily work both imaginable and possible. My mom, Sue Durlam Lucht, seemed to know what I should do with my life before I did. She believed in this book from the beginning and provided endless encouragement, even accompanying me to the archives when I needed to make yet one more trip. Likewise, I am indebted to my husband, Paul Soucy, who is a true partner in every sense. He listens to my ideas, reads my writing, and shares all aspects of our life equally—the joy, the work, and the responsibilities that come with a family. I consider myself fortunate to have a spouse who supports me both in theory and in practice, and I am grateful for the example he sets for our sons. That brings me to the two most important people in my life: Quentin and T. J. Soucy. These sweet boys inspire, entertain, and educate me every day. Thanks, guys. I hope you write your own books someday.

SYLVIA PORTER

Introduction

IN 1942 THE DIRECTORS of the New York Stock Exchange (NYSE) met to discuss who should be allowed on the floor of the exchange. The exchange floor was dirty, scuffed by the shoes of men racing one another for shares of the American dream. The furious trading that took place there resembled a testosterone-fueled scrum. The environment was unruly, loud, and aggressive. And it was strictly off-limits to women. The men all agreed this was how it should be. However, they faced a problem. It had recently become public knowledge that one of New York's most prolific and respected financial writers, S. F. Porter, was a woman. If Porter trained her eye on the all-male exchange, the NYSE might find itself the subject of unwanted controversy during the electrified "Rosie the Riveter" days of World War II. But should women really be allowed into the stock exchange? The board finally saw its way around the dilemma and voted on a resolution: "Sylvia is one of the boys. We hereby award her honorary pants."[1]

Sylvia Porter (1913–1991) originated the personal finance column, a specialized form of journalism—now a staple of major newspapers and websites—that has been overlooked in media history. At the height of Porter's success, she reached forty million readers in more than 350 newspapers as a syndicated columnist; published a monthly financial advice column in *Ladies' Home Journal*; and produced a shelf full of books, including the bestselling *Sylvia Porter's Money Book*. During her sixty-year career, she advised bankers on the bond market and also counseled half-a-dozen Treasury secretaries and three U.S. presidents. "Few journalists have done more to put financial news on the map than Sylvia Porter, and none has done more to advance the cause of women in this area of journalism,"

1

journalist John Quirt wrote in his history of the field.[2] Yet her story has never been told, nor have historians examined the development of personal finance journalism. There is no biography of Sylvia Porter to date. And despite writing many other books, including an unpublished novel, she did not write her autobiography.

In 1958 *Time* magazine published an article about Porter, who was by then a well-known newspaper columnist and frequent guest on radio and television programs such as *Meet the Press*. The editors claimed that Porter "bustles through the messy, male-contrived world of finance like a housewife cleaning her husband's den—tidying trends, sorting statistics, and issuing no-nonsense judgments as wholesome and tart as mince pie."[3] I discovered the article while I was in graduate school, studying postwar representations of American women in news magazines. I was immediately fascinated. Here was a woman who did not fit our cultural memory of the fifties. She was outspoken, she was respected, and she was not a housewife. Defying the decade's historical reputation for conservative gender norms, the article praised Porter's audacity and success. The editors did not hold her up as an example of a psychologically damaged career woman, they did not inquire about the well-being of her child, and they did not ignore her. They had, however, chosen metaphors that stuffed Porter into the mold of wife and helpmate. They had even titled the article "Housewife's View." In a type of rhetorical sleight-of-hand that would eventually be exposed for its sexism, the editors had made a woman with a reputation for heavy drinking seem as innocent as a new pair of white ankle socks. I began to wonder about the story behind Sylvia Porter. I wanted to understand how she had built a career in a field dominated by men and cultivated an overwhelmingly positive public image over the course of several decades, maneuvering her way around discriminatory gender norms and waves of ideological change.

When Porter began her career as a financial journalist in the 1930s, she hid her gender behind the byline "S. F. Porter" because the field was so inhospitable to women. Not only was it difficult for a woman to get hired—the Associated Press and *New York Sun* both told Porter they would never hire a woman to cover finance—but even if a woman could land a job, editors worried that readers would not trust the information published under her name.[4] That attitude would change over the next six decades, as more women entered the workforce and gender norms shifted to accommodate women's greater roles in the economy. Porter challenged the perception that women could not understand finance. By the end of her career, Sylvia Porter's name was so trusted in financial matters that esteemed investment authorities would plead for her endorsement of their books and products, knowing her stamp of approval would increase sales.[5] Porter had come a long way, indeed, but how had she gotten there?

This work contributes to the historical literature on women in journalism by using primary sources to examine Porter's career within the larger context of economic and social change. The analysis is confined to her work; there is very little in these pages about Porter's personal life. Rather, this is a professional biography of a woman who built a veritable empire in the male-dominated field of financial journalism. The longevity of Porter's career affords an examination of the relationship between her work and women's social status during a span of time that included the economic uncertainty and political radicalism of the thirties; the advances and exploitation of working women during World War II; the clash between conservative gender norms and women's increasing roles outside the home after the war; and the feminist activism of the sixties and seventies. I trace Porter's evolution from a curiosity—"the glamour girl of finance"[6]—to a nationally recognized expert, paying particular attention to the role of gender in her development of a populist form of financial news.

Personal finance journalism is a form of service journalism, often written as a column, that advises readers on financial matters directly affecting their lives. Common topics include saving, managing debt, shopping for life insurance, paying taxes, buying houses and cars, investing, and paying for college. This type of journalism helps readers decide what to do with their money and warns them what not to do. It exposes financial scams, blows the whistle on predatory industries, and reports on public policy issues—such as taxes, social security, and health care—that directly affect readers' bank accounts. Its target audience is the large swath of Americans in the middle class: people who are not wealthy, but who have at least enough money to wonder what to do with it. Personal finance has been described as a branch of consumerism that serves readers while remaining palatable to advertisers, who are the main source of revenue for traditional news outlets. "It appears to satisfy both the need of consumers to sort out the array of financial choices the deregulated marketplace has thrust upon them as well as newspapers' bottom lines," journalist Trudy Lieberman wrote.[7]

Personal finance journalism is both popular and profitable, but it also has a rich history that includes the enlistment of American consumers during World War II and the economic boom that followed. For decades, Porter's only direct competition was the Kiplinger family in Washington, DC. In 1947 Willard (W. M.) Kiplinger started the magazine *Changing Times* with his son, Austin, to help people make financial decisions newly available to them after the war. The magazine was a departure from *Forbes, Business Week,* and *Fortune,* whose outlook was business-oriented. *Changing Times* was written for individuals and used a personable style of writing. A staff memo told writers to "look an imaginary reader in the eye and write to him."[8] The Kiplingers, who published the only personal finance magazine in existence for almost three decades, kept a low profile relative to Porter and did not consider her a threat.[9] The Kiplingers were based firmly in Washington; Porter, in New York. Despite their similar approaches, they stayed out of each other's orbit. Porter's circle included bankers, public relations executives, Treasury officials, and tax specialists. Her influence did not come from her colleagues, who were reluctant to grant her that kind of authority. Ultimately, her power came from her readers, as she attracted a vast audience with her nationally syndicated newspaper column and multimedia presence. Her peers eventually took notice because the public took notice. Simply put, Porter built a circulation so large she could not be ignored.

Despite Porter's prominence in twentieth-century culture, her career must be properly situated within women's history. Any biographical study must address the question of why one person's life is worth such extensive research. Especially in women's history, which is often a story of subjugation, scholars must be careful not to extrapolate too much from one exceptional woman's success. The late Gerda Lerner articulated this concern when she described some of the earliest work in women's history: "The history of notable women is the history of exceptional, even deviant, women and does not describe the experience and history of the mass of women."[10]

Porter was, indeed, an exception. Only about one-fourth of all newspaper journalists were women when she entered the field, and very few of those women worked in financial news. In addition, the bankers and economic analysts who served as the sources of information for her reporting were almost all men. Porter battled deep-seated discrimination inside and outside the newsroom to position herself as a public authority on financial issues. That she was successful must be considered a major achievement. However, she also exploited the labor of other writers and was not as attuned to the average American as she wanted the public to believe. She offered a strong voice for professional women's rights throughout her career but was loath to recognize competition from other women in her field. By providing a comprehensive analysis of Porter's career, including her treatment of other women, I have tried to respect the limits of one woman's experience and offer a more inclusive history. I have concluded that Porter's experience may not be generalizable, but it is transferable. It foregrounds issues deeply embedded in the stories of women who succeeded as twentieth-century writers and journalists, even those whose work did not reach nearly 20 percent of the population.[11]

Porter's professional strategies—which I uncover in her correspondence, writing, media coverage, and marketing materials, as well as through interviews with people who worked for her—are surprisingly fresh. They could prove illuminating to a new generation of women journalists, who might not face the overt sexism Porter encountered but might be surprised by the lingering gender dynamics of the industry. Even today, the country's newsrooms do not look like its college classrooms. Women make up an overwhelming 65 percent of journalism undergraduates, but they comprise only about 36 percent of full-time journalists.[12] At newspapers, in particular, women receive far fewer job offers than men; and, if hired, they report lower job satisfaction and less support from their organizations.[13] Four times as many women as men say they intend to leave the newspaper industry entirely.[14] If women as a group are to succeed in traditional news organizations, they must either change the culture or find ways of coping within a historically masculine environment. By demonstrating how gender ideology functioned within one woman's exemplary career and within the field of journalism more generally, Porter's narrative historicizes the gender-charged workplace younger women face today.

Discrimination has led to innovation when determined professionals with demographic handicaps look for ways to circumvent traditional power structures. Many women journalists embraced the Internet at the turn of the millennium, sensing an opportunity to broaden their qualifications and restart their careers. Likewise, Porter also embraced new media throughout her career, cross-promoting herself on radio and television as well as in books, magazines, and newsletters.[15] She saw the importance of a multimedia presence before others did and could be considered a predecessor of powerful public figures like Martha Stewart and Oprah Winfrey. Reaching for stardom, Porter used an army of ghostwriters and assistants to construct her brand, which she crafted with the help of promotions experts and her friends in public relations. Just as a life-sized portrait of Porter presided over her Fifth Avenue apartment, her public persona was a towering presence in U.S. media culture, each brushstroke meticulously chosen to serve the cohesive whole. She wrote candidly but spoke carefully, attenuating her message while remaining true to the image she had cultivated as an enduring friend to the middle class.

My narrative of Porter's career emphasizes seven professional strategies she used to achieve unprecedented success as a woman in financial journalism. I have interwoven the strategies throughout the chapters—showing, if not always stating, how they functioned—and the reader is invited to consider these strategies as a framework for understanding Porter's work. Because I believe my analysis to be transferable to the experiences of other professional women, historical and contemporary, I hope these themes will resonate with scholars and journalists alike and perhaps revitalize a conversation about women and journalism that began decades ago. These seven professional strategies are as follows:

1. Porter entered a nonprestigious field in journalism.

Porter was hired at the *New York Post* in 1935 to cover the bond market, a low-status beat in a low-status section of the newspaper. Because she was willing to write about bonds, an unappealing subject, she avoided competition from male reporters and made herself indispensable to the organization. Ironically, writing about bonds gave Porter a professional edge by conditioning her to think like an expert and write like a journalist. Bonds were difficult to explain to the average reader, and taking on this challenge trained Porter to break down complex subjects into their simplest, most precise terms. Porter's specialization in bonds also gave her a broad, international perspective on the economy. By learning why governments and corporations indebted themselves, and to whom, Porter learned how the pieces of the global economic puzzle fit together. She developed a unique perspective on domestic and international economics, which allowed her to explain developments to the nonelite with refreshing clarity. Porter developed a strong, personal writing style that connected with readers, which persuaded the editors of the *New York Post* to keep her even as they fired the rest of the financial staff in 1938. She became the newspaper's financial editor on the condition that she would put out the entire section by herself. Again, Porter found hidden advantages in adversity. Working alone gave her editorial freedom, which she exercised to publish a daily column filled with ambitious reporting. The investigative articles she wrote during World War II earned her several journalism awards, cementing her position within the field.

2. Porter allied herself with her readers rather than her peers.

Realizing her career would not advance on the basis of peer recognition alone—the New York Financial Writers Association excluded her when it was formed in 1938—Porter instead sought the allegiance of readers. She developed a writing style that made readers believe she was on their side, shedding light on the inner workings of Wall Street. And, for the most part, she really was on their side. Porter enjoyed an upper-class lifestyle and sometimes overgeneralized her own experience, but she was a consistent champion for the middle class. She possessed a strong sense of fairness and believed it immoral for large corporations to profit at the expense of average Americans, so she set about educating the public about economics and money.

By appealing to the public rather than to her peers, Porter steered around traditional avenues of advancement in journalism. She never considered seeking a position in newspaper management, which would have required years of careful politicking and grooming at the mercy of her superiors. Instead, she carved a unique role for herself by identifying a growing market for understandable financial reporting and catering to it. She left the staff of the *New York Post* in 1947 to work on contract, which liberated her from the newspaper's hierarchy and allowed her to write for other publications as a free agent. Once Porter's column was syndicated in 1949, she consciously sought the audiences of more populist, less prestigious newspapers such as tabloids and afternoon newspapers. As *Post* publisher Dorothy Schiff would have phrased it, Porter chose the mass over the class. She did not compete with the *Wall Street Journal*, which barely acknowledged her before the 1970s, and wrote sparingly for the *New York Times*, which did not pay as well as magazines. Rather than compete with men for journalism's most coveted jobs, Porter simply outflanked them by appealing directly to the public. Because of her influence with millions of readers, Porter gained access to policymakers in Washington, who solicited her advice and goodwill and served as sources for her reporting. She advised President John F. Kennedy on his speechwriting, President Lyndon Johnson on his budget, and President Gerald Ford on inflation. In 1964 Johnson asked her to be president of the Export-Import Bank, which would have made her then the highest-appointed woman in a financial position, but she declined because of her commitment to being a columnist. In 1974, however, she proposed the idea for a Citizens' Action Committee to Fight Inflation. President Ford promptly implemented the plan and named her as the committee's chair. Political resistance to the committee's work (epitomized by the hapless slogan "Whip Inflation Now") illustrated why Porter had stayed out of politics for most of her career.

3. Porter formed alliances with men who could help her career.

Porter relied on many people throughout her career, but several relationships were particularly beneficial. Her marriage to second husband Sumner Collins, whom she wed in 1943, was "ahead of its time," she once said.[16] Collins, the promotions director for the *New York World-American* and later for the entire Hearst newspaper company, encouraged his wife to continue publishing under the same byline of "Sylvia Porter" after they were married because it was so well established (even though "Porter" had been the surname of her first husband). He also suggested Porter start a weekly newsletter, *Reporting on Governments*, rather than offer free advice to the individual bankers who regularly wrote to her. Because of their high-powered careers, Porter and Collins enjoyed a wide social circle that included many business acquaintances whom Porter could use as sources. Collins also made an effort to stay in the good graces of Dorothy Schiff, the publisher of the *New York Post*, occasionally sending complimentary notes to her. Collins was happy to let his brilliant wife have the spotlight, but he played the role of a strong business partner behind the scenes.

A second relationship that benefited Porter's career was her friendship with Henry Morgenthau, Secretary of the Treasury under President Franklin Roosevelt. Porter had written critically of Morgenthau's policies in *American Banker* in 1934, but the two became friends in 1938 after she exposed the practice of "free riding" on government bonds. Afterward, he sought her advice when setting the prices of new government bond issues, and she responded with unwavering support of his policies in her newspaper column. In 1940, Porter helped Morgenthau conceptualize a new savings bond to fund the impending American war effort. Protective of the investment she had helped design, Porter would tout U.S. savings bonds for the rest of her career as a safe, patriotic way for middle-class Americans to save.

A third relationship that furthered Porter's career was her friendship with tax expert J. K. Lasser, with whom she co-authored two books after World War II. By the time the United States entered the war, Porter already had published two monographs and had been solicited by dozens of publishers who wanted her to write a full-length book. Rather than publish a book on her own, Porter elected to pair her name with that of a male financial authority. She and Lasser published their first personal finance book, *How to Live within Your Income*, in 1948. "The next book must be your own!" one of her agents wrote to her that year.[17] Despite this encouragement, she decided to collaborate again with Lasser, publishing *Managing Your Money* in 1953. By linking her name with Lasser's, Porter probably believed she could reach a larger market. She had resisted publishers' suggestions that she write a book about finance specifically for women, not wanting to forfeit the male half of her potential audience. Despite the professional gains she had made, she likely feared that male readers would not buy a book about finance written by a woman. Male readers would, however, buy a book written by Lasser, and Porter helped establish her legitimacy by associating her name with his.

Porter was assisted by other men during her career, including her lawyer, Hal Meyerson, and her third husband, James Fox, a public relations executive who took an active role in Porter's career after they wed in 1979. Professional reliance on men was unavoidable, considering the fact that nearly everyone Porter encountered in financial journalism was male, leaving few women to mentor her. However, the fact that Porter was married for fifty-six of the sixty years she spent working also suggests she depended heavily on her personal relationships for professional and psychological support. Her second and third husbands were in a position to further her career because of their expertise in public relations, and she relied on their advice and assistance.

4. Porter used gender ideology to her advantage.

Historically, gender has been a disadvantage for professional women, a handicap to be overcome in a patriarchal society and in male-dominated professions such as financial journalism. However, Porter's career demonstrates that gender could be a source of power for individual women, if not for women as a group. Porter performed a delicate balancing act, capitalizing on her novel status as a woman writing about finance while assuring readers she was just as feminine as other women. Her mixed message implied that she was both different from other women and just like them. As a professional, she set herself apart, demonstrating to male colleagues that she was a fellow soldier, not the vanguard of an impending female invasion of the newsroom. At the same time, she emphasized her femininity during interviews, discussing clothes and domestic matters at length, which reassured contemporaries she had no interest in disrupting traditional gender binaries. As an outspoken, driven, and influential woman, Porter could have been perceived as a threat. Showing a savvy understanding of gender ideology, Porter played down her difference even as she profited from it.

In 1942 T. O. Thackrey, executive editor of the *New York Post*, decided "the time has come for us to make capital of the fact that S. F. Porter is a woman writing on financial subjects, rather than trying to disguise Sylvia as an old man with a long white beard."[18] He realized the *Post* could benefit from the publicity Porter would receive as a woman—and an attractive one at that—writing about the staid subject of finance. During World War II, the climate was right for the revelation of Porter's gender. Professional opportunities were opening to women while men were off fighting the war, giving women bigger paychecks and an expanded role in the economy. Advertisers promoted women's strength and ability as workers. The government tailored messages to women as consumers, appealing to their patriotism as it asked them to fight inflation and conserve precious commodities. Porter seized on the boost in women's status to widen her audience, portraying herself as a role model for other women. She addressed her newspaper columns about wartime financial management directly to women and wrote articles for women's magazines about how wives could manage their money in the absence of their husbands. She was a frequent guest on radio programs during the war, where she discussed the danger of inflation and encouraged women to buy savings bonds to help the cause. In interviews with journalists, she acknowledged her unique status, but she insisted the brain had no sex and said other women could do what she was doing. During the war, Porter's message was one of female empowerment.

After the war, Porter continued to seek the double exposure of female-only and mixed-sex readerships by publishing in both women's magazines and general-interest publications and newspapers. While she found women to be an important constituency, she was unwilling to be just "one of the girls." She refused to write a book about finance specifically for women, and she frequently spoke to groups composed of both men and women. Significantly, Porter's postwar audiences tended to be segregated: either all-male, such as when she spoke to economics clubs or bankers groups, or all-female, such as when she spoke to women's investing clubs or charity groups. She handled both audiences with ease, demonstrating her ability to bridge masculine and feminine cultures. Her gender consciousness helped her build a wide audience and maintain a positive public image even when her journalism threatened to breach gender norms.

5. Porter mythologized herself in interviews with other journalists.

Porter showed a talent for embellishing the stories surrounding her start in journalism. In 1942, for example, Porter had been denied entry to a shareholder meeting held by General Mills because the venue did not allow women. She had raised the issue with the company's executives and soon was permitted to enter. Then she wrote a positive story about the regional shareholder meetings the company was holding around the country and the large number of women who attended them, failing to mention that she was the only woman allowed into the company's meeting in New York City. Porter's column had been so complimentary, in fact, the company's president wrote to thank her for it. Years later, however, she told a more heroic story to a young feminist journalist. In that version, Porter claimed she had written a scathing column about the male-only General Mills meeting. She said this had been her lead: "The company whose customers are all women held its annual report meeting in a building which does not permit women."[19] That might have made a better anecdote, but it was not true. Another example of Porter's self-mythologizing was the story of her meeting with Treasury Secretary Henry Morgenthau, at which the two discussed the thirty-year, nonfluctuating Series E U.S. savings bond. Porter preferred to tell the story with dramatic flair, saying Morgenthau had summoned her in the days following the Japanese attack on Pearl Harbor. However, the Series E savings bond was first issued in May 1941; the meeting had taken place in December 1940, well before the attack of December 7, 1941.

As a journalist herself, Porter understood the power of a strong narrative. She knew stories that adhered to professional and ideological norms would garner positive media coverage. She also must have realized how little time most journalists had to fact-check a source's version of past events, so she felt comfortable engaging in some historical revision. By telling stories that used appealing narrative arcs, she allowed news articles about her to function as myth. She encouraged journalists to hold her up as an exemplar, transmitting and reinforcing American fortitude and individualism.

6. Porter used multiple media platforms to reach different audiences.

To achieve universal appeal, Porter used different outlets to reach different audiences and tailored her message to each group. She used the technical writing of her bond newsletter to maintain a toehold in the banking industry, enabling her to attend the convention of the American Bankers Association every year and claim insider status as a bond expert. She used appearances on *Meet the Press* and other issue-oriented television and radio programs to establish her legitimacy with Washington policymakers. She used her writing for women's magazines, such as *Ladies' Home Journal* and *Vogue*, to inspire female readers and promote financial literacy. She used her writing for general-interest magazines, such as the *Saturday Evening Post* and *Life*, to deliver a message of financial common-sense to homes that might not have received her column in their local newspapers. She gave hundreds of speeches over the years, carefully amending her message depending on the audience. For example, she told a meeting of car dealers in 1954 that it was "ridiculous to talk of 'overproduction,' to worry about the 'saturation' of the markets," but later told those convened at a foreign policy conference that the auto industry's overproduction that year had been unpatriotic.[20] Porter demonstrated in the twentieth century what would become common wisdom by the new millennium: To achieve superstardom, a media celebrity had to cross platforms and audiences synergistically, using each appearance and article to promote the others. This had to be done in such a way, however, that it did not disturb a celebrity's overall image, conceptualized even then as a "brand," if not labeled as such.

Porter's biggest accomplishment—and the vehicle for her rise to prominence—was her newspaper column, which put her name and face in front of forty million readers around the country five days a week. The column gave her legitimacy among newspaper publishers and convinced book publishers of her marketability as an author. It ensured readers would recognize Porter's name when they later saw it on books, on television, in magazines, and in the myriad products her organization branded in the eighties. By hitching her star to the middle class as it expanded after World War II, Porter tapped into the fastest-growing market of the twentieth century. Porter's multimedia strategy invites comparisons between her ubiquity and that of modern media stars, who have followed her path by putting their names on multiple media products geared toward middle-class consumers.

In Porter's case, this rampant branding also had a downside. Her products, often created by different sets of people, began to cannibalize one another. The syndicate that distributed her newspaper column came to believe her books and magazine articles duplicated too much content. Writers who helped produce her books found they did not always have the copyright permissions to repurpose her content, which created confusion and conflict. Furthermore, Porter's journalistic reputation suffered from some of the more formulaic content that appeared under her byline. What Porter gained in name recognition, she lost in authenticity as she shifted from a position of cultural authority to a position of cultural power.

7. Porter exploited the labor of other writers.

Porter achieved her celebrity status in large part because other writers—including many women—helped her. This is a delicate point to make because history is full of successful men who have trampled on the rights and feelings of others on their way to the top, and it would not be fair or logical to assume Porter was different because she was a woman. However, Porter's use of ghostwriters must be acknowledged (especially because she, herself, was reluctant to divulge how much assistance she received). She insisted to many interviewers that she did all her own research and writing, which allowed her to maintain a mythical, larger-than-life public image. To allow this notion to stand—that Porter's achievements were the result of an entirely individual effort—not only would be inaccurate but also would elide an important theme in women's history: the success of certain, privileged women at the expense of others.

Porter began using ghostwriters for her newspaper column in the late 1950s, which allowed her to focus on her media appearances and promotional efforts. One assistant, Lydia Ratcliff, wrote Porter's newspaper column and *Ladies' Home Journal* column for thirteen years without credit. The arrangement between Porter and Ratcliff culminated in the publication of *Sylvia Porter's Money Book*, which involved many writers whom Ratcliff organized from her home in Vermont. The writers were not allowed to claim credit for the book, even privately, and some of them found themselves with more work and less pay than they had expected. Shortchanging her writers might have helped Porter's bottom line, but her callousness alienated the leagues of writers who had worked for her. Her focus on short-term gain cost her long-term goodwill. As Porter's reliance on ghostwriters increased in the eighties, a joke began to circulate: *Half of America reads Sylvia Porter's column. The other half writes it.*[21] The woman who had battled her way into financial journalism, commanding the respect of presidents and eminent economists, was dismissed as a has-been. The lackluster end of Porter's career simply did not do justice to the brilliance and hard work that had preceded it.

* * *

A number of journalists remember Sylvia Porter as a pioneer in personal finance and a role model for ambitious women, although few scholars recognize the scope and impact of her career. This book traces Porter's trajectory, unpacking her professional strategies and exploring the socio-economic roots of a populist genre. I argue that gender indirectly influenced Porter's development of personal finance journalism and directly influenced the way she presented herself to the public. Researchers have long demonstrated the extent to which media constructions of successful women conform to normative conventions of femininity. My analysis here presents Porter as a chief architect in those constructions, as she cultivated a public image in keeping with dominant gender ideology even as it changed over the years. She took careful aim at the moving target of twentieth-century femininity. By doing so, she mitigated any perceived threat her authority posed and won the approval of conventional Americans.

However, this mode of gaining public acceptance did not drive the content of Porter's work. She differentiated herself from male financial writers by originating the genre of personal finance as a populist perspective on macroeconomics. But her writing initially gazed outward toward the global economy rather than inward toward the home, as she explained systemic developments in ways that would resonate with individual Americans. She did not, in other words, set out to domesticate finance. In my analysis, Porter's journalism was a direct response to the good fortune and ideological prominence of American citizen-consumers during and after World War II; a growing national emphasis on the individual over the collective; and, more pragmatically, Porter's reliance on others to write her column.

Porter's journalism began as a craft and ended as a commodity. Her newspaper column initially had been infused with her expertise, which had made it inimitable. As she began to employ other writers in order to further monetize her brand, her column necessarily became a product multiple others could write. It lost her idiosyncratic voice and perspective, which made it vulnerable to competition. As Porter generalized her column, the requirements for entry into the larger field of financial journalism became less specialized. Writers with no expertise in finance or economics were hired to satisfy the public's growing interest in money. Ultimately, the genre of personal finance became ubiquitous, spawning multiple brands and inhabiting entire sections of bookstores. "It wasn't a conscious decision," she insisted about her creation. "I just gradually arrived at a formula which says, 'Here is what is going on and here is what you can do to protect yourself.'"[22] This simple statement of Porter's formula belies the complexity of her career, which unfolds on the following pages as a story central to the history of American financial journalism.

1

Wall Street Crusader

SYLVIA PORTER was born Sarianni Feldman on June 18, 1913, in Patchogue, Long Island, the only daughter of Russian Jewish immigrants. Louis Feldman, a physician, and his wife, Rose Maisel Feldman, eventually settled the family in Brooklyn, where they raised Porter and her older brother, John, to appreciate music, history, and literature. "We talked from morning till night," John told an interviewer. "And we were a family that didn't think it was unfeminine for a girl to think. If anything, we rather thought that intelligence added to womanliness."[1] In this intellectually rich environment, Porter later recounted, she was reading Greek history while other girls her age were reading *The Bobbsey Twins*.[2] She skipped two grades and graduated from James Madison High School at age sixteen.[3]

Although she was obviously intelligent, any encouragement Porter received came solely from her mother.[4] Louis Feldman, Porter would say later, was a "chauvinist deluxe."[5] She told an interviewer: "The sun rose and set on my brother John. He was programed [*sic*] to be a doctor. He could crawl around my father's office and read his medical books—but not little Sylvia. I was just a girl."[6] In contrast to her father, Porter's mother insisted she pursue a career. Rose Feldman had given up her ambitions for paid work when she married Louis, yet she supported suffrage and other rights for women. Porter would come to view her mother's dreams—and regrets—as crucial to her success, telling an interviewer:

So—I became my mother's daughter, and that explains a great deal. Mother had been married at 17, immediately became pregnant with my brother and two years later with me. Her expectations of an independent career were pretty much stifled right then and there. So she poured it all into me—her frustrations, her disappointments, her regrets about all the things she wanted to be that she never could have become. I remember nothing else of my childhood so clearly as her singling me out and saying, "You! You will have a career!" That took a great deal of independence and spirit on her part, because my father was typical of the dominating male of that period.[7]

Porter was always grateful for her mother's influence. Without it, she believed, she might not have had the fortitude to resist cultural beliefs outside the family that pressured women to submerse themselves in marriage and motherhood. In one particularly emotional interview with a journalist, Porter broke into tears in a New York restaurant as she remarked: "Anything I am is due to my mother. I am living her life!"[8] Porter repaid the debt by finding opportunities to involve her mother in her busy life. She invited her mother to accompany her on business trips and vacations and tasked her with decorating the two homes Porter shared with her second husband. The two supported each other, the impressive achievements of one woman made possible by the insistent encouragement of the other.

Coming of Age during the Depression

Porter never had the opportunity to gain her father's respect—or perhaps she was freed of the burden of having to try—because he died when she was twelve. The loss of a male provider can be found in the biographies of many women who made names for themselves as journalists in the nineteenth and twentieth centuries, but in Porter's case this event had an especially poignant effect: it changed the way she viewed money.[9] Louis's death stripped the family of the professional status it had enjoyed when a physician was the head of the household. Rose scrambled to maintain their comfortable, if not luxurious, standard of living. She changed the family's name to "Field" and tried several occupations before establishing a business as a hat designer.[10] Porter, in particular, felt the loss of status very keenly. She had wanted to attend Vassar College, but the family did not have enough money. So she settled for Hunter College, the women's arm of the New York City university system, and lived at home while she attended.

Porter was a freshman in college when the stock market crashed in 1929, profoundly altering the lives and perspectives of her generation. The crash and subsequent depression were catastrophic to an economy powered by idealism, and the crisis revealed an information gap between the privileged elite and the manipulated masses. Few who had anticipated a market crash considered mentioning it to the credulous public. With the exception of the *New York Times* and specialized publications such as *Forbes* and the *Commercial and Financial Chronicle*, which sent out distress calls, the mainstream press repeated the rosy assurances of public officials and financiers that the market of the prosperous twenties would continue to roar.[11] As wealth skyrocketed, at least on paper, those who predicted stock prices would drop were vilified. It was believed that public predictions of a stock's decline would lead holders of that stock to sell, depressing its price, so those who suggested the market would fall were accused of *wanting* the market to fall—an accusation akin to aiding the enemy during wartime. Economist John Kenneth Galbraith wrote in his classic history of the crash: "In 1929 treason had not yet become a casual term of reproach. As a result, pessimism was not openly equated with efforts to destroy the American way of life. Yet it had such connotations. Almost without exception, those who expressed concern said subsequently that they did so with fear and trepidation."[12]

Financial journalists were pressured to cheer the market rather than level the investing field with balanced information. The month before the crash, a writer for the Hearst chain of newspapers dared to compare buying stock on margin to gambling. The *Wall Street Journal* wrote of that characterization: "Even in general newspapers some accurate knowledge is required for discussing most things. Why is it that any ignoramus can talk about Wall Street?"[13] The day before Black Tuesday, as October 29, 1929, came to be known, the *Wall Street Journal* acknowledged recent declines in the market but said investors should "not expect these to disturb the upward trend for any prolonged period."[14] For the most part, journalists were allied with Wall Street insiders, not with small investors whose debts had been called in when the market began plummeting five days earlier. Moreover, some journalists were getting paid for their optimism. A congressional hearing revealed that writers at the *Wall Street Journal* and the *New York Daily News* had been paid to tout stocks in 1929.[15] Peer pressure, financial gain, and sheer ignorance had led the American press to gloss over the house-of-cards precariousness of the financial markets. This massive failure by journalists who claimed to be independent would become obvious only after the bottom fell out.

The public outcry after the crash led to sweeping changes in how the market was regulated and how journalists reported on it. Congress created the Securities and Exchange Commission and required companies that sold shares to the public to file regular public disclosures about their finances. Commercial banks, which lent money to businesses, were separated from investment banks, which bought and sold shares in those businesses. Insider trading—buying or selling shares based on information unavailable to the general public—was made illegal, as was the "pump-and-dump" scheme, in which a group of investors teamed up to buy large quantities of a stock, artificially inflating its price, and then sold it en masse. Journalists began paying closer attention to businesses and the market. Despite the inhospitable economy, the magazines *Business Week* and *Fortune* were launched in 1929 and 1930, respectively, joining *Forbes*, *Barron's*, and *Kiplinger's Washington Letter* to cover business and finance. The crash demonstrated the power of the markets to affect everybody, not only the very rich, and journalists felt a responsibility to explain financial issues in language more readers could understand.

For example, the *Wall Street Journal*, finding its reputation badly damaged after the crash, began a resurrection under editors Casey Hogate and Barney Kilgore.[16] Hogate understood that all news had implications for American industry, and he sought to move the paper from its narrow focus on finance to a more general business orientation. Kilgore appealed to a general audience by ensuring the *Journal* was well written and understandable. He insisted that financial jargon be explained or that it not be used at all. He also broadened the newspaper's appeal beyond Wall Street by adding feature stories and expanding its coverage of government. The *Journal* eventually would achieve the largest circulation in the industry as America's first nationally distributed newspaper, and Kilgore would be remembered as the father of modern business journalism. Chris Roush, a scholar of business journalism, wrote: "Kilgore understood that the best business reporting was written for the broadest audience possible. A banker needed to understand the same information about the economy as did a consumer wanting to borrow money from the bank. A seasoned Wall Street investor needed to know why the stock market was falling in the same simple terms that a grandmother in Thomasville, Georgia, could comprehend."[17]

The increased attention to financial journalism in the thirties was also influenced by the ideas of the British-born economist John Maynard Keynes. In 1933, Keynes wrote an open letter to President Franklin Roosevelt in the *New York Times*. Three years later, he published his classic book *The General Theory of Employment, Interest and Money*, fueling a debate over how large a role government should take in regulating the markets. Keynes's radical idea was that governments could change the behavior of markets and businesses through strategic management of the economy. He believed that countercyclical spending—increasing government spending when the economy was weak and reining it in when the economy was booming—would prevent the kind of catastrophic collapse that had occurred after 1929. The concept of a cohesive national economy took shape as journalists reported on Keynes's ideas amid the ongoing depression. The word "economy"—previously used only in the sense of "economizing"—acquired a definite article (i.e., "the economy") and entered the general lexicon to denote the sum of all financial transactions within a defined body. Treating "the economy" as a singular, complex organism worthy of study and news coverage legitimized it within popular discourse and brought together the subjects of politics, finance, business, and labor.[18]

Attention to the economy coincided with a rise in interpretive reporting, colorful writing, and the departmentalization of news, all noteworthy characteristics of journalism in the thirties.[19] Journalism historian Maurine Beasley described interpretive reporting as "an approach to news, often provided by syndicates, that stressed interconnections between facts and permitted specialists in areas such as science, economics, and labor to share their expertise with readers."[20] Objectivity, promoted as a professional ideal in journalism during the early decades of the twentieth century, had suffered from the disillusionment caused by World War I and the market crash. Journalists who felt misled by government public relations efforts and who were caught off-guard by the depths of the economic disaster began to question whether simply reporting facts—such as who said or did what, at what time, and in which location—served readers.[21] It was becoming evident that one could report the facts without reporting the truth, such as when the daily press accepted President Herbert Hoover's contention on October 25, 1929, that "the fundamental business of the country . . . is on a sound and prosperous basis," a statement he had made at the request of the banks.[22] Recognition was growing among journalists that what officials pronounced on stage, for public consumption, diverged from what insiders whispered behind the scenes. Journalists believed it was their responsibility to decipher the truth, pulling the curtain back when it was appropriate and providing context for the facts they considered salient. Subsequently, the thirties witnessed a rise in the number and influence of syndicated columnists, such as Dorothy Thompson, Walter Lippmann, Walter Winchell, Doris Fleeson, Drew Pearson, and Robert Allen.[23] Columnists served as a bridge between the private and public realms of power, supplementing the straight factual reporting of the wire services with their individual, livelier writing styles.

These trends—increased interest in financial news, a populist emphasis on the average reader, and the rise of interpretive reporting—fatefully coincided with Porter's decision in college to unite her love of writing with a timely, pragmatic field of expertise. Driven by a desire to understand the market crash, she had changed her major from English literature to economics and graduated magna cum laude in three years. Her powerful intellect enabled her to master the new discipline without ceding her creativity. A classmate at Hunter once said, "She would sit down and glance over the textbook, and in a few minutes she would be better prepared than the rest of us could be if we studied all night."[24]

Her focus was not entirely on her schoolwork, however. During her junior year, she married Reed Porter, a banker she had met on the subway. She later described the relationship as romantic but inconsequential: "Instead of having an affair, we got married."[25] During her senior year, Porter wrote a novel, *Those That Never Sing*, which she tried unsuccessfully to have published. When she graduated in 1932, her mother appeared at the commencement ceremony on her behalf while Porter went on a joyride around the country with her husband and some of his friends. When she returned home, she set about finding work.

Looking for Work

The thirties were complicated years for women who sought paid work outside the home. A stressful clash of economic and cultural imperatives generated grave hostility toward women wage earners, who were accused of exacerbating the impact of the Depression on men cut down by job losses in construction, mining, and other heavy industries. Married women, in particular, were discouraged and even prevented from taking jobs, even though men's low wages and underemployment often made women's income necessary for their families' survival. Men were still considered the rightful breadwinners, a social norm legalized in Section 213 of the 1932 Federal Economy Act, which deterred a husband and wife from holding federal jobs at the same time (the practice being that if both were employed and the government downsized, the woman lost her job). Discrimination spread, fervently illustrated by a suggestion from Norman Cousins, then the editor of *Current History*, who believed there was an easy fix to the economic crisis: "Simply fire the women, who shouldn't be working anyway, and hire the men. Presto! No unemployment. No relief rolls. No depression."[26]

As the Depression wore on, gender segregation in the workforce and women's low status as workers began to create opportunities that were unavailable—but also undesirable—to men. Light industries recovered faster than heavy industries, and some women accepted jobs in manufacturing and service-related occupations. By the later years of the decade, married women were hired at rates relatively unchanged from before the crash. As the government grew into a welfare state—the culmination of decades of work by women social workers and activists—political appointments of women increased.[27] First Lady Eleanor Roosevelt ensured some women journalists in Washington did not lose their jobs by regularly holding women-only press conferences, where she addressed so-called women's issues but sometimes broke news about her husband's policies.[28] "Though some women were powerful in the thirties, women as a group were not empowered," historian Sara Evans concluded about the decade's bewildering turns.[29]

In 1936 about 12,000 women worked as editors, writers, and reporters in the United States, roughly 25 percent of all journalists.[30] However, newspapermen had not yet accepted women as colleagues, a vestige of the era's overt discrimination and scapegoating of working women. In an ostensibly supportive foreword to newspaper reporter Ishbel Ross's compendium of women's achievements in journalism, Stanley Walker, city editor for the New York Herald-Tribune, wrote: "A great many of the girls who have managed to get on newspaper payrolls have been slovenly, incompetent vixens, adepts at office politics, show-offs of the worst sort, and inclined to take advantage of their male colleagues."[31]

The landscape was even bleaker for women in financial journalism, although several women had made inroads over the years. Progressive muckraker Ida Tarbell publicized corporate abuses and promoted social justice through government regulation with her exposé of Standard Oil for McClure's Magazine. The nineteen-part series was born of Tarbell's childhood experience with the oil monopoly that had driven her hometown oil cooperative out of business.[32] Marian Glenn introduced a section called "Woman in Business" in the first issue of Forbes in 1917. Advertised on the cover as a "unique department," the section promised to give voice to "the Business Woman's problems and the expression of her points of view."[33] Cecilia G. Wyckoff wrote for the Magazine of Wall Street in the twenties, and Clare Reckert, the first woman to cover finance at the New York Times, began working at the newspaper during World War II.[34] Later, Joan Meyers and Eileen Shanahan wrote for the Journal of Commerce, and Shanahan later covered economics for the New York Times. On a list of the top one hundred business journalists of the twentieth century published by the Journalist and Financial Reporter newsletter, twenty-nine were women.[35] Women had maintained a small presence in financial journalism, but the field as a whole—and the industry it covered—was a den of masculinity. Women entered through the back door, usually as freelancers or part-time employees. This meant women were paid little for their early work and were expected to prove themselves competent before being hired as full-time staff writers, a professional and financial obstacle that was not in place for men, who were often hired on nothing more than a letter of introduction.

Financial journalism was a fairly vacant field when Porter began her career, a situation that worked to her benefit. Vermont Royster, who began working at the *Wall Street Journal* about the same time Porter began her career, said: "[T]he staff was small and I could freewheel and write about different subjects and reach out and do stories before anyone else got to them. That situation continued into the 1950s, and it gave me an advantage and a wider perspective than most people get when they go into journalism today."[36] Lindley Clark, a *Wall Street Journal* columnist who graduated from college in 1949, echoed that statement: "There were very few people then who were doing a decent job of writing about the economy, and very few newspapers that were doing a decent job of covering it. I remember thinking as I finished school that I was getting into a field that was wide open."[37] Even in the sixties, according to personal finance columnist Jane Bryant Quinn, who followed Porter into the field, the lack of prestige made financial journalism undesirable to men, which created opportunities for women. Quinn told an interviewer, "I started doing money stories because nobody else wanted to do them. Business reporting was a low-status job."[38]

By immersing herself in the seemingly dry subject of finance, Porter was able to piece together an unconventional start to her career. She told an interviewer she had been offered her first job on July 8, 1932, at the very bottom of the Depression, after responding to a job advertisement for the investment firm Glass and Krey.[39] She had recently graduated magna cum laude from Hunter College and had earned a Phi Beta Kappa key that she wore around her neck with pride. The firm's founder, Arthur William Glass, hired her immediately.[40] Porter and Glass formed an unconventional partnership, scanning the market for quick ways to make money without assuming too much risk in an uncertain time. "We used to spend days drinking coffee, studying financial pages and magazines and discussing them. It was a very unorthodox business office. We learned together," Porter said.[41]

The pair's most creative scheme involved the gold market, a trip to Bermuda, and British government bonds. Anticipating the United States would go off the gold standard in 1933, the pair made arrangements for a bank account and hotel accommodations in Bermuda, where they sold gold for British pounds. As recounted in a midcentury book about famous journalists, Porter traveled to Bermuda to make the arrangements and then returned to New York City. Glass then took $175,000 in gold coins to Bermuda.[42] As soon as the U.S. government's decision to go off the gold standard was announced, Glass sold the gold coins for British pounds and deposited them in the Bermuda bank. From New York, Porter bought British government bonds with the money in Bermuda, and the two sold the bonds for U.S. dollars in New York. The scheme netted them a profit of $85,000 for a week's work. Porter said she received a $50 bonus and a raise from $20 a week to $35 a week as a reward for the deal. In what would become a pattern of self-mythologizing over the years, Porter told a more dramatic version of the dollars-to-pounds story to a writer for *Time* magazine. She told the magazine that Glass had called her at home at midnight, ordered her to travel to Bermuda the next morning with ten Western Union messengers and suitcases full of gold, and instructed her to sit on them. According to this version, Glass then cabled Porter in Bermuda to say, "The expected has happened. Await instructions."[43] She sold the gold and bought the British bonds. In either case, the episode foreshadowed Porter's specialization in currency and exchange as she learned to analyze global economics and international trade.

Porter took several other jobs in the next two years, using each opportunity to further educate herself. She learned how to analyze the business cycle and how to make money in government bonds. She also pursued a master's degree in economics, which she never finished, at New York University. As a freelancer, she wrote book reviews for newspapers and articles on government bonds for *American Banker* magazine and the *Commercial and Financial Chronicle*. Always, though, she looked for something better. Porter was restless with ambition and sought a full-time job that would unite her love of writing and her specialization in finance. She began writing a regular column on government bonds for *American Banker* in 1934, hiding her gender behind the byline "S. F. Porter."[44] She was still only twenty-one years old when she attacked a member of President Roosevelt's Cabinet in an early column. Challenging one of Treasury Secretary Henry Morgenthau's policies, Porter questioned in print whether it was stubbornness, stupidity, or bad advice that drove him to make poor decisions.[45] When Morgenthau contacted the magazine, demanding to speak with S. F. Porter (who he assumed was a man), the editors—afraid of introducing him to an arrogant young woman—told him the writer was out of town.

Galvanized by what had happened to middle-class Americans after the stock market crash, and believing in her talent for comprehensible explanation, Porter wanted to write for a general audience. However, she had a harder time landing a job in the news business than she had at a Wall Street firm or a specialized publication. Perhaps editors in the financial press could sense immediately that she knew her material while general news editors, lacking specialized knowledge, were more skeptical. Perhaps journalists were simply more chauvinistic. Whatever the reason, the Associated Press rejected her application, saying it had never had a woman in its financial news department and never would. The *New York Sun* also denied her a job, saying much the same thing.[46] Finally, Harry Nason, managing editor of the *New York Post*, hired her in 1935 to write three articles a week under the byline S. F. Porter. She would be paid $10 per article. Later in her life, Porter would write to Nason, sentimentally remembering the beginning of their association and her prolific career:

> Oh, I remember, I remember . . . [ellipsis in original]. The morning in the spring of 1935—comin' on 40 years, Harry—when I walked into the city room, a thin, poorly dressed eager young girl looking for a reporter's job in the financial section and saw you in the corner office behind the glass partition with your feet on the desk and you beckoned me in and you laughed and laughed when I told you what I wanted to do—but you didn't turn me down with disdain and contempt as the Sun and AP had done (and the others). . . . And I used every source I had ever met without shame, searching for stories no one else could get, because I was USING friends and not giving a hoot what else the story did as long as it passed you and got into the paper. . . . I have never forgotten, not ever underestimated, not ever ceased being grateful. . . . You never permitted me to be part of the inner circle of Ike Gellis, others in the city room—whoever

from the upper floors joined in. I never got close to any of you, for those were indeed the pre–Women's Lib days. But you were thoroughly objective. You gave me the chance without thought of skirts or pants or sex or whatever. . . . Not being part of the inner circle, the intrigue and the ups and downs swirled around me and as I swayed with the changes and fought on—not knowing that I was pioneering and therefore not at all scared of it—you all faded away.[47]

New York Post

The *New York Post*, founded by Alexander Hamilton in 1801, did not have much to lose by hiring Porter. The nation's oldest continuously published newspaper had changed owners and outlooks three times in twenty years, swerving from a traditionally Democratic broadsheet under Thomas Lamont of J. P. Morgan; to a conservative tabloid under Cyrus Curtis of the *Saturday Evening Post* and *Ladies' Home Journal*; and then back to a liberal broadsheet under J. David Stern, who bought the paper in 1934. The *Post* was not a player in the tabloid wars and mergers of the 1920s, but that was more a reflection of its inconsequential status among the New York City newspapers than a credit to its management.[48] By the time Porter joined the staff, *Post* editors were sore with whiplash from the changes but desperate to keep their jobs, as consolidation and the poor economic climate made newspaper jobs hard to find. The paper was losing millions of dollars a year, and in just a few years Dorothy Schiff would be able to acquire it for the cost of its debt alone. Porter said of the *Post* during this time: "It seemed doomed to an early death, but I was determined to help turn its fortunes around by spectacular reporting in my chosen area and by writing that would combine the poet and novelist I yearned to be with what my editors at that time thought was an astounding specialty for a woman."[49]

Despite the financial legacy of its founding father and its reputation as "a wise old Mr. Stoxandbonds" under the conservative Curtis, the *Post*, like most papers, did not have much invested in its business pages in 1935.[50] The section had its own front, titled "Money, Industry, Economic Trends: The New Deal in Business" (reflecting the era's focus on President Roosevelt's economic policies), yet it appeared to be on life support.

The increasing interest in the economy during the 1930s had not made the financial pages a desirable destination for journalists—evidenced by the anemic output of the *Post*'s business section. On a typical day, the section featured two bylined stories (one of them often from Kenneth Crawford, the paper's Washington correspondent and not technically a business writer), two unsigned "special dispatches," five wire stories, an unsigned market overview, and a handful of press releases. Other days, not a single bylined story was published in the section. Undaunted, Sylvia Porter marched into the demoralized newsroom on West Street, notorious for its disrepair, and took a job no one wanted covering a subject few understood: the bond market.

S. F. Porter's byline first appeared in the *New York Post* on August 6, 1935. The article published beneath it read nothing like the work of a writer who one day would be famous for explaining the markets to the masses; rather, it read like the work of a writer who had never prepared a news story for publication. The article, about a series of bonds soon to be offered by the Canadian government, was dense with jargon, numbers, and bond market arcana. The first sentence of Porter's first news article read: "The real significance of the Dominion of Canada's $76,000,000 2½ per cent loan is that it is a 'feeler'—the first issue in a series of refunding operations to convert the entire Dominion and Provincial debt."[51] From there, the article only got more unintelligible. But the *Post*'s newest contributor rallied, learning in two days what took many writers two years: how to translate jargon for a general audience. She jazzed up her language and got to the point in her second story, which began: "The new issue mart is pausing for major repairs. With the spectacularly successful Kresge Foundation issue floated today, the calendar of offerings will be practically clean until after Labor Day."[52]

During her first year at the *Post*, Porter learned it was more important to write articles that would get past her editor than it was to impress competing journalists with her mastery of the market. Because she was a freelancer, she was paid only for what was published. The value of such an arrangement was that she learned quickly what worked and what did not. Market trends and exclusive information that other newspapers did not have, written in clear, simple language, appealed to the *Post*'s middle-class readers. Market minutiae, written in the special code of bond traders, did not. Porter learned to grab readers by "giving them news you think is important in words that will help them realize this is what they've been seeking without knowing they were."[53] She began to develop her "iceberg" theory of good financial writing: Two-thirds of what a reporter knows remains beneath the surface, but the visible one-third is so sharp and solid that her deep knowledge of the subject becomes apparent.[54]

Porter wrote about subjects few journalists understood and even fewer wanted to cover: corporate debt restructuring and the issuance of federal, municipal, or foreign bonds. Unlike stocks, bonds did not lend themselves to the up-or-down "horse race" coverage favored by journalists writing about any subject, whether it was sports, politics, or finance. Bonds were paradoxical—their prices moved opposite their yields—so one could not calculate sums made or lost simply by watching the ticker. Also, they were fixed-return investments, which meant they did not lend themselves to dramatic reversal-of-fortune stories or tales of aggressive exploits in pursuit of the next big thing—a narrative popular with American journalists. The irony, from a news perspective, was that the bond market was much larger than the stock market and had a bigger impact on the economy, government policies, international relations, and corporate finance. In December 1935, several months after Porter started at the New York Post, trading in the stock market totaled $45,590,420 while trading in the bond market totaled $315,473,600, nearly seven times as much.[55] The bond market, according to Lee Cohn, the veteran financial journalist who would later write Porter's newsletter, "was a weird culture, an absolutely myopic world," indecipherable to most outsiders but essential for understanding the economy.[56] The issuance of bonds—that is, the assumption of debt—was how governments and corporations financed their large-scale endeavors. To understand how countries, states, municipalities, and businesses operated, it was important to know how much they borrowed, where the money went, and—perhaps most important—to whom they were indebted. The 1930s were years of financial ferment, domestically and internationally. By learning how governments financed themselves, Porter acquired an impressive ability to glance at an economic puzzle and discern how all the pieces fit together. She developed such a unique, clear perspective on the United

States' economy and its relations with other nations that she could explain subsequent developments with refreshing clarity to the nonelite, earning her the attention of editors and readers alike.

Scrappy tabloids were more welcoming to women than staid broadsheets such as the *New York Times* and were a better match for Porter's populist disposition. Porter's allegiance was to middle-class Americans. Her talent was boiling down complex financial issues in ways the average reader could understand: translating the "bafflegab," as she called it, of the financial experts. "She knows finance and can humanize it," *American Magazine* wrote about her.[57] Early in her career, she described her mission this way: "I feel that I am conducting what almost amounts to a crusade to try to put these economic developments that affect everything we do into language which the average man and woman can not only understand, but will want to read because they are really interested."[58] Porter aimed at the nexus of economics, politics, and society in her writing, arguing it was essential for voters to understand the interconnections if they were to make informed decisions at the polls.

Porter was appalled by most newspaper coverage of the New Deal. The Roosevelt administration, demonstrating its media savvy, had begun releasing selective economic statistics to the press corps in an attempt to shape news coverage. Washington journalists, in Porter's estimation, would go to the White House every day "and jot down whatever they were told, and then they'd go off and write their stories. And they did that, day after day, with no clear idea of the international effects of the news they were reporting. To them, it was just another story."[59] Porter's disdain for shallow journalism and her allegiance to average Americans motivated her to educate herself about the consequences of government decisions so she could put the publicized statistics in perspective for her readers. Porter's approach immediately earned her the loyalty of readers who appreciated her no-nonsense, democratic perspective on finance.

Despite her populism, Porter's audience in those years of struggle remained people who had at least enough money to wonder how best to save or invest it. And despite her lifelong liberalism, she did not rally the unemployed, nor did she appeal to the government on their behalf.[60] She encouraged sound economic policy, achieved through calculated management of the bond market, careful government spending, controlled inflation, and a progressive tax structure. She criticized corruption and championed the small investor. "One of the things that turned me in the direction of personal finance was remembering how my ma and pa had lost money in Liberty Bonds by selling them at the wrong time, which is what a lot of people did after the First World War. Of course most of the Wall Street crowd knew what it was doing and sold the bonds when prices were high," she told an interviewer.[61]

A Woman on Wall Street

Under the cloak of a gender-neutral byline, S. F. Porter enjoyed the freedom to write about anything approved by her editors without giving readers the opportunity to dismiss her as "just a woman." Asked by Elsa Maxwell, a colleague at the *New York Post*, how she had gotten away with a story on corruption in the government bond market, Porter replied that nobody had known she was a woman. Her byline had disguised her, just as pseudonyms have disguised literary women throughout history.[62] Of course, if readers had paid careful attention—or considered the possibility that a woman could be writing about finance—they might have picked up on Porter's playful references to her gender, which she occasionally slipped into articles. For example, in a series about women on Wall Street, Porter hinted to readers that it was not safe to assume the initials at the top of the article were those of a man. The modern woman financier, she wrote, "scorns publicity, *seeks refuge behind an initial which hides her sex*, battles with men on a basis of accomplishment rather than personality" (emphasis mine).[63] As Porter's confidence and reputation grew, she became even more brazen. In columns addressed to women during World War II, Porter made overt references to her gender. After the United States entered the war in December 1941, Porter wrote, "there are certain things we—women—can do to help make the adjustment easier."[64] Six months later, she was writing with revolutionary zeal. "The first World War brought women into finance and the second World War is giving us our big chance. From this day on, you will write the story."[65]

Before the social upheaval created by World War II, professional women pursuing careers in male-dominated fields met heavy resistance from colleagues, friends, family, and the larger culture, which still idealized the "wife-companion" as the natural role for women.[66] Despite the hostility toward working wives, who were perceived to be stealing jobs from male breadwinners, the number of married women working outside the home continued to rise in the thirties.[67] A simple reason was that economics trumped ideology. Since the turn of the century, consumerism had overtaken production as the dominant function of the American homemaker. During the Industrial Revolution of the nineteenth century, manufacturers had focused on building infrastructure—the raw materials of capitalism that kept the factories humming. By the twentieth century, as production became more efficient, manufacturers were able to divert labor to produce goods for the household beyond the basics of food, fuel, and fabric. At the same time, workers' wages rose, giving them more money to spend on nonessentials. Businesses began pouring money into advertising to convince consumers such items were needed. As women shifted from making their household goods to buying goods already made, they started a pattern of earning money outside the home to buy what was used inside it.[68] In this way, women's work for wages was essentially an extension of their mission as homemakers: to care for their families, whatever it cost them personally. They were willing to suffer social disapproval and criticism for leaving their homes if it meant they could provide for their families financially. To these women, wage work was simply another form of caretaking, even if the larger culture did not see it that way.

A second type of woman continued to enter the workforce during the thirties: the educated woman, usually from an affluent family, who sought a career for self-fulfillment.[69] As women fought to enter and rise within the professions of medicine, law, science, and higher education, some of them eased the perceived conflict between their sex and their vocation by carving out specialties in line with women's traditional roles as caregivers. Women lawyers specialized in family law; doctors became pediatricians.[70] Drawing on a long history of women as social reformers, these women used their clout as potential mothers—and the idealized Victorian image of women as the better sex—to justify professional, even public, careers. However, in contrast to the working housewife, these women usually felt compelled to choose between marriage and a career or planned to work only until they were married. While the number and proportion of working wives rose overall during the thirties, professional women as a group found it difficult to justify their work.[71] Some journalists and progressive elites celebrated women's freedom to choose a career over marriage, but they did not question why the two were deemed incompatible. Freedom of choice in the thirties meant deciding between a career and marriage. But it did not protect professional women from the cruel judgment that could be heaped upon them—most keenly from other women.

Porter wrote of the ostracism and maltreatment she endured early in her career from other wives scornful of her choice. In 1939 she and Dorcas Campbell, vice president of the East River Savings Bank in Manhattan, were invited to speak at the annual convention of the Florida Bankers Association in Palm Beach. "We were viewed as freaks," Porter wrote of the experience twenty years later. She harbored resentment toward the bankers' wives, who had looked upon the two professional women with scorn and condescension. The married women, whose social status depended upon their marriages, assumed Porter and Campbell had resorted to working because they could not find husbands. Some of the men initially approached Porter and Campbell for conversation at cocktail parties, but then they quickly excused themselves, unsure of how to relate to professional women in a social setting.[72]

Feminine rejection was significant to women in the field because, as a bank cashier told Porter in 1936, "The future of women in finance depends as much on women on the outside of Wall Street as men on the inside."[73] If professional women could not gain the respect of other women, how could they hope to win over men? Of course, elite women were equally capable of showing hostility toward their sex. Emma Hemmes, a former vaudeville performer who, in 1936, became the first woman cashier on Wall Street, said women in finance faced no discrimination. "Ninety per cent of the time a fight between a man and a woman in business is the woman's fault," she told Porter.[74] Women as well as men believed that if women could not accept the mores of a masculine environment, they had no business being there.

Professional women thus faced a double bind. They might have been excluded from the upper reaches of their male-dominated fields, but if they organized or demanded better treatment as a group they risked losing what gains they had made as individuals. In addition, women who sought careers in traditionally masculine fields were more likely to identify with their work than with their sex. If this had not been the case when they started, it surely was after the intensive training, harsh socialization, and superior job performance required of ambitious women. The result was that many professional women fought their battles in depoliticized isolation, advocating for measures that would help them individually but failing to call for systemic change.

Porter was a strong advocate for the rights of professional women for the duration of her career, but even she pulled some punches when restraint would benefit her individually. In 1942 she arrived at the University Club in New York, on assignment for the *Post*, to cover an annual meeting of General Mills. The company, a large producer of cereal and other food products, had been holding regional meetings around the country with the hope of increasing shareholder attendance. Porter faced a problem as she tried to enter the meeting: women were not allowed in the University Club. She demanded to speak with the company's leadership and was eventually let in. Decades later, she would boast to a reporter that she had written a column vilifying the company for holding its meeting at a club that excluded women.[75] But that was not true. Instead, Porter had written a favorable column that noted General Mills' large number of women shareholders. "Women have been sprinkled liberally among those attending regional meetings of the company in the last 12 months. So here is another giant American company owned by 'little people' and 'small women investors' in addition," she wrote.[76] She never mentioned that women shareholders in New York had been excluded from the meeting in their city. The company was clearly pleased with the coverage. The president wrote to Porter eight days after her article was published:

My dear Miss Porter:

Despite the embarrassments occasioned by the rules of the University Club, I thought our little party came off very nicely. I certainly enjoyed it greatly and felt well repaid for my trip to New York.

My personal congratulations and thanks for your fine story in the
New York Post, which I have read with great interest. It is always a plea-
sure to talk with you and to read your warmly human comments, so
unusual in financial pages.

Kindest personal regards.

James F. Bell[77]

Women in finance—whether at investment houses, banks, or insurance companies—were both cursed and blessed in ways women in other
professions were not. They were cursed because the singular objective of
their work precluded them from arguing they were performing a noble
service. They were not shaping government policy, teaching, or minis-
tering to sick families; they were making money for their employers or
themselves, plain and simple. It was difficult to put a traditionally feminine spin on that, given the historical connections between money and
masculinity. However, this objective gave them one advantage over their
more reform-minded sisters. If they could demonstrate an ability to make
money, male business owners were likely to let them do so. Profit was
powerful. This special dynamic—the difficulty of establishing a feminine
claim to legitimacy on Wall Street, coupled with an inarguable bottom-
line goal—nurtured an environment that allowed exceptional women to
prosper but did not allow women as a group to succeed. Although Porter
was invited to social functions, such as a dinner for the president-elect of
the New York Stock Exchange, women as a group were excluded from the
New York Financial Writers Association until 1972.[78] In the early years of
her career, Porter told an interviewer, bankers would not talk to her, so
she relied on male allies: other financial reporters who were willing to
feed her information secondhand.[79] A few prominent women were able to
succeed in finance-related occupations, but the overwhelming majority of
women were not given—and did not pursue—the chance to try.

The larger culture was supportive, in theory, of individual women's
achievements in business after suffrage was won, as long as their stories were of the uncomplicated Horatio Alger type. Journalists painted
an attractive image of feminine achievement in the business world,
but it was one that bore slight resemblance to reality. Journalists made

little distinction between "working girls" in lower-level clerical jobs and women in the professions. Most articles minimized the effort, time, money, and talent required to secure and keep a good position. Writers also sidestepped the controversial issue of combining marriage and career by focusing on spinsters and widows forced by circumstances to support themselves or on young girls who planned to quit their jobs once "Mr. Right" appeared. Despite the distortions, omissions, and misinformation, however, the articles in popular magazines did inform the public about a variety of occupations women held and offered alternative roles to those of wife and mother.[80] Contributing to these portrayals of women's accomplishments, Porter wrote a staggering ten-part series on women in finance that was published in the *New York Post* from June 16 to July 9, 1936. The articles show that she, too, was more comfortable documenting the successes of women than reporting the discrimination they faced. Porter profiled ten successful women on Wall Street for the series, probing their career strategies, personalities, and beliefs about marriage and home life. In New York City, she reported in 1936, seventy-two women were partners at brokerages that held seats on the New York Stock Exchange, 250 were members of the Association of Bank Women, four were bank presidents, and two were bank vice presidents. Most of these women were not married, she reported, and despite their seriousness they all looked younger than their ages.[81] She interviewed ten women: two partners at investment firms, two bank executives, one investment broker, one publicist for a brokerage, two self-employed investors, one bond saleswoman, and one trust officer. Porter's series sheds light both on women's experiences in financial occupations and on media representations of successful women in the 1930s.

The bond market was a frequent point of entry for women on Wall Street, as it had been for Porter in the newsroom, suggesting bonds were considered a more suitable specialty for women than stocks—either because they were less volatile, and therefore a safer investment, or simply because fewer men wanted to work in bonds, so jobs were more plentiful. Indeed, bond saleswoman Marjorie Elizabeth Eggleston told Porter that women had made more progress in bond sales than in any other financial field, establishing bonds as a legitimate arena for women interested in a career on Wall Street.[82] Bonds also had a connection with the government, which—because of the social safety net it came to provide in the twentieth century—was likely conceptualized as more feminine than the competitive, masculinized private sector. Mina Bruere, founder of the Association of Bank Women, identified the U.S. government's sale of Liberty Bonds during World War I as the most significant event in the relationship between women and finance. "It taught women what bonds and stocks were," Bruere said.[83]

The overwhelming opinion of the women Porter interviewed was that it was not possible to have both a successful career and a successful marriage. Clara Taylor, president of the Women's Bond Club of New York and owner of her own investment firm, held beliefs typical of the period. Hardly discouraging of women's ambitions—she had started an apprenticeship program on Wall Street for women undergraduates—she believed in their right to choose a career. But choose they must, Taylor told Porter. "The married woman cannot concentrate on her home and her business at the same time and only the woman who recognizes this problem will really make a success of one of them."[84]

Orline Foster, the author of five books and hundreds of magazine articles on stocks and economics, reiterated this point, claiming that "a home and a successful career simply do not mix."[85] She had launched a career after her husband died by investing her inheritance.

Porter took special care to emphasize the Wall Street women's femininity, focusing attention on their looks, their surroundings, and their clothes. According to Porter, Foster's "red and white summer dress was definitely feminine."[86] Bruere was a "rare harmony of efficiency and womanliness."[87] A partner at an investment firm, Louise Watson, occupied an office decorated in the current style, "so fashionable in feminine living rooms."[88] Another partner at an investment firm was "incongruously womanlike"—so much so that "it was easier to imagine Ethel Mercereau seated at a garden party serving tea than working a full business day in the heart of Wall Street."[89] Likewise, publicist Elizabeth Ellsworth Cook, despite being "a militant, soap-box feminist," was "incongruously frivolous."[90] Trust officer Henriette Fuchs even found a way to feminize banking. She claimed bookkeeping was a natural vocation for women on the basis of their talents as homemakers, a perspective that would be echoed in media portrayals of Porter. "Banking is like housekeeping in a way. In a bank everything must be orderly, washed and nursed just as though the bank were a home with a good housekeeper in charge," Fuchs said.[91]

Porter cheered this notion that women might even be inherently better at banking because of their neatness, a trait stereotypically associated with femininity.

The series read as if it had been written by someone looking to these women as role models—which, of course, it was—but Porter was also carefully constructing these women for her readers. It was a legitimizing strategy that she would apply to herself in the next phase of her career. Porter championed the women's achievements while playing up their personalities more than their intelligence. She admired women who were carefully groomed, who dressed in the current fashions, and who popped with personality. The same characteristics that she noted approvingly in the women she interviewed would later drive how she constructed her own image: a bold personality tempered by an emphasis on clothes and appeals to notions of traditional femininity. Porter mitigated potential resistance to women's accomplishments in a male-dominated field by emphasizing their difference, satisfying readers who believed in sex segregation that, despite their employment, these women remained safely on the distaff side of the street.

This professional strategy, while effective for many women, was not deployed without risks or weariness. Eggleston reported that women were still "persona non grata" on Wall Street because men felt entitled to the financial kingdom while women were there because of a special interest. Viewed as interlopers, women had to be better than men to survive. The one advantage women had, Eggleston said, was their exceptionalism. They could charm their peers with their personalities and attract attention as a woman doing nontraditional work. "However," she told Porter, "that's more of a novelty than an accomplishment."[92]

One woman whom Porter interviewed displayed exasperation with her status as a novelty. Mary Vail Andress, an assistant cashier at Chase National Bank, gave terse, one-sentence answers to any question Porter asked her. Then she pulled out a clippings file bulging with all the articles that had been written about her as a woman on Wall Street. Tired of granting interviews, she told Porter to look through the old clippings for answers to her questions.[93] Another woman, Mary Riis, refused to accentuate her femininity. Riis, the ombudsman at a brokerage firm, emphatically told Porter: "The brain has no sex."[94] Porter liked that statement and made it one of her signature lines. She used it often in interviews with journalists, and she made it the title of a speech she gave frequently about women and money.[95]

By the time Porter's series on women in finance was published in 1936, she had graduated from freelancer to full-time staff writer at the *Post* and would soon have complete control over the business section. Under a new business editor, she had been given a wider range of assignments, having proved her competence and paid her dues. She had begun writing about the stock market, investment firms, and foreign currencies in addition to government and corporate bonds. She won total freedom in August 1938, when circumstances at the financially troubled newspaper led the editor-in-chief to fire every other journalist in the section. Porter kept her job by agreeing to do the work of all the men who had been let go, as long as she could have the title of financial editor.[96] With her new power to decide what went into the section every day, she began writing a daily column, first called "Financial Postmarks," then "S. F. Porter Says." She wrote the column five times a week and filled the remainder of the section—which had been shrunk to a single page or two, at most—with wire copy and press releases.[97] Porter's column enabled her to develop an interpretive style of reporting, a unique voice, and a personal connection with readers. She had found a platform, albeit a wobbly one in those early days, and began the slow process of building an audience.

Porter rarely named her sources, even before becoming a columnist, instead asking readers to trust attributions such as "four Wall Street firms are said to be," "the *New York Post* has learned today," "this is the opinion of a group of banks," and "it was learned authoritatively today."[98] Porter entrusted herself with the authority to impart knowledge she thought readers should know, as long as it would not do calculable public harm, and reserved for herself any information she deemed too risky to publicize. She would maintain this stance even as the press grew more adversarial toward government and business in the decades to come. Justifying her decision not to report a paperwork crisis that had closed several brokerages and threatened many others in the late 1960s, she told an interviewer: "If you're going to be an analyst and a columnist on economic life, don't you think you have a responsibility not to bring the whole structure down?"[99] She felt a deep, abiding responsibility for the economic life of the nation and held a strong belief in her own power to cause improvement or mayhem.

Friend of the Government

Porter's complicity with "the whole structure"—composed of government, the markets, and the economy—was never so on display as during World War II, when she became one of the nation's biggest boosters for U.S. savings bonds and supported regulations to control inflation. Having questioned Treasury Secretary Morgenthau's intelligence in *American Banker* a few years earlier, Porter caught his attention again in 1938, when she wrote an article for *Scribner's* magazine exposing the practice of "free riding" on government bonds. Insiders would make a down payment to the government on newly issued bonds, then sell the bonds at a premium to less informed investors before paying the government its full asking price. Of course, Porter had been railing against the practice of such "chiselers" for years in the *New York Post*, and Morgenthau had already asked that it be stopped.[100] Nevertheless, her article in *Scribner's* caused a run-up in bond prices, leading Morgenthau to call a press conference announcing the rules would be changed to disallow the practice. This time, Morgenthau insisted on knowing who S. F. Porter was. When he found out Porter was a woman, he sent flowers. The two struck up a personal friendship and a professional symbiosis. Morgenthau occasionally called Porter to ask what she thought the price should be on a new bond issue, and Porter responded with unwavering support for the administration's policies in her columns, a departure from her criticism of prior years. Later, Porter would deny she was privy to any more information than other journalists received from the Treasury Department. "It has been suggested that I had inside information on the Treasury's offerings, but I did not. What I wrote was simply my judgment based on my understanding of the bond market," she told an interviewer.[101] This specialization in bonds, developed in Porter's early work in journalism and cemented by her relationship with Morgenthau, formed the basis of her first book, *How to Make Money in Government Bonds*, published in 1939.

Porter's most significant collaboration with Morgenthau came when she helped craft a federal policy that would give Americans a safe investment and provide the government with a substantial source of revenue. In December 1940, anticipating America's eventual entry into World War II, Morgenthau summoned Porter from a banking convention in Florida. He wanted her to come to Washington, DC, immediately to discuss a new savings bond that would be issued to help fund the impending war effort. Flattered and not wanting to defy the wishes of the Treasury secretary, Porter immediately boarded a train for Washington, although she had only warm-weather clothes with her. As she later told interviewers, she arrived in Washington at 7 P.M. on a Saturday and frantically began looking for a clothing store. She found one bargain dress shop open and bought the only ensemble that fit: a black dress for $10.95 and a hat for $1.95. The clerk lent her a coat. At the meeting, Morgenthau told her he planned to issue savings bonds similar to the Liberty Bonds that had helped fund World War I. Remembering how her parents and many others had lost money on Liberty Bonds when the government defaulted, Porter refused to support the idea. According to Porter, the two of them hashed out a blueprint for the thirty-year, nonfluctuating Series E savings bond. The bonds helped the federal government fund the war, appealed to the country's patriotism and sense of common purpose, and encouraged Americans to save their surplus wages during the war, which helped offset inflation.

Given the extensive and slanted coverage in the *New York Post* in 1940, one might have thought the United States was already at war. As Porter's meeting with Morgenthau showed, the government was mobilizing and looking for ways to pay for U.S. involvement in World War II long before the Japanese attack on Pearl Harbor. The liberal *Post*—which had been made into a tabloid in 1940 under the ownership and management of FDR confidante Dorothy Schiff and her husband, George Backer—carefully followed events overseas but did not reflect the domestic debate between isolationists and interventionists. The premise of the *Post*'s coverage was that U.S. involvement in the war was inevitable; the only question was when it would begin. Porter analyzed the financial backdrop of the war, writing columns about where governments were stashing their money, which nations and companies were providing military supplies, and how U.S. banks and markets were becoming entangled in the drama.[102] In 1940 she predicted World War II would spark the biggest economic boom in U.S. history. She also warned men of draft age they were no longer eligible for car loans or other personal credit because banks assumed they would soon be sent to war. With inside knowledge she did not reveal to readers, Porter suggested the United States might pay for its role in the conflict by offering the same kind of small bond to its citizens that Canada was using to fund its participation. The "if" in the title of Porter's second book, *If War Comes to the American Home*, published in 1941, was specious; the United States was already fighting an economic war. Porter made it clear the nation's women and children, not just its men, would soon be called into service.

When the United States officially entered the war, the government took control of the economy in a way it never had, with a slew of new agencies reaching directly into homes and affecting how people lived.[103] Food, gasoline, and other products were strictly rationed; wage-price controls were instituted; and housing was built in locations where demand for workers was high. "War is hell. But for millions of Americans on the booming home front, World War II was also a hell of a war," historian Mark Leff wrote.[104] Needing the consent of citizens who generally favored a more limited form of government, U.S. officials relied on the news media to communicate their guidelines for consumers in ways that would resonate with the public's patriotism and self-sufficient spirit. Not wanting to be disregarded, advertisers also collaborated with the Office of War Information to present a unified message that Americans at home were just as important to the war effort as the men abroad.[105]

During World War II, "the American way of life" coalesced into an ideal that would be invoked during the Cold War and afterward to justify U.S. involvement in conflicts that were not fought on American soil. While Britons were defending their own front yards, Americans were fighting for intangibles such as freedom, democracy, and the American way.

American propaganda could afford to be—possibly had to be—highly emotional and manipulative because the war, while making demands of almost all Americans at home, was being fought largely in their imaginations. This presented an opportunity for the advertising industry, which used wartime propaganda to justify its own existence. In making references to the war, advertisers sought not to appeal to an existing altruism they perceived among consumers but rather to elicit the government's support of their industry in the form of contracts and spending on ads. Advertising executive Walter Weir called World War II "the greatest, the most golden, the most challenging opportunity ever to face American advertising. If we make advertising fight today, we'll never again have to defend its place in our economy."[106]

The war also raised the profiles of many journalists—including women, who found new opportunities in the absence of their male colleagues. Porter uncovered two scandals during the first year of the war, which earned her a National Headliners Club award for financial and business reporting.[107] One batch of columns exposed the actions of twelve senators, dubbed "the silver bloc," who were preventing the United States from using its silver reserves for war purposes. She also wrote a magazine article that was condensed for *Reader's Digest*, attracting wide publicity.[108] The article, originally published in *Barron's*, exposed an open secret in Washington: a dozen senators from Western silver-mining states had forced passage in the thirties of several laws whose sole purpose was to protect the value of silver as a backup, like gold, for paper currency. The laws stipulated that (1) the U.S. Treasury had to buy all the silver produced in the country for about 71 cents an ounce, far higher than the world market value of 45 cents; (2) after buying all the U.S.-produced silver, the Treasury had to buy foreign silver to maintain a silver–gold ratio of 25–75 in its reserves, which it would never be able to do because of its surplus of gold; and (3) the Treasury could not sell its silver for less than $1.29 an ounce, ensuring there would be no buyers. So the United States was sitting on a pile of silver that it could not use—and for which it had paid a premium—despite the desperate wartime need for silver to make parts for submarines, tanks, airplanes, artillery, torpedoes, and bombs. When Porter published this article, she was publicizing a long-standing beef of

Morgenthau's; he was as "indignant as anybody else" about the policies, she wrote.[109] Porter did not report the senators' side of the issue and used the words "scandal," "crime," "preposterous," "laughingstock," "indecency," "disgraceful," and "outrageously extravagant" to describe their actions.[110] In response, Senator Edwin Johnson, a Democrat from Colorado, took the floor of the U.S. Senate to call Porter "the biggest liar in the United States."[111] A telegram from Senator D. Worth Clark, a Democrat from Idaho, to the editor of *Reader's Digest* showed how acutely the legislators had felt the impact of Porter's story:

> Four weeks ago I submitted to you on behalf of Senator [Pat] McCarran [D-Nev.] and myself an article entitled Silver Goes to War. This was sent pursuant to our exchange of telegrams and to my letter to you in connection with your previous article Twelve Men Against the Nation. Since then I have heard nothing from you. The repercussions of your first article have as you know been enormous and frankly a rather serious situation is developing here. I wonder if you would be good enough to advise me by wire if possible what your decision is as to the publication of my article.[112]

Reader's Digest never published the senators' response. Marc Rosen, the magazine's associate editor, wrote to Porter that he had ignored the senators' request out of journalistic independence and that he stood by Porter's article as written.[113] It appeared the senators' outrage, expressed so publicly, helped Porter more than it hurt her by garnering the respect of her peers.

The other batch of columns that earned Porter her Headliners Club award had to do with the U.S. subsidiaries of the German industrial war-making machine I. G. Farben. In November 1941 Porter began tracking the government's efforts to uncover the true ownership of one company, a leading producer of chemicals and dyes in the United States. In several front-page stories, she noted with suspicion that the company's board of directors included a number of German names.[114] But her pièce de résistance was an eight-part series in March 1942 that was doggedly meticulous in its dissection of I. G. Farben and its holdings in the United States. She laid bare the economic maneuverings common to all wars and warned readers the Germans' infiltration of U.S. business was as alarming a prospect as if their military had landed on Long Island. The men who controlled I. G. Farben, she wrote, were "enemies even more powerful and important to America's future than the soldiers in the Axis armies, for they made Hitler and they intend to 'win' their war—whether or not that means a Hitler victory, too."[115] Porter wrote a chilling account of a group of German businessmen who had decided well before Hitler rose to power that their nation would achieve European dominance, first economically and then militarily. They began planting businessmen in Europe and the United States to infiltrate corporations, including Ford and Standard Oil, and to marry American girls in order to become U.S. citizens. Within the ranks of U.S. business, Porter wrote, the Germans had access to patents and trade secrets that helped their armies fight American soldiers.[116] Hitler was merely a puppet for these industrial powerhouses, Porter concluded.[117] She gave no indication of her sources, and not a single person was quoted in the series. An editor's note indicated Porter would turn over her research to a congressional committee investigating Farben's U.S. activities.

Porter's columns became more strident and instructive during the war, reflecting a charged atmosphere in which journalists did not remain detached from the news they covered. Three marks of her signature writing style began to emerge: an unambiguous point of view presented as plain common-sense; a distinctive second-person voice that addressed the reader as "you"; and a preference for superlative statistics. For example, in January 1942, Porter wrote about a government plan to sell U.S. bonds directly to the Federal Reserve (a practice that would remain after the war as a permanent staple of U.S. monetary policy).[118] The headline alone declares her approval from the top of the *Post*'s financial page: "Direct Sale of U.S. Bonds to Reserve Banks Is Logical; Disaster Cries Unjustified."[119] Porter also began to write directly to the consumer, developing an assertive, imperative voice, as in: "Stop Withdrawing Savings to Buy Bonds and Hoard; You're Hurting the Country."[120] The third mark of her writing style, the superlative statistic, emerged as the government increasingly relied on select data in its public relations campaigns and the polls of George Gallup gained force: "Never before in American history"—one of her favorite phrases—"has the cost of food been as cheap for the average working man's family as today."[121] Porter extended her superlatives to laws and trends, which maximized the potential impact of what she wrote and matched the *Post's* sensational way of presenting news.[122] The cultural permissiveness allowed to writers who supported the cause of World War II helped Porter develop a crusading, decisive voice of authority.

"To the Women"

Porter's emerging voice was most on display in the columns she began writing directly to women in November 1941, just before the United States entered the war. *Editor & Publisher* identified this series as the first financial column addressed specifically to women.[123] Each column carried the address line "To the Women" as part of its headline. The first one, published November 21, 1941, contained tips for buying holiday gifts, but Porter's agenda for the column expanded quickly.[124] Still under cover as S. F. Porter, Porter said it was women's duty during the war to: (1) buy defense bonds; (2) use substitutes for rationed foods when cooking; (3) watch prices and notify authorities if a retailer was violating price controls; (4) tell lawmakers a tax increase was the best way to pay for the war; and (5) pay off debt, which would help stave off inflation. She offered the same prescription in speeches to women's groups and on radio programs, highlighting inflation as the wartime enemy women should be most concerned about.[125] In the early days of the war, Porter was a tough taskmaster, delivering dire, unequivocal warnings about what would happen if women did not comply with her instructions.[126]

By addressing women as a monolithic group and providing instructions on how to spend their money, Porter was tapping into a growing sense in government and financial circles that women, in their capacity as homemakers, were an economic force that needed to be controlled.[127] The women's pages of newspapers promoted the government's campaign to draw women into the war effort, highlighting the social effects of their individual decisions. Framing food rationing as a way homemakers could help the men fighting abroad "helped officials concerned with civilian resistance reframe rationing as an issue of female patriotism rather than government intrusion," according to researcher Mei-ling Yang.[128] The

Office of War Information sent press releases to women's pages and distributed a news budget to editors every two weeks, outlining the stories the government hoped the women's page editors would publish. The editors dutifully ran recipe substitutions for restricted ingredients and tips for making rationed foods last as long as possible. "Unlike the attempt to regulate market behaviors of women as consumers, which was aided by more formal means of control such as quotas, price ceilings, and judicial processes, the government's effort to coordinate their non-market behaviors as homemakers with a national interest had few resources to depend on other than the media," Yang wrote.[129] Even so, the government relied on columnists such as Porter to spotlight women's behavior as consumers and adhere to structural mechanisms. By linking women's traditional roles as household caregivers to the national war effort, the government was able to enlist women who were unable or unwilling to adopt more unconventional roles by working outside the home. Women not only could produce for the war; they could consume for the war. In this way, authorities upheld traditional ideas about femininity during a time of social upheaval and appealed to as many women as possible.

Porter did not restrict her coverage of women to homemakers, however. She wrote vividly and enthusiastically about women's changing roles in the workforce and reminded her readers what had happened during World War I, when women had made significant progress in the workforce only to be sent home afterward. Before the bombing of Pearl Harbor, Porter attended a conference in Columbia, Missouri, on the changing status of women. Her columns about the conference carried the message that, like it or not, in the future women would have more financial responsibility and a greater presence outside the home. Furthermore, the current education system was not properly preparing them for their new roles.[130] Porter wrote from the pragmatic, capitalistic perspective of an American economist. The demands of the economy would require more women to enter the paid workforce, which would give them more financial independence. That meant they needed to be taught what to do with their money. In fact, Porter was optimistic that opposition to women's work outside the home was fading. She reported that of one thousand people attending the forum, all appeared to be supportive of women's employment. No one raised his or her voice in opposition or showed concern for traditional gender roles.[131] She reported that 25.5 percent of women fourteen and older worked for wages in 1940, compared with 24.3 percent in 1930. She also said one-sixth of married women worked in 1940, compared with one-eighth a decade earlier. With some eagerness, Porter quoted Thomas Beck of Crowell-Collier Publishing: "We won't have a man's world after this war, but neither will it be a woman's world. It will be a people's world."[132]

Porter followed her reporting on the conference with a ten-part series on women and war that began January 7, 1942, and announced, with Roosveltian flourish, a "new era for women," "a social revolution," and "more equality in marriage."[133] She welcomed the independence this would create for women and imagined a future in which men and women worked side by side and new services emerged to help families with their child care and household responsibilities.[134] However, Porter was not blind to the social dislocations women's economic liberation would cause. Recalling the hurtful expulsion of employed women after World War I, when they had been shunted aside once their emergency labor was no longer needed, she cautioned readers to plan for women's continued employment and to approach related social issues with care. "The home, children, the 'heart of America'—all are involved in this problem," she wrote.[135]

Porter advocated the greater availability of child care to accommodate working mothers and a "community living" approach to social policy, similar to measures that had been adopted in Britain. She noted that women had always worked for pay; what was revolutionary was they now had more diverse opportunities and access to higher wages.[136] Porter argued forcefully and valiantly that moralistic rhetoric over whether women *should* work outside the home was moot; they *were* working outside the home, they would continue to do so, and Americans ought to start planning for a new workforce after the war. She wrote that both the United States and Britain should anticipate the social dislocation created by war while honoring women's capability and motivation as wage earners. She acknowledged the problem was dicey because it would involve an emotionally charged discussion of gender roles.[137] Some women would resent giving up their financial independence after the war, others would not be able to afford to quit their jobs, and still others who had found outside work stimulating would be psychologically depressed as home-makers. She predicted 50 percent of women would be working for pay by 1950.[138] "There's no longer much point to arguing whether women can work or should work. Women are working at every type of job, and after this war, countless thousands will try to hold their positions," she wrote.[139] Her predictions about the plight of employed women after the war would prove prophetic, overwhelming her appeals for pragmatic, forward-looking thinking before the workforce tightened.

The proportion of married and older women who worked for wages dropped when the soldiers came home. The proportion of white married women working outside the home hovered between 20 percent and 30 percent in the fifties and did not reach 50 percent until the mid-seventies.[140] Nevertheless, Porter's assessment of working women's status during the war—and the backlash that awaited them—was impressively accurate for the time. Historian Alice Kessler-Harris has shown that while the war pulled about five million women into the workforce, this was a mere blip in the long march of women into the paid workforce during the twentieth century.[141] As Porter predicted and historians later confirmed, the trend would continue into the fifties as the nation enjoyed an unprecedented economic boom that required the labor of women. The greatest jump would be seen in the paid work of married women, a fact that would launch extensive debate about women's proper roles. Porter's optimism that resistance to women's paid work had broken down for good would prove naïve, as the country moved into the conflicted cultural terrain of the Cold War.

What was significant during World War II was the larger culture's ebullient encouragement of women's work outside the home, as well as the expanded opportunities available to individual women who replaced men in jobs that carried more prestige and higher wages. In 1936, a Gallup Poll showed that 83 percent of respondents opposed paid work for women; in 1943, only 13 percent opposed paid work for women.[142] As Kessler-Harris wrote: "Wartime appeals to patriotism turned the defensive posture these arguments [in favor of women's paid work] had in the depression into an aggressive stance. Where the depression had prompted women to apologize for paid work—to present it as a last resort to preserve family life—the war focused attention on women's positive contributions to labor force needs."[143] As it did for other women journalists, World War II ignited Porter's career. Having delivered hard-hitting scoops that established her reputation as a serious journalist, she continued to develop her voice of plainspoken authority that addressed average readers directly.

Porter also extended her reach into American homes through a medium that could not mask her gender: radio. During the war, Porter moderated a radio forum on the investor's role in national defense, served as an occasional guest on *Opinion Requested*, and began a weekly radio series on women's roles in the war effort. Producers loved booking the lady economist who livened panel discussions with her astute barbs and quips. She was a frequent guest on the ABC radio program *America's Town Meeting of the Air*, which published an ad in 1944 that read like a boxing promotion. In one corner was economist Beardsley Ruml, ready to defend his new tax proposal; in the other corner was Sylvia Porter, whom the ad made sure to identify as the nation's only female financial editor.[144] The dueling experts even had their own seconds: tax attorney T. N. Tarleau for him, Harvard economist Alvin Hansen for her. Porter frequently spoke to women's groups about the danger of wartime inflation and how best to control it, telling both the Federation of Women's Republican Clubs of New York State and the Daughters of Pennsylvania that a price bill before Congress would cause inflation because of the farm bloc's selfishness.[145] Alongside former government officials and economists at the New School for Social Research, she argued that higher taxes were unavoidable to pay for the war and recovery. In general, Porter argued in favor of a federal sales tax and other government interventions but against protectionism for specific industries. These opportunities to make her case fed Porter's expanding audience, providing additional venues in which she could showcase her financial expertise and unique perspective.

Seven months into the war, the *Post*'s executive editor, T. O. (Ted) Thackrey, recognized his financial editor's star power. In July 1942, Thackrey wrote a memo that would change Porter's career. He suggested the newspaper treat Porter the same way it did its male columnists. He also believed the paper should highlight Porter's gender. "I believe very definitely that the time has come for us to make capital of the fact that S. F.

Porter is a woman writing on financial subjects, rather than trying to disguise Sylvia as an old man with a long white beard," Thackrey wrote.[146] Porter's full name appeared in the *New York Post* for the first time on July 20, 1942.[147] She enjoyed telling reporters that one longtime reader who had been addressing his correspondence to "Dear Mr. Porter" began his next letter "Darling—."[148] Unveiling her gender in the newspaper launched a period of manic activity in Porter's career that would take her from a print columnist known by a relative few to a multimedia phenomenon known by many. This growth phase of Porter's career would be accompanied by a shift in professional strategy. No longer would she hide behind her initials, minimizing any perception of gender difference. She was about to start accentuating her femininity, playing gender to her advantage.

2

Glamour Girl of Finance

WHENEVER SHE WAS ASKED to speak to one group or another about women and finance, which happened frequently, Sylvia Porter liked to tell the story of her encounter with the Wisconsin Bankers Association in June 1940. She had been invited to speak at the group's annual meeting but could tell from the correspondence she received that the group's leaders assumed S. F. Porter, the esteemed big-city financial columnist, was a man. She chose not to tell them otherwise. Upon arriving at the convention hall, the doorman refused to admit her, explaining that a very important dinner for bankers was about to begin and that women were not permitted. "Well," Porter replied. "That's going to be a problem. I'm the keynote speaker."[1] The association's befuddled president was consulted, and Porter was allowed to give her speech to a stunned, though eventually receptive, crowd.

Once Porter's name and photograph began appearing with her column in the *New York Post*, the reaction to her changed from shock that she was a woman to amazement that she was an *attractive* woman—which made her a prime object of media attention. Most articles raved about her looks, style, and charm, drawing a contrast between her sex appeal and the boring reputation of finance. Most also recognized her powerful mind, finding incongruence between her looks and her brain. Others simply could not believe a woman could put two cents together, let alone master the bond market. Reporters of both genders inundated Porter with requests for interviews, labeling her "Princess Charming of Wall Street,"[2] the "glamour girl of finance,"[3] and "Wall Street 'Joan of Arc.'"[4] One headline announced: "A Financial Editor Can Be Beautiful!"[5] The writer of that article quoted a convoluted passage from Porter's speech and added:

53

"Coming from someone who looked as feminine as an unbalanced check-book, this was an astounding statement."[6] However, the reporter noted, the men in the audience hardly cared what Porter said as long as they could keep looking at her. A profile of Porter in *Newsweek* opined that as a "pert, pretty, smartly groomed brunette," she was an "unlikely source" of financial information.[7] The editor of the *New York Herald Tribune* wrote especially colorfully about Porter, the only woman profiled in a book about prominent journalists of the 1950s: "Yes, there is Sylvia. Journalism is tough enough for a woman, but Sylvia made it even tougher for herself. She became a woman business-economics writer (her column seems to appear almost everywhere), and she made the complex subjects she writes about as vital as she is. Frumpy, one might guess about a woman writer on economics. Not so. Not so."[8]

If Porter recognized the sexism inherent in journalists' emphasis on her appearance, she did not let it bother her. On the contrary, she found a certain power in it. She was pleased and flattered by her new status as the pinup girl of finance, apparently having decided it was better to be looked over than overlooked (a perspective once voiced by Hollywood actress Mae West). She did not mind comments about her hats, hair, and heels if the cultural approval meant she could speak her mind.[9] As the *Atlanta Journal and Constitution* declared in a headline: "People Stop to Look at Sylvia Porter, Then Stay to Listen."[10] Even in private correspondence, Porter was coquettish with the men she knew professionally. For example, after Lester Merkel of the *New York Times* had repeatedly solicited Porter to write an opinion article for his newspaper, she responded: "If you're as persistent in love making as you are in getting articles at a minimum price for your worthy publication—all I can say is Wow-Wow!"[11]

Porter began to craft a public image that would neutralize any negativity the public might feel about a woman writing with authority about finance. Beginning in the forties and continuing for the rest of her career, Porter positioned herself in accordance with prevailing gender norms. In the forties, this meant exuding Hollywood glamour; in the fifties and sixties, it meant projecting a cozy ideal of family togetherness; in the seventies, it meant asserting her independence. Porter developed her own principles of marketing that would give her license to write what she wanted. Years before "multimedia" and "convergence" became buzzwords, she used a strategy of triangulation that took advantage of the expanding media landscape in the mid-twentieth century. The years 1947–1960 embody the growth phase of Porter's career and correspond with a period of enormous change in the media industry. Three of Porter's tactics during this time stand out: (1) She made use of multiple media platforms, including newspapers, magazines, books, radio, television, and a specialized newsletter; (2) she constructed a public image of herself that she adapted to changing gender norms and different audiences; and (3) she cultivated the middle class as her core audience and consistently aligned herself with its interests.

In 1943 Porter entered into the most beneficial partnership of her career: her marriage to Sumner Collins, the director of promotions for the *New York World-American*. She had divorced her first husband, Reed Porter, two years earlier by traveling to Reno, Nevada, where one could file the paperwork after establishing residency for six weeks. The only meaningful consequence of that first, youthful marriage was Porter's byline. Her marriage to Collins, on the other hand, had a profound personal and professional impact. The two met on a cruise and immediately got into an argument about a strike at one of the Detroit newspapers. A member of the Newspaper Guild, Porter defended the workers, while Collins, a staunch Republican, took the side of management. Spirited political discussions would be a hallmark of the Porter-Collins union. The couple even hung a sign on the door to their Fifth Avenue apartment that read, "No matter what you believe, one of us agrees with you."[12]

In an era when other professional women experienced conflict between their marriages and their careers, Porter viewed Collins as a business partner. Porter told an interviewer that most of the guests the couple entertained were acquaintances and colleagues of Collins's, whom Porter cultivated as sources.[13] "Our marriage was way ahead of its time," she said.[14] Collins had even encouraged her not to change her byline when they married because it was so well established. While Collins was described as a shrinking violet by some who knew the couple, the marriage worked precisely because he accommodated his wife's spirited personality and high profile.[15]

Multimedia Blitz

As a business executive for the *New York World-American* and later for the entire Hearst enterprise, Collins had strong ideas about how Porter could profit from her status as a financial authority. One of his contributions was the suggestion in 1944 that the two of them start a weekly newsletter about government bonds for a specialized list of subscribers. Collins told acquaintances he was tired of waiting to start dinner while Porter responded to letters from bankers who sought her advice. He also believed it was foolish for her to give free advice.[16] The enterprise, called *Reporting on Governments*, quickly became profitable—"our little gold mine," Porter would call it.[17] Collins was publisher; S. F. Porter was editor.[18] They initially charged $40 for a yearlong subscription. (Nearly twenty years later, they would charge $60 a year and have 2,500 subscribers.)[19] Early in the newsletter's existence, Porter sent a copy to her literary agency, noting the contrast between the writing in the newsletter and her writing for newspapers and magazines, which targeted a general audience.[20] According to Lee Cohn, who would write for the newsletter in the sixties and seventies, the audience for *Reporting on Governments* included Wall Street investors, bond houses, traders, and bankers.[21] The significance of the newsletter for Porter's career was that it gave her a forum to demonstrate her technical knowledge to a specialized audience. It allowed her to show that she could talk finance to insiders, not just to the public. By earning the respect of the banking elite, Porter launched an early defense against the presumption that populists who wrote for the masses were intellectual lightweights. An advertisement in 1953 highlighted the success of this strategy. The copy in the ad called Porter an "authority on family financial matters" but also said she was "constantly consulted by economists, bankers and government."[22]

By the mid-1940s, Porter was an accepted presence on Wall Street, where she was even allowed to visit sources at the male-only New York Stock Exchange after the board voted to make an exception for her.[23] The University Club—where she initially had been turned away for General Mills' annual meeting—permitted her to attend a dinner held by Standard Oil, which had invited her.[24] Her gender even helped her get scoops. Male sources, trying to be gentlemanly, invited her for tea or coffee; in such a relaxed situation, she could draw more information out of them than they had planned to give. They often underestimated her, assuming her to be less threatening than her male colleagues. And she was less noticeable, which worked to her advantage. In 1956, for example, she broke the news of Ford Motor's plan to issue public stock after overhearing bankers at a convention. They had assumed the bathing beauty in the two-piece swimsuit was somebody's wife, she recounted, and were stunned when a story about the stock offering was published in the *New York Post* the next day.[25] Asked by a journalism student at Columbia University whether men ever made passes at her while she was reporting, she hedged a bit: "Well, when you're discussing international finance, it's quite a jump to 'Watcha doin' tonight, babe?'"[26]

Porter continued her radio presence after World War II as a frequent guest on *Author Meets the Critics*, *People's Platform*, and *America's Town Meeting of the Air*. (The latter program devoted its broadcast on November 17, 1947, to a lineup of female luminaries, giving Porter a rare opportunity to share the microphone with author Evelyn Millis Duvall, photojournalist Margaret Bourke-White, and *New York Times* editorial writer Anne O'Hare McCormick.[27]) Porter also experimented with the fledgling medium of television, appearing with Edward R. Murrow on *Person to Person* in 1956 and with Mike Wallace on *Night Beat* in 1957. She increased her presence in national magazines such as *Life* and the *Saturday Evening Post*, an important way for financial experts to gain influence in the forties and fifties as the nation debated the terms of its new economy. She rounded out her portfolio with articles in women's magazines such as *Good Housekeeping*, *McCall's*, *Vogue*, and *Ladies' Home Journal*.

Indeed, Porter seemed to be everywhere. On November 9, 1952, she sat before senator-elect John F. Kennedy of Massachusetts on *Meet the Press*. Her co-panelists were Maury Davis of the *New York World Telegram & Sun*, Ogden Reid of the *New York Herald Tribune*, and Robert Riggs of the *Louisville Courier-Journal*, all of whom were invited to question Kennedy before she was. On camera, Porter hummed with contained energy, reflexively reaching for a cigarette that was not there while the others grilled the newly elected senator. When it was finally her turn, she lightly dismissed the "superficial issues" that she said had dominated Kennedy's campaign and instead asked what he would do to prevent deflation, which she called a "pressing concern." Kennedy agreed that deflation would be a bigger threat than inflation over the next four years and said he supported measures to offset such a predicament, such as cutting the budget more slowly. This answer set off the most fiery exchange of the show as the other panelists tried to nail down Kennedy's position on a balanced budget: was he, or was he not, in favor of one? He tried to finesse a response, saying he was in favor of a balanced budget as long as economic conditions allowed it.[28] As Kennedy battled with the insistent newspapermen, Porter sat back—no longer fidgeting—clearly pleased to have started a fight.

As Porter's star rose, she hired a literary agency in New York to handle the contracts for her books and freelance writing. The agency, Brandt & Brandt, was a husband-and-wife team composed of Carl Brandt, who founded the agency, and Carol Brandt, who later joined him. During the period immediately after World War II, the agency was inundated with requests for articles and books by the financial guru with a gift for language. One solicitation, representative of the many requests her agents received over the years, seemed to anticipate *Economics for Dummies* at least fifty years before that series would explode onto bookshelves. A publisher had suggested Porter write an economics primer that would simplify basic principles for readers who might be new to the subject, even suggesting they market the book as "economics for the unintelligent."[29] Porter was the only person capable of writing with enough clarity to appeal to the masses, this publisher believed.

In 1948 Porter produced a self-help book, coauthored with J. K. Lasser, titled *How to Live within Your Income*. In discussing the project with the book's publisher, Simon & Schuster, Porter articulated her allegiance to the middle class, along with her belief that a plainspoken approach would lead to higher sales. "Simplicity, real simplicity, should be our 100% goal, don't you think? . . . I'm afraid of complication in any part of the book, for fear it'll scare off the readers."[30] The book offered spending models to guide families in their decisions about money—even though Porter believed each family was unique and should tailor its financial planning to its own needs. "Our belief was that if you try to make your income-outgo match that of the 'average' family, you are pursuing a myth, for the 'average family' is a myth invented by the statistician for the convenience of the statistician," she said in one of her famous observations.[31]

As American families got their financial affairs in order after World War II, the market was growing for concrete advice. People wanted to know what proportion of their income they should spend on each item in their family budget and how to navigate increasingly complicated government regulations. Lasser had been publishing a do-it-yourself tax guide since 1939 and wanted Porter join him in that endeavor. Porter initially agreed but soon backed out of the project, writing to Lasser: "I'm bitterly ashamed and terribly sorry. But after hours of time—and I mean hours—I can't rewarm myself on our 'tax bible' book. Hell, this was supposed to be fun—not agony. Maybe you'll want to give this to someone else who will collaborate with you on it. But me . . . me . . . I'm back to my other world. I gotta. As of now, I'm just wasting your time and mine."[32]

That year, Porter published her last collaboration with Lasser, a book similar to their first one, titled *Managing Your Money*. Simon & Schuster had been disappointed with the performance of *How to Live within Your Income*, which sold 150,000 copies as a dollar book, and the next book, published by Holt, sold only 35,000 copies at $3.95.[33] Porter and Lasser were making inroads with publishers and the public, although some older Americans—perhaps bitterly recalling the assurances of financial experts immediately before the Depression—remained wary.

While promoting *Managing Your Money* in 1953, Porter and Lasser told radio host Mary Margaret McBride that they had tried to imagine all the major financial transactions of a middle-class life and explain how to handle each one.[34] However, this particular interview was less notable for its discussion of the book than for the audible tension between Porter and McBride, two diametrically opposed personalities. Their interaction provided a poignant and somewhat humorous illustration of the competing claims on womanhood after World War II. The two women were different in every way. McBride took an intense interest in her listeners and responded to their letters personally; Porter cared about her readers only in the aggregate and delegated her correspondence to an assistant. Porter's voice was low, resonant, and husky from smoking, oozing sophistication; McBride's high warble reminded listeners of an older aunt or family friend. McBride thought marriage and a career did not mix; Porter's husband played an active role in her career. Throughout the interview, McBride insisted that finance was just too difficult for her to understand, "a subject to me that is utterly Greek." During one of these self-effacing interludes, Porter interrupted to point out McBride's financial success: "But you've done such a superb job of it!" McBride just as insistently demurred: "Oh, no, I've bought government bonds, that's it." Porter insisted women could manage their money. She said she was no longer the only woman writing about finance because the war had helped women onto the financial pages. "There are some mighty fine girls coming up—and they'd better! After all, we do balance the budgets, Mary Margaret, and you can say it's hard—fine. But I think we do it better than the men would."[35]

World War II had made publishers eager for a book about money written specifically for women. In a letter to one of Porter's agents, one publisher alluded to the timeliness of the subject and the marketability of Porter's writing among women, in particular.[36] Such a book would pay off handsomely, the publisher believed, and he wanted to take advantage of the visibility the war had given to the subject of economics and to women workers and consumers. However, Porter did not want to parse her books the way she did her newsletter, magazine articles, and speeches. Her books, she insisted, should have mass appeal. When a different publisher's representative, Jacqueline Parsons of Julian Messner, made a similar request for a financial primer specifically for women, Porter replied to Carl Brandt, her primary agent at the time:

> She told me that the firm got the idea a couple of weeks ago after noting how successful the recent appeals to women investors had been, and the first person they thought of for writing it was me. I . . . went into the spiel that . . . you and I thought any book I did on this subject now would, of necessity, duplicate "How to Live Within Your Income." . . . I thought you ought to know about this so you would have the information in your files and also so that you would know the sort of interest there apparently is in this book. I have no doubt that someone is going to write such

a good one that it will destroy my chance to do something I've wanted to do for so many years. But I do hope they don't do such a good job that it will hurt our market because some day, Carl, that book, the way I envision it, is going to buy you and me an awful lot of Coca-Colas![37]

When Porter's full name and photograph began running with her column in the *New York Post* in 1942, her editors had made a key discovery: not only was the "girl wonder" of Wall Street a marketing phenomenon, but the nation's women were a phenomenal market. Women's labor had been the main engine driving the U.S. economy during World War II, and women continued to control most of the nation's wealth after the war. Personal finance was as important to women as it was to men—perhaps more so, Porter thought. "Women are interested in everything and they control the money. There is the working woman and the independently wealthy woman. The housewife is usually handed the family paycheck and does all of the household spending," Porter told one journalist, who credited her with translating "financial gabgloob" to Mrs. Average American after the war.[38]

Porter's status drew attention to women's coiled power as holders of wealth. She frequently noted that if women were to assert their economic power as a unified force, they could demand whatever change they wanted—as investors, consumers, or voters. Doris Lockerman of the *Atlanta Constitution* accurately reported in 1950 that women controlled 70 percent of private wealth in the United States. They owned more than half of American Telephone and Telegraph and the Santa Fe Railroad; nearly half of the Pennsylvania Railroad, U.S. Steel, and General Motors; and 40 percent of public utilities. They also were the beneficiaries of the vast majority of life insurance policies. "Girls are beginning to know that the hand that rocks the cradle likewise packs a financial wallop," Lockerman wrote, criticizing banks for failing to recognize women as a potentially lucrative market.[39] Edith Olshin of *Magazine Digest* predicted that finance would never be a woman's world, but noted that Porter was having an impact: "Miss Porter was the first of her sex to break through the sacrosanct barriers of Wall Street. Others have followed and have found the going a lot easier because Sylvia Porter preceded them. Women are not flocking into finance in droves, and they probably never will. But they are there and they're making themselves heard."[40]

Porter was performing a clever balancing act. She did not allow herself to be pigeonholed by publishers and editors, demonstrating that she could write for men and women, the masses and the elite, investors and consumers. However, she did allow journalists to construct an image of her that was finely tuned to prevailing gender norms and would serve to mitigate potential resistance to a female voice of authority. In the late forties and fifties, print-media portrayals of Porter were of two types: either they had a breathless, cinematic excitement to them or they invoked images of a traditional, if public-spirited, homemaker. This dichotomized vision of ideal white womanhood—Hollywood glamour versus domestic conservatism—underscored deep conflicts over gender ideology that marked the postwar era.

Whichever feminine stereotype they chose, every journalist who profiled Porter commented on her appearance and seemed eager to reassure readers that even though she held what most considered a masculine occupation, she still met traditional standards of femininity. "Sylvia, who measures 36-26-36 and wears a perfect size 12 at age 49, worries constantly about her weight and appearance. She would much rather discuss clothes, diets and make-up than finance," wrote one reporter.[41] According to another journalist: "Slim and pretty, with a sophisticated taste in hats, she looks like Hollywood's idea of the lady reporter but she attacks her job like a hard-boiled newspaper man."[42] A coworker's description of Porter's manic arrival in the newsroom every morning made it clear that she wasted little time before rolling up her sleeves, yelling for coffee, and getting to work—but also that she always powdered her nose before she started banging on her typewriter.[43]

Just as Porter had emphasized style over substance when she wrote about women in finance in the thirties, the women journalists who were now covering Porter emphasized her obsession with fashion and the attention she paid to her appearance. Olga Curtis of the *Denver Post* claimed the expensive clothes in Porter's closet meant more to her than all the awards and honorary degrees she had earned professionally.[44] Allene Talmey of *Vogue* called Porter an "egghead" who "likes the feel of newspaper power" but also told readers she was "clothes-loving" and "nuts about pink."[45] Judy McCluskey of the *Providence Journal* described Porter as a "high-strung, outspoken, hard-driving professional woman" but also noted her "passion for haute couture clothes and other feminine luxuries."[46]

Such depictions presented conflicting expectations for women after World War II. It was acceptable, even desirable, for women to have a public presence—the culture celebrated women's "firsts," as evidenced by the attention heaped on Porter—as long their private selves (their *true* selves) were safely feminine. While men were encouraged to wield power both in public and in the home, professional women were expected to leave their authority on the doorstep—or at least to pretend that they did. For instance, Curtis told her readers there were two Sylvia Porters: the hard-nosed financial expert and an "an ultra-feminine female named Mrs. G. Sumner Collins who thinks of money as something to spend on pretties."[47]

Many who wrote about Porter held up her feminine charm as an attribute that would earn the approval of more traditional readers. Others, however, wielded gender as a weapon, creating a discursive cul-de-sac familiar to women with public careers. Antagonists focused attention on Porter's gender to discredit her when she said or wrote something they considered out of bounds. Saying her "slip was showing" was a pun popular with writers who no doubt thought themselves clever. For example, Ferman Wilson, real estate editor for the *Miami Herald*, castigated Porter for a series of columns she had written suggesting housing was dangerously overvalued in Florida (echoing a circumstance that had preceded the market crash of 1929). Wilson, a loyal booster for local real estate companies, derided Porter's "soprano squawk" and "sad sack Sylvia's sour song of sorrow." He referred to her as "Sylvia, dear," and said she was "talking through her Easter hat." He even scolded her as one would a child: "Why, Sylvia, go wash out your mouth." Criticizing Porter's failure to name any of her sources, he concluded: "Miss Porter, your slip is showing—in fact, several of your slips are showing."[48] Wilson's venomous tone left no doubt that he was attacking Porter not as a journalist, but as a *woman* journalist whom he considered out of her element. The *St. Petersburg Times*, which published Porter's column, ran a more measured response to her assertions about a possible downturn in the housing market. The *Times* simply reported that the St. Petersburg Chamber of Commerce had complained to the newspaper and said it would print any facts that rebutted Porter's arguments.[49]

Another gendered attack on Porter occurred during the weekly radio program *America's Town Meeting of the Air* in 1950 as Porter debated Leslie Gould, financial editor of the *New York Journal-American*, about which was better for small investors: government bonds or stocks. Gould argued that the savings bond made an impractical investment because the bond yields did not keep up with inflation and encouraged government spending; anyone with the means should invest in the stock market, he said. Porter, of course, came down on the side of bonds, arguing they were a safe saving method for the less affluent; the least inflationary way to finance the government; and a way of encouraging Americans to take ownership of their government. It was a high-minded debate until the question-and-answer period. That's when Gould, who had already noted Porter's attractiveness to listeners, said: "Miss Porter, your speech is what I call the emotional, not the factual, approach. Maybe if your slip were showing, I shouldn't call it to your attention, but if the roof of your new house were on fire, I would be dishonest if I didn't ring your doorbell. Do you get what I mean?" Porter replied: "Yes, I get what you mean, Mr. Gould. And I might say that if I were taking the emotional approach, which I'm not, I would have said, 'How many people ever jumped out of a window because they held United States Government Bonds?' That would be an emotional approach." She continued: "I think the most practical approach you can take is this. You spoke about the savings banks and their $3 million and their $6 million, and so forth. Well, I'm talking about the guy with $25."[50]

Porter responded to milder, though still gendered, treatment when she debated the president of the Executives' Club of Chicago on a radio program called *Wake Up America*. The debate—over the government's assumption of debt—was intense for the first twenty-five minutes. Then her opponent, the economist Alfred Haake, said: "Ladies and gentlemen of the radio audience, I wonder if you know the girl with whom I'm debating, I wonder if you know what she looks like." Recalling the episode in a speech to the Executives' Club, Porter insisted she had lost the debate not because she was angry but because she was flattered. "I just melted. I couldn't answer and for the next twenty-five minutes Dr. Haake won, hands down."[51] Porter faced a classic double bind while she built her career as a financial expert. She had to convince both colleagues and readers that although her authority was as valid as a man's, she was not trying to overturn society. Historian Nancy Cott described this dilemma elegantly, writing that after women had obtained the right to vote, "feminism constantly had to shadowbox with two opposing yet coexistent caricatures: the one, that feminism tried to make women over into men, the other, that feminism set women against men in deadly sex antagonism."[52]

Historians who study journalistic portrayals of women sometimes work from the perspective that gendered constructions have been imposed on women by a sexist media industry, with little to no input from the women themselves. However, there can be no question that Porter was an active participant in media constructions of her. She encouraged categorizations that suited journalists' need for established narratives because those images furthered her career, a tactic used by other public women. Historian Daniel Horowitz argued that feminist icon Betty Friedan adopted the persona of a frustrated suburban housewife to publicize *The Feminine Mystique* in 1963 because she knew the narrative would sell books and draw attention to her message.[53] This type of image manipulation drew on midcentury gender ideology to serve the interests of individual women. While it is true the normative ideals Porter invoked had originated in an oppressive culture that subjugated women as a group, Porter was not cannon fodder on the midcentury battlefield of gender; she was a savvy and aggressive warrior with an arsenal that included extensive knowledge of gender ideology.

Journalists' over-the-top characterizations of Porter's femininity would not have happened without her encouragement. After all, it was Porter who told Olga Curtis that she was really no stock expert at all and that she deferred to her husband at home. The world was his domain, Porter said; he was the one who kept tabs on public affairs and foreign policy while she tended to their personal life.[54] Likewise, Porter told Judy McCluskey of the *Providence Sunday Journal* that she wouldn't dream of doing her own taxes; and she told Katherine Hill of the *Louisville Courier-Journal* that she had just as much trouble balancing her checkbook as other women.[55] In 1958, *Time* magazine wrote that Porter "bustles through the messy, male-contrived world of finance like a housewife cleaning her husband's den—tidying trends, sorting statistics, and issuing no-nonsense judgments as wholesome and tart as mince pie."[56] At first glance, it might appear as if the male writers at *Time* could not resist dressing Porter in an apron even as they praised her brilliance as an economics writer—except that Porter frequently referred to *herself* as a housewife in her newspaper column and speeches. Speaking to a group of car dealers in 1954, for example, Porter said her financial perspective developed from her experiences as an "individual citizen and wage earner, a consumer, and a housewife."[57] To businessmen at the Executives' Club, she presented herself as little more than an intelligent wife who made astute observations to help her husband advance in his career. She was not part of the action, she assured them, and she was no expert. She was just "sitting on the sidelines and watching the wheels go round, while you are out making those wheels go round. . . . No, I would scarcely call myself an economist."[58] Porter cultivated a self-deprecating image that neutralized the electric charge of her gender. On a trip to an international financial conference in San Francisco, she had been approached by the viscountess Nancy Astor, who asked her: "Why do you make fools out of men? Why don't you try making men out of fools?" Porter recalled saying: "Lady Astor, all I'm trying to do is make something."[59]

Feminist in the Fifties

Postwar American culture is often characterized as deeply conservative and best embodied by television shows such as *Leave It to Beaver* or *The Donna Reed Show*, and Porter's media portrayals and self-presentation lend ammunition to feminist critiques of that era. Historian Elaine Tyler May has argued that the focus on traditional values after the war was fueled by the American foreign policy of containment. In May's analysis, foreign policy was aimed not only outside the nation's borders but also within them, reaching into homes to enlist husbands, children, and especially wives in the fight against communism. May analyzed surveys of white middle-class married couples during the 1950s and found that many of them had blamed Depression-era dysfunction as the source of the emasculation of men unable to find work and the fortitude of strong-willed women forced to provide for their families. Determined not to repeat that pattern, they expressed a total belief in the sanctity of the home and in traditional roles for men and women.[60]

Other historians have argued that gender roles after World War II were not fixed, but contested. "To state the obvious, many women were not white, middle-class, married and suburban; and many white, middle-class, married, suburban women were neither wholly domestic nor quiescent," historian Joanne Meyerowitz wrote.[61] Nancy Walker, in her book about women's magazines, argued that even the white middle-class domestic sphere of the forties and fifties was not prescribed and constricted but expanded and debated as part of a social restructuring that had been taking place since World War I.[62] Like May, Walker believed the American home had been drafted in the country's fight against fascism and communism. The home was rhetorically tied to democracy, and democracy was tied to capitalism; homemakers were encouraged in their role as consumers to validate and promote the American way of life. However, where May viewed this enlistment as constricting for women, Walker viewed it as expansive. The home extended outward, and the domestic sphere was given more prominence in the culture. Portrayals of women in the popular media often rendered their work away from the home invisible, however, choosing instead to emphasize their role as household spenders.[63]

While some journalists ignored the revolution occurring in many women's lives, not all of them did. Anyone reading Porter's column, for example, knew that white middle-class married women were rushing headlong into the paid workforce in the forties and fifties. Between 1940 and 1960, the number of women in the workforce doubled, and most of the growth came from educated women in middle-class families. By 1960, women's employment was increasing four times faster than men's, and the number of mothers working outside the home had jumped 400 percent since 1940.[64] In a speech to women journalism students in 1959, Porter actually expressed fatigue with *excessive* media coverage of working women, saying, "Women combining careers and marriage is no longer news."[65] She thought it asinine that women with successful careers were considered unusual, whether they were married or not. In another speech, she said women working on Wall Street had not been news since nineteenth-century financier Hetty Green roamed the district. "Actually," she said, "finance is a woman's field."[66]

The change in women's employment patterns of the 1950s drew sharp media attention to the issue, leading to a debate over the proper roles for women. However, the debate was not one-sided, as some feminists and historians have suggested. According to historian Susan Hartmann: "What scholars have tended to overlook is the public reconsideration of women's status and the support for women's employment expressed by leading decision makers and opinion shapers. In an era dominated by the celebration of domesticity and women's traditional roles, experts and opinion leaders not only recognized and approved of women's increasing employment but also sought to adjust public opinion and public policy to accommodate women's greater participation in the public sphere."[67]

Media historian Susan Douglas noted that it has been convenient to think of the stretch between World War II and the modern women's movement as a sort of Dark Ages for women. "Because the contrast between the Rosie the Riveter campaign and the virulent antifeminism that followed it was so stark, it is easy to paint a black-and-white, before-and-after portrait of this period. It is common to think of the post-war backlash as beginning with a vengeance in 1946 and reigning in a monolithic and uncontested form until the late 1960s. But this is not the case."[68] Instead, the period between World War II and the second-wave feminist movement witnessed the continuation of complex gender negotiations rooted in the labor crisis of the Depression and the national emergency provoked by the attack on Pearl Harbor. When Betty Freidan wrote about "the problem that has no name" in 1963, she was joining a public discourse that had been going on for years.[69]

Porter spoke and wrote passionately about women and work during the fifties, recognizing that the influx of white married middle-class women into the paid workforce was the economic story of a generation. A staunch individualist, Porter believed in freedom of opportunity for women and equal pay for equal work. She wrote about balancing work and family and advocated a tax deduction for child care to help dual-income homes. In 1950, she wrote a piece called "Woman's Place?—'In a Job,'" and told one of her agents: "Carl, maybe I'm cockeyed—but I think this is a very important subject and piece." She reiterated: "The working woman, Carl, is becoming an increasing social, economic and political force. If you want to see a couple of examples of it, look into your own home and then take a look at me, too."[70] She frequently pointed out that women controlled 70 percent of the nation's wealth and deserved respect from bank lenders and company executives. She pushed magazine editors to publish progressive articles on public policy. In 1952, she wrote to an editor of *This Week* magazine: "I also wondered whether or not we might not put in a paragraph or two covering specific 'reform' proposals. For instance, one of the bees in my bonnet is that it's rank discrimination for a working wife not to be able to take a deduction for the maid or nurse she must have to take care of the children in her home while she is away earning a living (on which she must pay taxes). Bills for this have been introduced and undoubtedly a law of this sort eventually will be passed. Why shouldn't THIS WEEK take some credit for emphasizing it?"[71]

Porter's pitch to *This Week* revealed her identification with elite, professional women rather than working-class women. She passionately believed in a woman's right to be brilliant but made no allowance for mediocrity—an important distinction because such an ideology privileged exceptional women rather than women as a group. Porter believed women who chose to enter male-dominated occupations should prepare themselves for criticism and offset it by turning in work that was above reproach. Unless a professional woman could prove herself above average, Porter told an interviewer, "there's no reason for being in a man's job."[72] In her speech to women journalism students, Porter claimed specialization would be their key to success. She urged them to identify a niche and become the best journalist within it. If a woman could not be the best at what she did, Porter told the students, she should not do it at all.

In all of her speeches about employed women, Porter emphatically asserted their emergence as the biggest economic story of her time. "The fact is that in my generation alone, a complete revolution has taken place and the married woman now dominates the working force," Porter told graduates of the Tobe-Coburn School.[73] Countering the domestic discourse of the period, she warned them, "If you are under the illusion that marriage and children will settle everything for you and you will live happily ever after in the twentieth-century equivalent of the rose-covered cottage, you're wrong."[74] Porter also spoke about discrimination and what she viewed as unfair laws and unequal pay. Eighteen million women worked outside the home in 1949, she said, but they held inferior positions and were paid about 60 percent of what men were paid for the same work.[75] Much of the blame fell on women for not exerting their clout, she said, noting they owned 74 percent of suburban homes, 65 percent of savings accounts, and two-thirds of savings bonds. Furthermore, they were in charge of most household spending, she said.[76] Women could demand economic change if they called buying strikes, refused to put their money in banks that did not cater to them, and asserted their rights as shareholders. "We may sound as though we own the world, but it's a paper world and a paper moon. For while the brain has no sex, men think it has and we let them. . . . Until we show we want to be capitalistic in more than name only, America's financial matriarchy, with its potential power, will exist just in the statistics," she said in her speech "The Brain Has No Sex."[77]

Porter repeated her claims about women's financial leverage in her newspaper columns, delivering her egalitarian message to a broad audience. She insisted after World War II that money was as feminine as it was masculine—perhaps even more so. Women's labor outside the home was driving the economic growth of the era, she wrote, and women controlled most domestic spending. "Why are we so quiet about it?" she wondered, noting that women owned the majority of the nation's wealth, savings, and blue-chip stocks. Advertisers had long identified women as the primary decision-makers when it came to consumer spending; why shouldn't they flex their capitalistic muscles as investors, also?[78] Porter wanted women to make their economic power known, but that would mean battling decades of discrimination.

In 1949 Porter castigated the New York Financial Writers Association for its blatant sexism. The group had excluded her when it was founded eleven years prior, and it still would not allow the president of the Federation of Women Shareholders to attend a dinner at which the poor woman was to be lampooned in a skit. In the same column, Porter took note of men's displeasure that the Chamber of Commerce for the State of New York had allowed women to attend a different dinner, one at which British economist Barbara Ward was speaking. "How silly! As though there aren't many women in business today who are far more important and powerful than most of the Chamber's members," she taunted them. She concluded it was high time for men to see businesswomen as people.[79]

Porter was an emphatic and eager participant in the postwar discourse about women's proper roles. During the fifties, as postwar economic advances took root and the nation's middle class grew, Porter shined a spotlight on wives who worked outside the home. There were 8.7 million married women in the workforce in 1950 versus 5.7 million single women, she reported.[80] Recalling the prediction that married women would dash back home after World War II, she noted "there actually are a million more husband-and-wife working teams today than in 1947."[81] Before the war, 14.5 percent of wives worked outside the home; by 1950, that had risen to 22.5 percent. She hailed the development as historic but predictable, a split characterization echoed in her references to her own working status: "I am typical. I am a symbol," she wrote.[82] This dichotomy reflected Porter's self-conception as both the same as and different from other women. It was true that millions of women were, like Porter, working outside the home, but it was equally true that very few of those women would achieve the status of a cultural icon. Porter was an active participant in the intersecting postwar discourses related to gender and finance while simultaneously functioning as an object of those discourses.

The stress of managing multiple strands of a public career weighed on Porter's personal life. In 1949 she and Collins adopted a baby girl, Cris Sarah Collins, from an adoption counselor in Kentucky who later would be accused of placing babies without the legal consent of their birth mothers. As Porter achieved greater success, she alluded to personal conflicts between her and her daughter, who might have found Porter's public image as a down-to-earth, supportive counselor to the masses incongruous with her personal tendencies toward self-involvement and insensitivity. However, Porter related to her readers through her roles as a wife and mother.

Citing her own difficulties juggling a career and a household, she predicted a growing market for easy-to-prepare meals, nannies, housekeepers, and household appliances. Porter ridiculed arguments that women were not important to the nation's economy and should confine themselves to raising children, keeping their homes clean, and pampering their husbands. As the nation went to war again in Korea, she said, women's labor would be needed as the male workforce was depleted. Furthermore, women's work was helping drive the economic expansion that was raising the standard of living for the middle class. Because of that, she argued, women should be forgiven for not meeting unrealistic gender expectations. She mocked a report on the "ideal corporate wife," which instructed women to advance their husbands' careers by keeping the home relaxing and calm, burying any qualms they might have about relocating, resisting the temptation to gossip or drink excessively, and keeping up with their husbands' intellect. "Well, there she is—an angelic person indeed. (Revoltingly so, if I may be permitted a biased judgment.) Also seriously . . . I flunked."[83]

Porter clearly took issue with media coverage of gender roles, accusing male journalists of trying to stuff the genie back into the bottle when it came to women's economic power. Male pundits were simply ignoring the facts about women's ownership of wealth, she said. Instead, they were trying to delude the country into believing the myth of the dependent housewife, too frightened to go shopping unless she had her husband's permission. "So they're huffing and they're puffing and they're trying to blow us down," she wrote.[84] Ever the economist, Porter was emphatically a realist. She was less interested in what should be the reality than in what was the reality. By the end of the fifties, she implored her readers to stipulate women's work outside the home as a fact no longer worthy of debate. Whatever one's personal opinion, the social and economic revolution of women's paid work would reverberate for years to come, and she thought it better to deal with the issues that resulted than continue to pitch battles over old prejudices. A hysterical movement to force women back into their kitchens would not change the economic realities that were driving the demand for more American workers and stoking women's desire to earn an income. Women earned a third of bachelor's degrees in 1958, and 81 percent of them would be employed within six months, she predicted. "Please understand my bias in favor of the graduate of 1958," she wrote. "You see, ever since I was a girl graduate myself, I've been trying to make possible what is happening to them today."[85] Porter also railed against pay discrimination. Milk cost one worker as much as the other, but men's and women's wages were not the same even though equal-pay legislation had been introduced in every Congress since 1945.[86] Male secretaries in New York City made $83 a week to female secretaries' $71.50 in 1953, she reported.[87] She also called for child-care expenses to be tax-deductible, treated like any other business expense.

Porter's assertion of the rights of professional women to a large, middle-class audience during the fifties shows the decade was neither as simplistic nor as uniformly conservative as scholars and cultural critics have portrayed it. Porter's column was syndicated in 1949 and, according to news accounts, was published in 171 daily newspapers by 1957. Within four years, her distribution had nearly doubled to 333 newspapers. Clearly, Porter's outspoken support of professional women did not poison her popularity with more conventional readers, probably because she mitigated her message of female empowerment with a public image that conformed to prevailing gender norms—telling interviewers she deferred to her husband at home, calling herself a housewife, and insisting she was just as feminine as women who did not have high-powered careers. By marketing herself in a way that did not offend more conservative audiences, Porter was able to assert women's rights without generating hostility. From this carefully constructed platform, she argued vehemently and consistently that women should have the same rights as men in business, finance, and the workplace.

Despite her entreaties to women to act collectively as consumers and investors, Porter practiced an androgynous feminism that was more rooted in the ideals of individual freedom than in the power of sisterhood. Historian Susan Ware, in her biography of radio host Mary Margaret McBride, described a "three-sex theory," which she wrote was common among women with successful careers in the early 1940s.[88] Professional women often presented themselves as a special case so as not to offend the more traditional members of society who believed women should marry, have children, and keep house. Such a strategy, whether it was conscious or not, "deflected society's attention away from the thorny issue of what would actually happen if vast numbers of women did indeed follow such paths. Accordingly, the choices made by exceptional women did not necessarily appear as an outright assault on traditional gender roles."[89]

Porter did not present herself as doing anything other women could not, or should not, do—and she encouraged those who tried—but she carried the feminist banner carefully. While she was a member of the New York Newspaper Women's Club and spoke to women's groups frequently, she was not an active link in feminist networks.[90] And she could be tough on her gender. Writing about the mobilization of the civilian workforce before the Korean War, Porter pleaded with women not to make the mistakes they had made as workers during World War II. She quoted anonymous male bosses who said that during that war, women frequently had been late or absent and had dragged down morale. While acknowledging the shortcomings of management and a general lack of support, she urged women to do better the next time they were called into service. "But you too, Tillie and Rosie, must think and prepare. For you're coming back. There's no question about it."[91]

Porter's writing for women's magazines was more traditionally gendered than her writing for newspapers, reflecting the judgment of mid-century women's publications that housewives needed practical advice that would harmonize the home, not revolutionize it. "Whereas in earlier decades the magazines had tended to emphasize individual choice and aspiration, by the 1940s the focus had shifted to a sense of collectivity and common purpose," Nancy Walker wrote of this period.[92] Porter wrote articles for women's magazines during World War II that addressed what would happen if their readers' husbands died in combat and instructed these women how to borrow money, buy savings bonds, and otherwise protect themselves and their homes. The visual presentation of these articles was striking; many were accompanied by illustrations of women who looked worried and overwhelmed by bills. Contrary to Porter's insistence in other forums that women were capable of making sound investment decisions and should seize ownership of their finances, she took a more condescending approach when she wrote for female-centric publications.

Porter's advice in postwar women's magazines reinforced male dominance and competence on financial matters. She advised readers in *Good
Housekeeping* that a life insurance policy would best protect them if their
husbands died "because it protects you from making a fatal financial mistake and from worrying about investing money."[93] In the same article, she
told women to "write down the names of one or two men to whom your
husband would wish you to turn for advice and financial counsel if he
wasn't there."[94] In side-by-side columns after the war expressing different viewpoints on what women should do with their money—save it or
spend it—Porter naturally came down on the side of saving, after chiding
wives and daughters for not holding on to their inheritances. (The other
writer, Louise Paine Benjamin, said, "no one ever got rich just from saving" and urged women to spend their money to become more interesting
people.)[95] In *Redbook*, Porter told young wives that even if they worked
outside the home, their household bills should be gendered: wives should
pay for household expenses, groceries, and entertaining at home. Husbands should pay for the home mortgage, the car, and eating at a restaurant. "The reason I say this is that certain expenditures seem masculine
and certain expenditures seem feminine. I cannot see myself picking up
a check when we're at a restaurant and saying, 'Well, that's out of the
household budget,'" Porter said.[96] Finally, despite her staunch support of
working women in her newspaper column, she told readers of *Redbook* to
"think of yours as a supplementary income because, happily enough, it
will disappear at childbirth time."[97] At the same time that Porter was writing about the national debt, international finance, and the business cycle
for mixed-gender audiences, her writing for women's magazines reflected
and upheld conventional gender norms.

Porter approached newspapers and general-interest magazines such
as *Life* and the *Saturday Evening Post* with more unconventional articles
about women's issues, but she was not always successful in getting her
work published. Based on her own difficulty in finding a good housekeeper, Porter wrote a passionate article in 1950 about the need for agencies that would hire and train domestic workers and send them to homes
once or twice a week. Titled "What 18,000,000 Women Want"—an apparent allusion to Rheta Childe Dorr's pro-suffrage book *What Eight Million*

Women Want, published forty years earlier—Porter's article anticipated the proliferation of cleaning services such as Merry Maids years in advance.[98] But despite several years of trying, she simply could not get the article published. "Boy, what a controversial subject this is turning out to be!" she wrote to an editor at *Look* magazine, which eventually bought the article but did not publish it. "I shudder at the thought that after my long, long years' serious endeavors in the sphere of economics, I may go down in the obits as 'the girl who tried to industrialize the American home.' Horrors!"[99] She asked her agency if they could get the article back: "Really, I do think that piece deserves the light of day."[100] She asked again three years later. Finally, Carl Brandt gently responded that mass-circulation magazines were reluctant to publish the article because the vast majority of households had no help and never would.[101] He suggested she write an article on equal pay instead—which he thought editors would find less controversial than the idea of a woman not cleaning her own home.

Porter failed to recognize her own lifestyle as elite and unattainable for most women, a blind spot she would have most of her career. About the article on household help, she replied to Carl: "I think the central idea is important and new, and inasmuch as I am now struggling with the servant problem in Pound Ridge—and getting god-damn nowhere fast, I feel the piece would have an even wider appeal than when I originally wrote it."[102] In 1950, Porter and Collins bought a thirty-two-acre estate at Pound Ridge in Westchester County, New York, where they swam, hunted, and socialized on the weekends. Their daughter would come to prefer it to the Fifth Avenue apartment they maintained in Manhattan. Porter called Pound Ridge the best investment she ever made; she and Collins had bought the property for $200 an acre, and she watched it appreciate to about $187,500 an acre for a total value of $6 million. However, as a child of the Depression, Porter never viewed her wealth as entirely secure.

Macroeconomics for the Middle Class

Porter's financial wariness was shared by millions of others in her generation who would be haunted by the horror of the thirties even during the heyday of the fifties. The postwar period was a pivotal moment in America's economic history. The country had shifted from an industrial to a consumer economy, making business investment relatively less important than consumer spending as an indicator of economic health.[103] Incomes were more equitably distributed, expanding the swath of workers who were considered neither rich nor poor.[104] In 1929, the top 5 percent of earners received 35 percent of the income; in 1951, the top 5 percent received 18 percent of the income. The middle class had risen from 31 percent of the population before the Depression to almost 60 percent by the mid-fifties, adjusted for inflation. More companies offered investment plans, drawing middle-class workers into the stock market. Mutual funds redeemed themselves after the checkered history of investment trusts as a way for small investors to leverage their assets while minimizing their risk. The United States began importing more finished goods than raw materials, reflecting the rising cost of labor at home compared with that of other countries, thus charting a course toward an economy based on the service sector rather than manufacturing.[105] Meanwhile, the postwar baby boom launched entire industries that catered to teenagers and their needs (as prescribed by advertisers) and cultivated a mass culture driven by television, fast food, box stores, and interstate highways.[106]

Amid such pronounced and possibly destabilizing growth, Porter believed economic vicissitudes should be moderated. She advocated the use of voluntary corporate measures and collective consumer action before resorting to government regulation. She also outlined a "charter of economic rights" on the premise that U.S. businesses and government officials could have avoided or at least mitigated the Depression that followed the market crash of 1929. As part of this economic bill of rights, she argued that people had a right to plan for steady economic growth, a right to "challenge all those at any level who would tell any of us that 'all is well, don't you think about it, Papa knows best,'" a right to protect small businesses, and a right to demand higher standards of living around the world.[107]

In 1951 Porter gave the commencement address at Hunter College, her alma mater. She told graduates the United States was fighting a war on two fronts: against communism abroad and against the high cost of living at home. Since World War II, Porter had been rallying the nation against inflation—a new worry for Americans because of the consumer-driven economy, war mobilization, and postwar boom. Porter not only thought rising prices hurt individual consumers but also viewed inflation as the largest threat facing capitalism and American democracy. She linked the fight against rising prices to the fight against communism. "A master plan of Stalin is to so weaken the American nation through successive inflations and deflations that it will be an easy plum, a cinch for the picking at the Politburo's will," she told the Hunter graduates. "A basic tenet of Russian communism today is that the democracies will destroy themselves and their way of life through their own economic weaknesses and stupidities."[108]

Porter thought that Americans had a personal responsibility to educate themselves about the economy, and she passionately believed economic literacy was a requirement of self-government. "Economics is the most neglected field in journalism, and my main contention is that this is terribly dangerous," she warned.[109] If the U.S. economy was not managed properly, she said, its booms and busts would shake the foundations of capitalism and undermine the democratic system of government. After World War II, she wondered why it was that "so great a nation as ours seems determined to push itself into an economic mess" and called on all Americans to stop the dangerous creep of higher prices.[110] Because of that fear, she began a tradition of reporting the cost of the same food items from year to year to demonstrate the effect of inflation. She also called on consumers to initiate buying strikes and other actions to show they would not accept higher prices. Given the natural tension between supply and demand, she believed in the power of consumers to offset economic forces beyond their control.[111] Individuals could serve their own interests by taking steps to control inflation, but such actions were also necessary for the collective good.

Anti-inflation measures also appealed to Porter's sense of fairness. Lower prices could be enjoyed by everyone, unlike tax breaks for the rich or wage increases for union workers. For example, Porter was furious about the automobile industry's frothy overproduction in 1955, when dealers were stuck with cars they could not sell and manufacturers laid off workers because they had miscalculated the market. Her anger even led her to write to Treasury Secretary George Humphrey, questioning why the administration had not asked the leaders of the car industry to steady their production rather than swing wildly between working employees round the clock and laying them off. "Does not giant industry, when it is so powerful, have a responsibility to help even out the ups and downs even though it means a little less profit one year in order to make just as much profit the next year?" She wrote. "Can the ruthless competition between General Motors and Ford in 1955 . . . be justified on economic grounds? It seems such a darn shame."[112] Humphrey replied with more than a little condescension, rebuking Porter for her idealistic vision. "It seems that our economy cannot grow on a nice, even basis in just the right amount each month or year," he wrote. "If everything was always nice and even . . . the thing that has made this country great would be lost," he wrote.[113] Not one to be disregarded, Porter fired back that she was not asking for Utopia: "I was just wistfully envisioning a real world in which things would be more even than in my entire adult experience."[114]

Porter carried her anti-inflation diatribes and big-picture economic analysis into her newspaper column. She had clearly identified her audience and wrote for the largest market force in the country, using a folksy writing style that made it clear whose side she was on. Her readers were "Mr. and Mrs. America," "you, the small businessman," or "we, the consumers." She began her practice of translating economic "bafflegab" and sounding the alarm when politicians or financial officials were being disingenuous. She offered average Americans a look inside the control hub of the buzzing economy and showed how movements in the international markets affected their household finances. A typical column began: "Would you like to know what the stock market is going to do? . . . Come along with me—while we visit the 'insiders.'"[115] She piqued readers' interest in economics and finance with vivid, creative writing that showed how individuals were directly affected by larger issues.

Porter explained her approach by invoking classic Cold War rhetoric, which took the fight against communism directly into the American home. The success of U.S. foreign policy rested on the shoulders of American consumers, she wrote.[116] It would not be enough to assist other nations through efforts such as the Marshall Plan; Americans would have to demonstrate the superiority of capitalism if they were to beat back communist expansion. After the communist takeover of Czechoslovakia in 1948, Porter became even more strident, insisting her fellow citizens "understand—thoroughly—the unbreakable relationship between the future economic stability of America and the future political peace of the whole world."[117] In speeches, she told her audiences there had been an economic cause behind every war and social change in history.[118] She presented a convincing argument that global stability required an educated populace and a vigorous financial press that looked out for the interests of the middle class.

Following those principles earned Porter a powerful enemy in 1955: popular radio commentator Walter Winchell, who was incensed when she wrote about allegations that insiders were profiting from stocks he mentioned during his broadcasts. On Monday, January 10, a particular stock, Pantepec Oil Co., opened 31 percent higher after Winchell had touted it during his radio program the day before.[119] It turned out a large number of people had bought 1,000 to 2,000 shares the previous Thursday and Friday and sold them after the price jumped Monday, indicating they may have known Winchell was going to promote the stock. The *New York Times* reported that 357,600 shares of the stock were traded on Monday, the largest volume for a single stock recorded on an American market.[120] By March 3, the stock's price had fallen about 20 percent. The activity in the stock before and after Winchell's broadcast attracted the attention of the U.S. Senate and the Securities and Exchange Commission, which launched separate investigations but took no action other than to ask Winchell to stop touting stocks. Porter examined other stocks that Winchell had mentioned on the air and arrived at an inconclusive result: some were up and others were down. She even wrote in her column: "Winchell is not alone in this. He's just the most sensational and best-known performer."[121] Despite her evenhanded coverage, Porter later told an interviewer, "Winchell never forgave me for writing about that. We had a sharp exchange of words about it one time. . . . I was outraged by what he was doing on the air, and I felt that people ought to be told about the situation."[122]

Porter's allegiance was clearly with the little guy: the American householder and small business owner. She criticized tax policies that benefited the wealthy at the expense of those less fortunate, and she was not persuaded by the argument that tax breaks for large corporations provided incentives for business investment. "I don't want to carp. But what about the incentive of the little man? I mean, the incentive to eat?" she wrote.[123] In 1947, she slammed the findings of the Committee on Postwar Tax Reduction, which she accused of ignoring the needs of middle-class Americans as it served up recommendations that would help the rich. Elite policymakers should educate themselves on the finances of average American families, many of whom had to plan their spending carefully just to afford bread and milk, she wrote.[124] Porter also believed the professional class was getting squeezed between capital and labor. This was dangerous, she said, because the educated, professional middle class provided the nation's political leaders and embodied America's idealistic promise of class mobility and self-betterment. "As we belittle and neglect this class, we belittle and neglect America itself."[125]

Porter believed in government protections for individuals and small businesses—but she also thought people had a duty to protect themselves. On February 16, 1951, Porter used the term "personal finance" for the first time in her newspaper column, urging every high school and college to offer a course on the fundamentals of household finance.[126] Based on lessons from the Depression as well as the war, the concept of personal finance rested on the assumption that it was both necessary and possible for individuals to make smart decisions with their money. As the American middle class exploded after the war, so did authoritative advice stressing financial responsibility, generally defined as a family's preparedness for economic contingencies. Americans were encouraged to think about the future—not the present, or even the past—as they modified their financial habits.

During the fifties, as the economy boomed and the GI Bill drove up homeownership, Porter gained an appreciation for the relevance of household management. She arrived at a "how to" formula for personal finance that mattered to average people. Thus, in addition to explaining the intricacies of the trade balance, she told her readers how to save, how to buy life insurance, how to buy a house (and why they should have flood insurance), when to get clothes on sale, and how to pay for college. However, she would say later that personal finance was not the same field as consumerism because she was telling people what they could do to survive financially rather than coaching them on how to spend their money.[127] She continued to write about public policy, especially the tax and budget proposals of each presidential administration, and she blew the whistle on anything she considered unjust or unsound: inequities in the law, industries that preyed on consumers, "planned obsolescence" in home appliances, and wasteful government spending. But Porter's gaze also included individual Americans and how they could take control of their financial circumstances. She later explained this two-pronged approach to an interviewer: "If I can get the readers on Monday by telling them how to save twenty percent on clothes, the chances are they'll still be with me on Wednesday when I tackle the dollar."[128]

Porter's personable approach drove her circulation higher as readers heeded her calls to action. Directors of U.S. savings bond divisions reported that sales skyrocketed whenever Porter promoted the bonds in her column.[129] According to *Editor & Publisher*, when Porter once offered to mail a free unit-price chart to anybody who wrote for one, she received more than 100,000 responses from readers who wanted help calculating the cost of their groceries.[130] Another time, after Porter had visited Louisville, Kentucky, and wrote several articles criticizing the city for developing its suburbs at the expense of its downtown, city officials took out large advertisements in the *New York Times* and the *Wall Street Journal* to counter the negative publicity by promoting their rejuvenation efforts. Their ads began, "Hi-Ho, Sylvia! (Miss Sylvia Porter, That Is)," and invited Porter to return as the guest of a new commission looking for "some expert planning brains" to save their city.[131]

From a journalistic standpoint, the years 1947–1960 were the apex of Porter's career, even though she had not yet published a bestseller, she had not yet enjoyed her celebrity status of the sixties and seventies, and her sources in the administration were still at the Treasury rather than in the White House. In short, Porter did not yet have cultural power. She did, however, have cultural authority. She received complimentary letters from Treasury secretaries and renowned economists, who appreciated her ability to communicate their ideas to the public.[132] She received four annual awards from the New York Newspaper Women's Club between 1945 and 1951, at which point the Boston Chamber of Commerce named her one of twenty-five outstanding women in America. She even had the honor of seeing a racehorse named "Sylvia Porter," which demonstrated her populist appeal. Porter's work and voice were authentically hers, and she delivered a unique economic perspective to tens of millions of newspaper readers five days a week. She maintained a significant presence on radio and television programs. She supported rights for professional women, battled inflation, and spread economic literacy. She explained the wide world of economics to average Americans, empowering them to make better decisions with their votes and money. Porter's message was still more important than her name, but that was about to change. On November 28, 1960, *Time* magazine put Sylvia Porter on its cover.

3

Expert with an Empire

THE ILLUSTRATION ON THE COVER of *Time* magazine's November 28, 1960, issue portrayed a young-looking Porter as she might have appeared in the 1930s: hair upswept, wearing a beret and an art deco necklace, in front of a vague cityscape resembling Park Row in Manhattan. But while the *Time* cover might have appeared to celebrate the early years of Porter's career, it actually marked a new beginning as Porter evolved from an authoritative financial journalist to a national celebrity and the head of an editorial team that published content under her name. From 1960 to 1975, Porter relied on a team of assistants who wrote her syndicated newspaper column; a question-and-answer column in *Ladies' Home Journal*; an annual series of tax books; her newsletter, *Reporting on Governments*; and occasional magazine articles. Porter also began writing an annual economics overview for the *World Book* encyclopedias and continued her numerous television and radio appearances. She also published a personal finance book, *How to Get More for Your Money*, in 1961. This period in Porter's career culminated in the publication of the compendious *Sylvia Porter's Money Book*, a collaborative effort by Porter and numerous other writers. The book was an immediate bestseller, reaching the market just as the public's interest in personal finance exploded. By leveraging her hard-earned reputation, exploiting the labor of others, and participating in government endeavors, Porter propelled herself from a recognized expert to a marketable brand.

As the 1960s opened, *Time* used its punchy, idiosyncratic writing style to express awe toward Porter, who embodied the kind of individual achievement the magazine's editors loved to trumpet.[1] She was—and still is, more than fifty years later—the only financial journalist ever to appear on the newsweekly's cover. Titled "Sylvia & You," *Time*'s revealing profile took note of Porter's personal writing style, her commitment to explaining economics to average readers, and her impressive influence.[2] The article reported that 16,000 readers had recently written to the New York Stock Exchange asking for pamphlets on investing after Porter had advised them to do so. It also claimed her newspaper column was published in every state except New Hampshire and Alaska, an expansive network of distribution that contributed to her estimated annual income of more than $250,000. Casting her as a force of nature, the magazine published photographs that showed Porter speaking to the Detroit Economic Club and said the men in attendance were "well aware that more car buyers, more stock market investors and more plain everyday consumers listen to Sylvia Porter than to any other economics writer."[3] After the article was published, Porter's column gained thirty-four subscribing newspapers, including one in New Hampshire, which made Alaska the only state in which she did not have a presence by 1961.[4]

Time portrayed Porter's success partly as a reflection of the increasing interest in business and finance. Decades before, she had entered the changing field of journalism with the expertise to meet a need nobody had quite realized was there.[5] Americans' demand for understandable writing about economics had been driven by the expansion of the middle class after World War II, by which time Porter was in a position to capitalize on it. However, the article also credited Porter's unique wisdom and unapologetic talent for self-promotion. To get the *Dallas Times Herald* to publish her column, for example, Porter had torn a dollar bill in half and given one half to the editor, promising to give him the other half if his newspaper subscribed to her column.

One of Porter's most celebrated lines came from this 1960 interview in *Time*: "One of the soundest rules I try to remember when making forecasts in the field of economics . . . is that whatever is to happen is happening already."[6] This sort of sound bite, a hallmark of Porter's simplified approach, did not necessarily earn the approval of Wall Street insiders, one of whom described her writing as "economics by the eyedropper." According to *Time*, insiders preferred the columns of Joseph Livingston of the *Philadelphia Evening Bulletin*, who was more sophisticated and respected.[7] (Livingston's column ran in 87 newspapers at the time, compared with Porter's 331.) Quite rightly, the article painted Porter as the people's economist, one who commanded the attention, if not the readership, of the financial elite. Even critics of Porter's writing admitted following her opinions because she had a sharp eye for economic trends.[8]

Time also captured the darker facets of Porter's personality, which were rarely revealed in journalists' profiles of her. The piece made reference to her chain smoking, excessive drinking, and difficulties in personal relationships:

> Existing in a chronic state of tension, she smokes Kent cigarettes, one after another, gulps Scotch raw in man-sized quantities, pursues an elusive slumber with sleeping pills or murder mysteries. . . . The apartment maid has been fired so many times that it has become a ritual. Even the Collinses' daughter, Cris, has learned to be wary during "Mama's thinking moments"—the oppressive periods when Sylvia is having difficulty with a story. "I think that's a ridiculous present," snapped Sylvia last week, on the occasion of her daughter's eleventh birthday, when Cris proudly exhibited a life-sized doll, the gift of a friend. "You've never wanted dolls before, and you're too old for dolls." At this uncharitable observation, Cris was on the threshold of tears—where she was shortly joined by her mother.[9]

Paradoxically, the magazine painted Porter in colors that were both more masculine and more feminine than those she used to portray herself. The portrayal of her as something of a mad genius contrasted with the empathetic, maternal image she projected to the public. At the same time, the rare glimpse of Porter's emotional temperament undercut the insistent rationality she expressed in her economic analysis. The accuracy of the account was a testament to the rigor of the magazine's army of female fact-checkers and to the commitment to originality that drove the newsweeklies at the middle of the century. Porter welcomed the article despite its less-than-flattering depiction of some of her mannerisms, and its impact extended beyond the expected to the serendipitous. (The primary researcher who had fact-checked the article, Mary Elizabeth Friend, introduced Porter to Lydia Ratcliff, another *Time* researcher, who would become Porter's longest-serving assistant.) Of the hundreds of articles written about Porter over the years, *Time* offered the truest, most balanced account of her nature as a public and private figure.

Fights with the Flagship

Porter's volatility was legendary, especially among executives of the *New York Post*, where Porter kept an office for twenty years after becoming syndicated. Porter left the *Post* staff to become an independent contractor in 1947, and her column had been syndicated since 1949, but she maintained an uneasy relationship with her home newspaper. She continued to consider herself a *Post* staff member and threatened to leave whenever she felt disrespected, even though the paper paid much more for her column than it did for others and also provided her with office space. The newspaper's executives were proud of having launched Porter's career and considered her column an asset. However, she never felt comfortable in the newsroom, and staff reporters and editors resented the special treatment she received.

It fell to publisher Dorothy Schiff to referee conflicts and soothe Porter over such issues as whether the *Post* promoted her column adequately, furnished her office stylishly, or answered her phone willingly when she took one of her frequent vacations. Porter and Schiff were guaranteed to have an interesting relationship, given the pressures each faced in a male-dominated field. Neither of them was easily bullied, resulting in several well-matched standoffs over the thirty-seven years of their professional association.

Schiff was born in 1903 into a wealthy family dominated by her grandfather, the banker and philanthropist Jacob Henry Schiff. She was a self-described socialite until her second marriage to George Backer, a writer and liberal activist who encouraged her involvement in Democratic Party politics. Backer persuaded Schiff to acquire the struggling *New York Post* in 1939, which she did for the price of the newspaper's debt. Backer then took control as president and editor. However, Schiff became frustrated with her husband's ineffective management. The newspaper lost $2 million in the first two years under Backer and required a tremendous amount of investment, forcing Backer to ask his wife for money every month.[10] Backer became ill and retired in 1942, and Schiff took over as publisher. She subsequently divorced Backer and married her new editor,

T. O. Thackrey. Several years later, she divorced Thackrey and gave him control of the newspaper, only to take it back almost immediately. Finally, ten years after she had acquired the newspaper, Schiff learned to trust her own vision and assumed full control of the *Post*. She transformed the newspaper from a money-weeping, strident broadsheet into a profitable tabloid that separated news and opinion.

Schiff remained publisher of the *New York Post* for twenty-seven years, operating it as a lively, populist vehicle for news that catered to readers' thirst for sex and crime while trying to stay inside the boundaries of good taste. She employed serious-minded columnists to balance the sensationalism of the headlines and viewed the newspaper as a business entrusted with the public's interest. In her opinion, readers were not only voters but also consumers, a view reflected in her perspective on the use of advertising. She told her biographer: "The idea that advertising isn't of value in itself is absurd. The consumer is overwhelmingly a woman—she buys for the family, except the car, the color of which she chooses—and we are here to serve the public, which includes the consumer. Even on welfare, she is the consumer; she loves most ads, and so do I."[11]

Despite occasional deference to Porter's expertise, Schiff maintained the upper hand in their relationship. Letters between them, in which Schiff asked Porter to explain the economic details of political developments, indicated they generally agreed on economics and politics. Schiff was active in the Democratic Party but was also a staunch capitalist—a political orientation she shared with Porter. However, Schiff had things Porter did not: a family fortune, a prestigious bloodline, and access to the most elite social circles. In a note thanking Schiff for helping her daughter get into the Brearley School, an exclusive prep school in Manhattan, Porter wrote that their relationship was "one of the nicest, warmest friendships I have ever known."[12] Schiff behaved more coolly toward Porter. She kept their correspondence on a professional plane, writing only to compliment Porter on her media appearances and thanking her when she promoted the *New York Post* in interviews. The *Post*-Porter union, Schiff once reminded her famous columnist, was "strictly a business proposition." Still, the partnership suffered its share of emotional flare-ups, usually over the *Post*'s contract for Porter's column.[13]

In 1954 Schiff requested a history of the *Post*'s contract with Porter's syndicate, wondering why Porter was being paid so much more than other columnists. According to an internal memo, the *Post* was paying $35 a week for columns by the renowned political journalist Doris Fleeson. It was paying $235 a week, plus overhead expenses, for columns by Porter.[14] Schiff's accounting investigation revealed the following: In 1947, when Porter had been on the *Post*'s payroll, she was paid $155 a week. On May 3, 1947, she became an independent contractor and was paid $175 a week, plus $60 for a secretary, for a total of $235 a week. Then, when her column was bought by Robert Hall in 1949 as he started the New York Post Syndicate, the *Post* began paying $235 a week to the syndicate and continued to provide an office, a telephone, and other services for Porter. The newspaper was also paying Porter $100 to write an annual business review.[15]

Despite this relatively lucrative deal, Porter had been trying to get out of her contract almost since she signed it. In December 1949 Porter met Schiff for lunch and sought her permission to leave the *New York Post*. The next day, she wrote to Schiff: "I do want to thank you for the promise you gave me of relieving me from my contract—when and if. It is good to have this assurance of freedom."[16] She gave her syndicate six weeks to find another New York City outlet for the column. However, she must have been divided over her course of action, because she told her team of literary agents during the same period that she wanted to quit newspapers entirely and focus on writing for magazines.[17] In a letter to Carl Brandt, her primary agent, Porter wrote, "I'm not quite sure how rooked I was in this deal. . . . [Y]ou seem so pleased at my statement at last that I am ready to go. Carl, I am."[18] Nothing would come of this—Porter kept her contract with the *Post*—but the sequence of events would repeat itself over the years. Porter would always be ambivalent toward the newspaper that had made her famous.

She was not satisfied with her office in the *Post*'s building at 75 West Street, finding it unbefitting a columnist of her stature. In 1956 she asked for more office space to house a second assistant, whom she called a "legman." She thought she might use an empty office in the accounting department, but the head of the department responded that he had other uses for the space and "didn't want Sylvia in his department anyway," according to Schiff.[19] Part of the conflict appeared to be that Porter still considered herself a *New York Post* staff member, and thus entitled to keep a prominent presence in the building, even though she had been syndicated for years. "[Executive editor] Paul Sann tells me that she insists that she is the Financial Editor of the *New York Post*. He insists that she is not an employee of the *New York Post*, that she works for the Syndicate and we merely buy her column from them," Schiff wrote in a report for her files.[20] The blowup resulted in a telephone conversation between Porter and Schiff, which Schiff described at length in her report:

> Sylvia was indeed very, very angry when she spoke to me. She demanded to know whether it was true that I had turned down her request for additional space, explaining that it was necessary because of her new employee, that the office she now had was enough for two but "not three women." She said she was renting a desk at her apartment to do some of the work and only needed another desk and telephone here. I told her that she should have made arrangements for office space for her assistant before signing with the Syndicate.
>
> . . . She told me that as Financial Editor of the *Post* she was handling an enormous amount of material for the newspaper. . . . I was careful to remain calm and told Sylvia that I didn't think it was fair to ask the *Post* to bear this burden, that it was really not our responsibility, that she not only wrote a newspaper column but had her own business—the newsletter.
>
> . . . I asked her please not to be emotional about this. It was a business problem and surely she could understand that the *Post* could not take over her office expenses; that in fact the room she was now occupying eventually would have to be taken from her because the space was needed. She said, "Am I to understand that you don't care whether I am at the *Post* or not?" I told her it really didn't make any difference to us where her column was produced, we were interested in her very fine product only.
>
> . . . She pointed out that she had been loyal for 21 years but would never feel the same loyalty again after this. I then got a little angry, I guess, and compared what we pay her to what we pay Doris Fleeson. . . . This really made her sore and she repeated her crack about the same

loyalty would no longer exist. She said this was a fine thing to do to her just before her vacation.[21]

Five years later, in 1961, Porter again told Schiff that she wanted to transfer her column to another New York City newspaper. Porter and Schiff had met for lunch the week before, and the publisher had told Porter that if she could get a better deal at another newspaper, she should do it: "It's strictly a business proposition," Schiff reiterated.[22] After their meeting, Porter had contacted the *Post*'s newsroom and asked the reporters to answer her phone while she and her assistant were on vacation. She had been told no one in the newsroom had time to do that. The combination of those two events was "devastating," Porter told Schiff, and brought to mind other reasons she wanted to leave. First, she no longer felt a personal connection to anyone at the newspaper. "Although I have had the illusion that I was a real part of the paper, I'm considered just another syndicated columnist who happens to be on the 15th floor," she wrote.[23] Second, she complained, the newspaper did not promote her column, despite her repeated requests: "The response has been either zero or so close to zero that I have become numb with frustration or worse."[24] Third, she said, the *Post* was not the crusading paper it once had been: "I'll always be grateful and always will boast that the *Post* had the courage to try me when I was a pioneer in the field of understandable financial reporting and a young girl to boot—but those who were responsible have been off the paper for years."[25] Finally, she believed she could get more money from another newspaper even though the *Post* paid more for her column than anyone else's. "I'm expensive and let's admit it," she wrote. She also felt she had been at one paper too long.

Schiff responded with a compassionate and lengthy letter complimenting Porter on her recent work and expressing sadness at the prospect of her leaving. The publisher appealed to Porter's Democratic politics and insisted the *Post* was the right place for her column. The newspaper had not stopped crusading, Schiff wrote, but as publisher, she had simply insisted that news and opinion be separated. She conceded that the *Post*, as an institution, was not as adept at self-promotion as Porter was. As for Porter's feeling that she was not well regarded by the newspaper's reporters and editors, Schiff responded with an intimate perspective on fame and those who achieve it:

> Don't you think that they may feel that you are not interested in any-thing they might have to say, that you live on a different plane, that you are a national institution, not a *Post* staffer? A sense of being alone is not unusual for people at the top of their profession. FDR, as you know a warm man who loved company, used to tell me he was lonely. Adlai Ste-venson said his friends stopped telephoning him after he had been a pres-idential candidate. Old friends become over-awed, are afraid to intrude in what they imagine is a too-busy life. And others are just plain envious.[26]

Schiff could have pointed out that earlier in the year, the *Post* had revamped its financial section and sought Porter's advice on issues such as how much space to allow for the stock tables. Porter refused to help, saying she knew nothing about such matters but could recommend some-one.[27] However, Schiff chose not to draw attention to Porter's cognitive dissonance toward her home paper. Instead, Schiff highlighted her own accomplishments—"a successful liberal newspaper has been achieved by this lone female publisher"—and said she had no intention of retiring, as Porter had suggested during their lunch.[28] This revealing exchange between the two women happened as the *Post*'s contract for Porter's col-umn was about to expire. The contract was renewed, but with an unusual proviso: The newspaper would pay $100 a week more for the column, for a total of $335, but the raise would be paid by the *Post*'s advertising depart-ment, which had told Schiff that losing Porter's column would hurt rev-enue.[29] The paper also agreed to do more to promote Porter's column.

Within a month, executive editor Paul Sann was frustrated with the deal. His concerns revealed the sometimes-conflicting interests of a nationally syndicated writer and a local publication. Porter had written a series on scams and swindles, and the *Post* was obliged to promote the first installment of the series—in color—on the front page. The problem was the series began with a column about homes and land, a topic of little concern to the *Post*'s New York City readers living in cramped apartments. Sann was angry his newspaper had to use expensive color ink to promote journalism better suited to rural broadsheets than a city tabloid. Adding to his distress, the *Post* paid much more for Porter's column than smaller newspapers did, especially after the recent contract negotiation. Sann wanted to change the order of the articles in Porter's series so that the first installment, the one the *Post* would promote, would be of more interest to city readers. Sann did not think this was too much to ask, given that the *Post* was essentially subsidizing the column for other newspapers. The syndicate, however, would not allow it.[30]

None of the parties involved in the contract for Porter's newspaper column was satisfied with the arrangement. A newly hired advertising director at the *Post* was furious when he learned his department was paying close to $5,000 a year for an editorial feature. Porter was still dissatisfied with her office; she told Sann she wanted a new lamp, new carpeting, and someone to hang a mirror and pictures for her. In addition, she had installed an air-conditioning unit at her own expense and did not believe she should have to pay for the electricity to power it. "I believe there was also some unpleasantness over a hole in the rug," Sann wryly told Schiff.[31] Nevertheless, the editor had decided Porter's column was a keeper, so he was reluctant to make a fuss. He was concerned the newspaper would lose a significant number of loyal readers if it dropped her column.[32] But by then, Schiff's patience with Porter was running low. She wrote to Sann: "I do feel it unfair for us to have to pay such a large amount for Sylvia when other papers in metropolitan areas pay a few dollars. As for her readership, I don't think it as large as you do. People know the name but it is hard to find anyone who reads the column. Forget the Sylvia business. I will tackle her myself."[33] In 1968 the *Post* canceled its expensive contract for Porter's column, saying it would pay no more than $125 a week and would not pay her expenses. The *Post* was moving to a new building, and Schiff made it clear there would be no space for Porter's office in the new location.[34] The syndicate bowed and agreed to the new terms. Schiff would later say she had kept Porter's column for sentimental reasons, even as she grew uneasy with Porter's activities outside the column.[35] "It is questionable in my mind whether Sylvia is worth anything to a newspaper when she is promoting WIN buttons and seems to have gone into politics," Schiff wrote to Sann in 1974, referring to Porter's work on President Gerald Ford's anti-inflation campaign.[36]

Indeed, Porter's focus shifted in the sixties from providing unique and authoritative information on economics to polishing her brand and making the most of her celebrity status. Weary of the grinding pace of daily journalism, Porter sought financial rewards in other endeavors, including an annual tax guide, an annual economic outlook for the *World Book* series of encyclopedias, and a question-and-answer column for *Ladies' Home Journal*. She also published *How to Get More for Your Money*, her first personal finance book in eight years. Porter's business and marketing acumen became apparent as she established a publishing empire and an identifiable brand of journalism. Widely recognized by women's groups, Porter was named Outstanding Woman of the Year in the Field of Journalism by *Who's Who of American Women* in 1960 and received numerous achievement awards, including an honorary medal from the General Federation of Women's Clubs alongside former first lady Eleanor Roosevelt and Senator Margaret Chase Smith.[37] Maximizing her exposure, Porter gave speeches around the country to anyone from homemakers to bankers and accepted invitations to serve on the boards of several organizations, including the American Red Cross.[38] By 1971 it was only logical that Porter—the nation's best-known financial columnist—would be named a director of the Society of American Business Writers (SABW), an organization founded to unite the growing number of journalists concentrating on business and finance.[39]

Ladies' Home Journal

Although Porter was read and admired by readers of both sexes, her women readers felt a special connection with her and looked to her as an important role model. In 1965 Porter began publishing a feature in *Ladies' Home Journal* titled "Spending Your Money." The monthly advice column answered letters, purportedly from readers, who were given a mailing address at the bottom of each column and invited to submit their questions. Porter was paid $16,000 a year to produce twelve question-and-answer columns, with her assistant, Lydia Ratcliff, receiving a portion of the annual sum. Porter's literary agents were not pleased with the deal, which Porter had negotiated alone. Carol Brandt, who had joined her husband's agency in 1955, was now the primary agent representing

Porter and believed she could have persuaded the magazine to pay more for the column (even though, she conceded, Porter's income was already "astronomical").[40]

The questions posed in Porter's *Ladies' Home Journal* column did not really come from readers. Ratcliff and Porter wrote their own questions, based on what they considered the most important issues facing middle-class women.[41] Reading the columns back to back, the repetition of the questions and the uniformity of their wording are apparent. For example, a question about a daughter who wanted to be an engineer appeared in June 1968 and again in November 1969; similar questions about daughters who wanted to go into other occupations also appeared throughout the period. A question about what a woman should do if her husband did not want her to work outside the home appeared in December 1966 and again, with similar wording, in November 1969. A question about a disabled Air Force test pilot appeared with identical wording in June 1969 and August 1969. However, despite the repetitive and formulaic nature of the questions, they offered a fairly accurate representation of larger social issues regarding women's roles and participation in the booming postwar economy.

The column reflected the era's conflict over married women's steady march into the workforce, raising questions about how to manage a two-income budget and how to share the financial responsibility for a family. One issue frequently discussed was who in the family should pay which bills. In Porter's calculation, husbands should pay for housing, taxes, insurance, and eating out, while wives should pay for the utilities, telephone, groceries, at-home entertaining, and the housekeeper.[42] In addition, every couple should establish a joint savings account, she wrote.[43] Addressing whether it was worthwhile for a woman to work outside the home, given the higher expenses she would accrue, Porter advised that it depended on each woman's situation and her reasons for holding a job.[44] Responding to questions that addressed whether the stock market was off-limits to women, Porter said absolutely not; women outnumbered men in the market, and housewives were the fastest-growing group of investors.[45] Other questions involved how much it cost to have a baby, raise a child, and get a college degree, as well as whether to invest in mutual funds or participate in investment clubs. In all matters, Porter's advice tried to address the realities of traditional middle-class family life while encouraging women to educate themselves about money and take charge of their finances.

In the debate over women's employment, Porter took a practical rather than an ideological stance. She summed up the controversy by posing as a conservative homemaker worried about the integrity of the traditional family and shocked by the number of mothers leaving their children to work outside the home. "What are they trying to achieve?" this letter asked. Given Porter's passionate belief that women and men should be given equal opportunities, her response to this objection was rather bland. Rather than assert every woman's *right* to work for wages, she simply reminded readers of some women's *need* to do so, writing it was "mainly economic security" that led women to work outside the home. "In short, the mothers of young children work because their families cannot manage without their earnings," she wrote.[46] Four years later, she made the same argument following a reader's statement of disgust toward mothers who left their children in the care of grandparents or babysitters to find employment. Porter responded: "You're likely to find that most of these young women are working not so much because they want to as because they must, financially."[47] In yet another column, after posing as a woman whose husband did not want her to get a job after the children had left home, Porter suggested she simply compromise by working part-time.[48]

Porter steered carefully, respecting the traditional gender ideology promoted by the magazine while nudging society toward acceptance of women's paid work. She was reluctant to offend readers, editors, or advertisers by flatly declaring women could and should work outside the home. Instead, she urged tolerance of women's wage work by reminding readers it was a financial necessity for many families. This argument allowed readers to negatively judge women who chose paid work if their families did not need the money—which undoubtedly was the case in many middle-class homes that subscribed to *Ladies' Home Journal*.

Heaping judgment upon a different socioeconomic group, Porter gave voice to criticism of low-income families struggling to feed a large number of children. She posed a question about "reckless women" who had children they could not afford, casting blame on these women for contributing to the world's unsustainable population growth. Failing to address why women, alone, would be responsible for this problem, Porter allowed the stereotype of low-income families to stand but steered her disapproval toward the middle class. Families with three or four children—instead of the more financially manageable one or two—were the ones damaging the nation's safety net, she said. She also left no doubt about her stand on social security and benefits for wage-earning women versus homemakers, writing it was unfair that an employed, married woman who had paid into social security for years would end up with the same retirement benefit as a wife who had stayed at home, supporting her husband.[49] Porter's column clearly reflected a number of the era's social and ideological divisions: between professional women and homemakers, between America's liberal-democratic promises and unequal expectations, and between assertions of women's domestic work as crucial to the nation's social fabric and judgments that this work was unworthy of financial compensation.

Porter's *Ladies' Home Journal* column served as a moderate voice in support of employed women's rights but upheld many social practices that a new generation of feminists had begun to protest. She asserted women's rights in the workplace but did not prescribe a revolution in the home. She consistently supported women's choice to hold a job or to be homemakers; insisted girls be given the same education and encouragement as boys; and addressed issues previously not considered from a financial standpoint, such as divorce. She also educated women about their rights under Title VII of the Civil Rights Act, passed in 1964.[50] However, while Porter argued vehemently in favor of women's right to work outside the home, she continued to promote a gendered view of the home itself.

Porter had articulated a gendered view of household finances for many years, explaining to interviewers that she, herself, had assigned a gender to each of her family's bills. For example, her husband paid the mortgage and the insurance while she paid for their groceries and laundry service. Both partners thus could imagine they were fulfilling their traditional roles—he providing shelter and protection, she taking care of domestic chores—even though she was employed outside the home. This system maintained order in the finances and peace in the marriage, Porter asserted.[51] Tellingly, Porter's characterization of bills as either "masculine" or "feminine" conformed to prevailing binary gender norms. This sustained the notion that even if a woman's career left her unable to complete her household tasks, she was not relieved of responsibility for them. Even if it meant paying a housekeeper, a woman was obligated to take charge of her family's care and upkeep. This mode of thinking normalized women's "second shift" of household work, an expectation that would burden future generations of women expected to juggle full-time employment with their traditional duties as wives and mothers. Dividing the bills along gender lines left the veneer of a traditional family intact. Although Porter advocated women's right to work professionally, she supported—at least publicly—strict gender roles within the nuclear family.

Even in her newspaper column, written for the widest possible audience, Porter recognized women's primacy in the home. But in this context, she won the gratitude of homemakers everywhere by treating them as economic producers rather than dependents. She periodically calculated the price of a homemaker's services, reminding the public that homemakers contributed to the economy as much as men and women who were employed outside the home. The child care, housekeeping, and food service a homemaker provided for her family were as legitimate an economic endeavor as if her family had paid to obtain those services elsewhere, Porter argued. In 1966 she used data from the Bureau of Labor Statistics to estimate that a homemaker's services as nursemaid, housekeeper, cook, dishwasher, laundress, food buyer, gardener, chauffeur, maintenance man, seamstress, dietitian, and practical nurse were worth $172.96 a week. She also noted such work added up to nearly one hundred hours a week, acknowledging that one barrier to getting more women into high-level professional positions was the domestic burden they carried for their families.[52] While her generation had made remarkable advances in the workplace, she wrote, they remained "the pivot of the family, the wife and mother."[53]

Porter's column in *Ladies' Home Journal* was more conflicted about women's social progress than her newspaper column, reflecting the period's ambivalence toward middle-class women. The magazine column's title, "Spending Your Money," focused readers' attention on how money should be spent, rather than saved or earned, while the word "your" gave women ownership of their finances. Portraying women as entitled actors in the financial sphere countered the stereotype of women as spendthrifts who played fast and loose with their husbands' money and provided a conceivably empowering image to readers who could not obtain a credit card without their husband's approval. However, the emphasis on spending reinforced the treatment of women in *Ladies' Home Journal* and other service magazines as consumers rather than producers.[54] The very fact that Sylvia Porter—a powerful, professional icon who advocated women's social and economic equality—addressed her readers foremost as consumers gave cultural cover to magazine executives who thought of women *only* as consumers. Furthermore, the way Porter structured the production of her column undermined readers. By inventing the questions rather than answering real ones, Porter denied women their opportunity to shape public discourse, sticking them with a passive role in relation to a magazine that was supposed to represent their interests. This paternalistic approach, in addition to the arrangement Porter had with her writing assistant, was anathema to second-wave feminists' dream of an anti-elite, collaborative culture. Porter was emblematic of the hierarchy at women's magazines, which feminists would protest at *Ladies' Home Journal* in 1970.[55]

Twentieth-century feminism generally has been defined by three characteristics: (1) opposition to sex hierarchy, (2) belief that gender is a social construction, and (3) identification of women as an interest group.[56] In theory, Porter subscribed to all three. She considered herself a liberal feminist, committed to ensuring that Enlightenment ideals of equality extended to women as well as to men. She believed the brain had no sex, which implied that gender was a social construction, and promoted public policies that would benefit women as a group. In practice, however, Porter's career revealed the fault lines of any far-reaching ideology. Intensely competitive, she had no qualms about exploiting other women's labor to further her own career. She promoted the rights of elite, professional women over those of lower-status women. Blind to structural inequalities, she believed idealistically that anyone who wanted to succeed had the opportunity to do so. She could be classist and insensitive to women whose situation did not match her own, failing to recognize that many of her personal irritations, such as finding good housekeepers and paying their payroll taxes, were problems of an upper-class life.[57] For example, she frequently wrote about the issue of domestic help in her newspaper column, arguing that housewives should not have to pay the employer's half of their housekeepers' social security taxes. She reasoned that the housewives would end up paying the entire amount due every quarter—their portion, plus the workers' portion—because domestic workers could not be trusted to save the money on their own. Domestic workers deserved the protection of social security, Porter believed, but she did not clarify who should pay into the system on their behalf if they could not be trusted to do so.

By the 1960s, women's economic status had fallen, despite the entrance of many older married women into the paid workforce. More than 40 percent of all women held jobs by the end of the decade, including 50 percent of mothers with children ages six to eighteen.[58] Women were also more educated: from 1960 to 1965, the number of women earning undergraduate degrees rose 57 percent, compared with an increase of 25 percent for men. By 1968, women earned a third of master's degrees and 13 percent of doctorates.[59] Despite these strides—and passage of the Equal Pay Act in 1963—women's full-time pay was only 60 percent of men's in 1966, down from nearly 64 percent in 1955.[60] Most women were confined to low-status, low-paying jobs as secretaries, clerks, and domestic workers. Fewer than 1 percent of federal judges, 4 percent of lawyers, and 7 percent of medical doctors were women.[61] Even in the traditional "women's fields" of education and social work, men had replaced women as administrators, librarians, and case supervisors.[62] As media coverage of the civil rights movement focused attention on the jarring contrast between America's shining democratic ideals and its shady realities, a new feminist consciousness awakened among white middle-class women.

Throughout the sixties, as the feminist movement gained momentum, Porter continued her pattern of carefully pressing for women's rights without going far enough to stir controversy.[63] In 1962 Porter published a series of newspaper columns about the New York Stock Exchange (NYSE) that dripped with vivid details. She reported that she had been stopped from touring the floor of the exchange because women were not allowed there, despite the fact that more than half of all shareholders were women and there was no official rule prohibiting women from being on the trading floor or becoming full members of the exchange. "It's tradition," she was told, but an NYSE vice president assured her he would get permission from the chairman of the board for her to visit the floor (the same type of permission she had been granted twenty years earlier). The official asked that she not publicize the flap in her column, a request Porter found laughable. "Women can't visit the NYSE floor without 'a note from daddy,'" she wrote. "Don't bring it up? Not 'embarrass us'? How little that VP knows Sylvia!"[64] Desperate to quell the controversy, within days the president of the NYSE had invited Porter to tour the trading floor and have lunch in his private dining room, which allowed her to give readers a behind-the-scenes look at the most prestigious stock exchange in the world. She gave readers a detailed glimpse of the inner sanctum of America's top financial institution. It was noisy, she wrote, and surprisingly messy. The floor was strewn with discarded gum wrappers, food packages, and small pieces of paper, artifacts of the manic temperament of the traders and the second-by-second pressure of moving markets. "It is both antiquated and automated, logical and paradoxical. It's fascinating," Porter wrote.[65] Three years later, Porter again reported on women's status at the NYSE, pushing the exchange to accept women as members. She went so far as to receive assurance that if she applied for membership and paid the $220,000 required for a seat, she would probably be accepted. "Yes, probably you . . . you . . . could. The implication was that very few other women could," she wrote, adding there was no women's restroom near the trading floor.[66] Having made her statement, Porter backed off the issue, and she never applied for membership to the NYSE. It was a savvy way to construct a public image: pushing hard enough on an issue to get noticed but stopping short of a radical demand for change. This strategy made her a favorite speaker, writer, and media personality. She could be counted on to provide a provocative sound bite but would never be perceived as a threat to the social order. Porter exhibited care and thoughtfulness in crafting her public persona; her private behavior was another matter.

Gaggle of Ghostwriters

It seems obvious that Porter could not have managed to write a daily newspaper column, a weekly financial newsletter, a monthly magazine column,
an annual economic review, and several books—all while making frequent
media appearances and giving speeches—without receiving assistance
from other writers. But exactly how much help she received was never
made clear to her readers, and it is difficult to pinpoint when this assistance
began. It might have begun as early as 1942 with the publication of Porter's
investigative series on I. G. Farben, which was dense with details derived
from painstaking research and did not read like Porter's other newspaper
articles. A letter from Porter to one of her agents indicates her magazine
contracts included expense money for a researcher as early as 1951.[67] That
same year, Marshall McClintock, a writer for *Collier's* magazine, solicited
Porter to write a book about the stock market with him. Porter wrote to
Carl Brandt: "He also said and suggested that he didn't care about publicity and seemed to imply that he wanted to perform the function as a
ghostwriter. I am most unenthusiastic about this sort of thing and would
much prefer to go along being honest about the picture and doing my own
stuff."[68] This unambiguous pronouncement on the question of ghostwrit-
ing is somewhat curious, considering the tone of Porter's newspaper column changed distinctly five years later with her hiring of a new assistant.

Before 1956 a typical column had begun this way: "It's god [*sic*] news,
Mrs. and Miss America. In a couple of months, you'll be able to buy some
of the prettiest, best-made spring and summer clothes in years."[69] Another
began: "Do you remember Mary and Mac, folks? The young couple I told
you about last June 4?"[70] These columns gave readers the feeling that Porter was sitting across the table from them, telling a story. The friendly
writing style was typical of a columnist who had spent twenty years getting to know her audience and honing a colorful, conversational voice.
Her columns often began anecdotally, introducing a real person to exem-
plify a statistic, and used a folksy second-person voice that spoke directly
to the reader.

In contrast, Porter's column of March 13, 1956, began with a straightforward, "newsy" lead, more typical of a news reporter than a columnist:

"The bright, ambitious son of a laborer who marries the daughter of a laborer will on average reach the top level in big business 26.1 years after he begins his career. If the same man marries way above his social or economic level, he'll get to the top only two months earlier."[71] It was a perceptible change in writing style, and it came after Porter had discussed her decision to hire a reporting assistant for her newspaper column. Typically, a reporting assistant—or a legman, as the position was called—would have hunted down facts and sources, conducted interviews, and provided the raw ingredients for copy; the writer then would have synthesized that information and presented it to the public in a piece of presumably original writing. However, according to assistants who worked for Porter at various times, they wrote the columns without credit and Porter lightly edited them.[72]

For the most part, Porter hired seasoned journalists who had developed their own sources and could work independently. For her newsletter, she hired the best financial writers in Washington: Joseph Slevin, who covered finance for the *New York Herald Tribune* and eventually published his own financial newsletter; Ben Weberman, a writer for *American Banker* and later the economics editor at *Forbes*; and Lee Cohn, an economics writer for the *Washington Star*. For her newspaper column, Porter hired writers who might not have specialized in finance but who shared her allegiance to the middle class.

Lydia Ratcliff, the assistant who helped produce Porter's *Ladies' Home Journal* column, was also one of the first writers to collaborate with Porter on other work. Ratcliff had been a researcher for *Time* magazine since 1954 and began working for Porter in 1963 after being introduced to the famous columnist by the woman who had fact-checked *Time*'s cover story about her.[73] For Ratcliff, a politically liberal consumerist, writing under Porter's name was a way to participate in the social activism of the sixties. She worked with Porter for about thirteen years, until the publication of *Sylvia Porter's Money Book* ended the women's professional relationship and led to a long legal dispute over royalties. Coming from *Time*'s meticulous fact-checking department, Ratcliff was appalled that Porter published statistics from press releases without verifying them and maintained personal relationships with public relations executives.[74] Ratcliff tried to make the column more journalistically rigorous while contributing to the environmental and consumerist movements launched by Rachel Carson's *Silent Spring* and Ralph Nader's *Unsafe at Any Speed*. Ratcliff's politics marked a departure from Porter's more neutral, analytical stance. "Sylvia wasn't really interested in social movements. She was interested in Sylvia," one of Porter's other assistants would say later.[75]

The two women worked across from each other at the dining-room table at Pound Ridge, Porter's country estate in Westchester County, New York. They would chain-smoke and discuss ideas for columns, which Ratcliff would write and Porter would edit. Ratcliff felt empowered by the wide reach of Porter's columns and was given the freedom to write about her favorite topics, although Porter insisted the columns carry her stamp. For example, when Ratcliff wanted to write a column about water pollution, Porter said she had to give it an economic angle. So Ratcliff wrote a column about how it would cost less in the long term to purify the nation's waterways than to deal with the effects of pollution. Ratcliff would eventually serve as a head writer for Porter, hiring others to work under them in a sort of umbrella organization. Porter took credit for a lot of work she did not do, and she was less than generous toward those who worked for her.[76]

As Ratcliff assumed more responsibility for Porter's writing, she hired Brooke Shearer, a freelance journalist who had returned to Washington, DC, from Eastern Europe in the mid-1970s and was looking for work she could do from home after having her first child. Shearer's husband, Strobe Talbott, had worked for *Time*; acquaintances at the magazine put her in touch with Ratcliff. "I couldn't imagine a better job in journalism," said Shearer, who worked for Porter for seven years. "I had a wide range of topics. I could write about whatever I wanted to write about."[77] Porter's writers found that other journalists would share tips with them because they did not consider Porter a threat. Advertisers, it seemed, held a different view. A series of columns Shearer wrote about milk marketing and price fixing in the industry threw the dairy lobby into high gear.[78] The dairy companies called the editors of newspapers that ran Porter's column and insisted they drop the column or lose dairy-industry advertising. Porter stood by the columns, and the crisis soon passed.

Porter was sensitive to the business side of journalism and usually tried to keep advertisers and subscribing newspapers happy. For example, after she had written a column about the financial problems of the movie industry caused by the arrival of television, the *New York Post* received letters from angry movie executives and movie theater owners, who advertised heavily in the *Post*.[79] The newspaper's director of advertising, Harry Rosen, drafted a response that he wanted the publisher to send to one theater executive. Rosen's letter said the *Post* wished the theaters the best and would cooperate in efforts to improve their businesses.[80] Dorothy Schiff was appalled by the draft and wrote her own letter, which said that as publisher, she would never censor a columnist.[81] To settle the conflict, Porter wrote a second column giving voice to the movie industry's perspective, which drew an approving letter from the Motion Picture Association of America.[82] Porter also made sure newspapers that subscribed to her column received at least as much advertising for her books and appearances as their competitors, if not more.[83] She wrote to a publicist as they designed a promotion for *Sylvia Porter's Money Book*: "I understand the pull of the *New York Times* and of such papers as *Chicago Tribune* and [the *Washington Post*'s] *Book World*. But I also know a great deal more about the sort of readership that the *New York Post* has and this readership's belief in the newspaper, and I think in this area that my knowledge may be more trustworthy than even your top notch experts."[84]

When Porter traveled on the speaking circuit, she gave interviews to the newspapers that published her column. And if a newspaper picked up her column, the editor received a personal letter from Porter: "I think you might underestimate the sense of pride with which I reacted to the news that you have reinstated my column," she wrote to the editor of the *Houston Post* in 1974. "I am convinced that rarely has there been a period during which my sphere of journalism has been so much in the forefront and during which what I am trying to do has been so important to so many millions of people."[85]

Porter's wide influence came from her ability to write cogently about issues few were covering at the time. However, Porter was not as personable as her writing style. "Sylvia was a fighter, imperious, a stingy person. She had fought to get what she had," Shearer said. "She wasn't going to let anyone take anything from her, even close friends, unless you fought like hell, too."[86] Those who worked for Porter had to demand fair treatment because she would take advantage of anyone who did not stand up for herself. Shearer believed Porter began using ghostwriters simply because she realized she could get away with it, and she wanted more exposure than writing a daily newspaper column would have allowed. "The fact is there is no way you can be on TV, writing five columns a week, and do all this, be a media star, and do it yourself," said Shearer, who understood the pressures faced by public figures more than most. She would later assist Hillary Rodham Clinton on the campaign trail in 1992 and work in the White House after Bill Clinton became president. "If you're going to merchandise yourself, to mass-market yourself, you have to have help."[87]

Shearer and Ratcliff developed a writing process that would eventually extend to Porter's other writers. The two would get together and discuss a column schedule. Writing far in advance of publication, Shearer would draft a batch of columns, usually three per week, and mail them to Ratcliff. When one of her columns was about to be published, Shearer would get an early version of it in the mail. If the column included any mistakes, she had only enough time to make corrections in the *Washington Star*, the local newspaper that carried the column. Shearer considered Ratcliff the column's "guiding intelligence," and she wishes Ratcliff had received more recognition. Shearer said she "fundamentally disagreed" with Porter's refusal to give others credit. Some people with name recognition "are fearful that giving anybody else credit will diminish their name. Sylvia was one of those," Shearer said.[88] However, Porter's writers devised their own way of getting their names into the column, which was necessary if they hoped to demonstrate to future employers that they had written for Porter. They would ask for internal credit in the form of an offhand, anecdotal reference slipped into a column. For example, Ratcliff gave herself internal credit once by imagining a conversation between her and Porter. The column began by posing a question—"'What's a blue chip?' asked Lydia while we were scanning a batch of stock market letters from brokerage firms recently"—which it then answered.[89] This was a modest form of credit, but at least it acknowledged Porter had assistance.

Future writers would include their first and last names, so, in the absence of a byline, they would have writing samples with their full names to place in their portfolios.

In the sixties, Porter's newspaper column could be categorized into six general themes: government policies, consumer trends, business trends, investing, question-and-answer sessions with experts, and the economic status of women. Paradoxically, as the decade progressed and the public's interest in financial issues expanded, the focus of Porter's columns narrowed. Her wide-ranging perspective as an economist became less evident, and the columns became less intellectual and more practical. Porter believed Americans' interest in so-called pocketbook issues rose during this decade because people had more money to spend and were looking for answers during a complex period in the nation's history.[90] But Porter's columns became more standard after others started writing them. They lacked her unique perspective on the large economic questions of the day, focusing instead on quotidian issues related to financial management. They became formulaic, which allowed multiple people to write them but resulted in journalism that was more like a commodity than a craft. The inimitable Sylvia Porter had become a brand and a business—a business nurtured by other writers.

By 1970, most columns could be summarized with a "how to" or "beware of" statement.[91] Readers were told how to buy a new car, shop for a mortgage, save on air conditioning, invest in mutual funds, save on income taxes, apply for a scholarship, or blow the whistle on a nonconforming nursing home. They were warned to beware of all sorts of scams, swindles, and quacks. They were advised how much to budget for babies, weddings, retirement, houses, or college. The woman who had once believed the average family was "a myth invented by the statistician for the convenience of the statistician"[92] began publishing one-size-fits-all financial advice. No longer was Porter tying political developments in Prague to the price of bread in Peoria. Rather than explaining what large economic developments meant for the individual, her column lionized the individual. This type of journalism, which developed into the genre known as "personal finance," provided a valuable service for readers but lacked Porter's brilliance as an economics writer.

Sylvia Porter's Money Book

In 1975 Porter published the book that solidified her status as the nation's foremost expert in personal finance and created a new genre in journalism and book publishing. *Sylvia Porter's Money Book: How to Earn It, Spend It, Save It, Invest It, Borrow It—and Use It to Better Your Life* was the first book that attempted to answer every possible question a middle-class reader might have about money. It was an unprecedented tome of information that described in plain language every milestone or purchase in readers' lives and advised them how to make smart decisions. It also elucidated mysteries of the financial markets for those who did not work on Wall Street or in a bank. "The American marketplace is an economic jungle," the book's foreword warned. "As in all jungles, you easily can be destroyed if you don't know the rules of survival. . . . But you also can come through in fine shape and you can even flourish in the jungle—if you learn the rules, adapt them for your own use, and heed them."[93] The book was 1,105 pages long and weighed almost five pounds. It quickly rose to the top of the *New York Times* nonfiction bestseller list and became a popular graduation and wedding gift, selling more than one million copies.[94] As the baby boom generation matured, its elders—who had survived the Great Depression and the economic turmoil of World War II—believed young people could use some commonsense advice from one of their own.

The success of *Sylvia Porter's Money Book* signaled a new fascination with money management, which began with the economic challenges of the seventies and culminated in the competitive individualism of the eighties. Television and print outlets rushed to meet the growing demand for economic and financial news, long considered a wasteland for journalists who started—or ended—their careers there. "Nobody wanted to cover the economy," said Lee Cohn, who wrote about economic policy for the *Washington Star* in the sixties and moonlighted on Porter's bond-market newsletter. "People were scared. They were intimidated by it."[95]

President Richard Nixon's institution of wage-price controls, a measure to stem spiraling inflation that the U.S. government had not taken since the Korean War, motivated journalists to pay more attention to the administration's economic policies. In 1970 the Public Broadcasting System

(PBS) launched *Wall Street Week,* the first television show wholly devoted to financial issues. Not to be outdone by PBS, other networks enhanced their own coverage, launching the careers of broadcasters such as NBC's Irving R. Levine and CNN's Lou Dobbs, well respected for their knowledge of business and economics. News outlets quickly learned that financial insiders were not the only audience for this kind of information. Middle-class Americans were struggling to maintain their financial position as credit markets tightened and wages lost ground. For the first time since the rise of Keynesian economic thought, inflation and unemployment—believed to occur on opposite ends of the business cycle—were happening simultaneously. Those most affected were people without sufficient capital to weather the storm.

Print outlets, most of which had aimed their financial content squarely at the business community, came under pressure to cover money management as it related to the middle class. In 1972 Time, Inc. began publishing *Money* magazine, its personal finance counterpart to *Fortune. USA Today,* from the moment of its debut in 1982, covered personal finance as one of its core beats; the newspaper snatched up journalists who had been writing for newsletters and gave them a national audience. Personal finance became a lucrative publishing genre, merging American's growing interest in finance with the individualistic trends toward self-help and self-interest that would characterize the seventies and eighties.

With all this new energy surrounding personal finance, Americans might have been surprised to know *Sylvia Porter's Money Book* had been in the works for decades. The *Money Book* grew out of her newspaper columns—but not the columns that explained large macroeconomic and political developments. Porter and her agents had discovered a far greater market for the columns she and her assistants wrote that provided commonsense financial advice for individuals and families.[96] In 1964 Robert Hall, the president of Porter's syndicate, wondered whether they should hire a writer to organize Porter's columns into a book.[97] Porter's immediate response was negative. "I just don't want to come out with a quickie which I am not proud to have above my name—and I think this is all that would result from the suggestion that you make," she wrote.[98] Porter might have found Hall's terms unacceptable, or she might have thought

Ratcliff was not ready to tackle the project. Whatever the reason for her early reluctance, by 1968 she had changed her mind. She wrote to her agents: "Finally, as a result of all the churning, I have zeroed in on the sort of book I am ready to start right now. It should take about a year to finish. It will be the best book I can turn out on all aspects of consumer/family finance. It will be designed to take everyman and everywoman by the hand and help them through the mysteries of money."[99] Porter suggested calling the book *The Money Mystique*, a sly reference to Betty Friedan's *The Feminine Mystique*, published in 1963.[100] Instead, the publisher tentatively titled Porter's book *The Economics of Your Personal Life* before arriving at the simpler and more authoritative *Sylvia Porter's Money Book*.[101]

The book was a five-year collaborative effort between Porter and her freelancers. Ratcliff coordinated writers working on different chapters of the book from her farm in Vermont. The freelancers were paid a flat fee, while Ratcliff was paid a percentage of royalties from book sales. Porter dedicated the book to her husband but also credited Ratcliff: "Leading all acknowledgments must be mine to Lydia Lawrence Ratcliff, my associate for twelve years. She and I worked together on this book from start to finish. Whatever success it earns, I share with Lydia."[102]

Despite the warm acknowledgment, the book unraveled the relationship between Porter and her lead ghostwriter. Ratcliff accused Porter of not paying all the royalties she was owed for the *Money Book* and subsequent versions of it. Under Ratcliff's contract with Porter, she was to receive a percentage of royalties from sales of the book, minus Porter's promotional expenses. Ratcliff accused Porter of manipulating her expenses in order to pay Ratcliff less in royalties. The accusation was corroborated by Shearer, who was caught in the middle after Porter claimed in her expenses to have had lunches with Shearer that never took place.[103] Three months after the book was published, one of Porter's agents, Carol Brandt, wrote to her regarding the dispute with Ratcliff. Brandt said both she and Porter's attorney, Hal Meyerson, believed that Porter's contract with Ratcliff had been too generous and that Porter owed her nothing.[104] But Ratcliff was persistent. The dispute, which began in 1975, would not be resolved until 1986. In one attempt to persuade Porter's attorneys to settle the case, Ratcliff's attorney hinted at the unwelcome publicity a court battle would bring. "I sincerely feel that possible public exposure of a contest to secure Ms. Ratcliff's rightful share of the *Money Book* and in the upcoming book could be very damaging," he wrote in 1983. The conflict ended in an arbitration agreement that awarded Ratcliff $15,000 of the $26,000 she believed she was owed.[105]

None of the *Money Book* writers, including Ratcliff, had signed contracts with the publisher, and thus they had no legal claim to their work on the book. Furthermore, because Ratcliff had hired the writers, Porter could maintain plausible deniability if a problem arose with any of them. Porter had cushioned herself with layers of people who handled her affairs and could claim ignorance if a conflict arose with someone who worked for her. Porter's attorneys fiercely protected her ownership of the writing published under her name, most of which involved self-employed freelancers whose resources were no match for her deep pockets. One writer received a letter after he had listed two chapters for the *Money Book* on his résumé. The letter demanded the writer cease to make the claim he had written any material for the *Money Book*, saying Porter did not even know who he was.[106] The writer responded that he would remove the book from his résumé, but that he was insulted by the assertion that he had not done the work. He had proof, he said, that he had written more than 80 percent of the two chapters. While he would take the work off his résumé, he also hoped that anyone involved with the effort would acknowledge his role. He seemed to imply it was a breach of ethics for Porter and her team of handlers to act as if he and the other writers who had contributed to the *Money Book* did not exist.[107]

Disagreements over the book's authorship never reached the public, which responded enthusiastically and drove the book to the number-five spot on the *Publisher's Weekly* nonfiction bestseller list for 1975.[108] Porter received letters from readers who appreciated her straightforward explanation of money matters and her allegiance to middle-class people like them.[109] A young man from Norfolk, Virginia, wrote to say he had found Porter's advice helpful after he had completed his doctorate and finally had money to spend.[110]

Porter characterized herself as a teacher for the masses and viewed the publication of the *Money Book* as the fulfillment of her earliest career objective to promote financial literacy. In a letter to the author Sterling Noel, a close friend, she reflected on her reasons for the massive endeavor: "WHY? Because I simply had to summarize that part of my life—as a teacher via newspapers and books—in the field of consumer economics. The pressures on me to write it became so intense I finally said yes and then, I could not compromise by turning out another pot boiler for publicity, prestige, and more cash. It had to be a good job because I shall not go this way again."[111] But Porter continued to publish in the tradition she had established—as would many other writers. Jane Bryant Quinn published *Everyone's Money Book* in 1979;[112] Richard Phalon published *Your Money: How to Make It Work Harder Than You Do* in 1979; and Grace Weinstein published *The Lifetime Book of Money Management: Your All-Purpose Financial Planner* in 1984. An ill-informed reviewer for the latter noted: "Somehow the writing of comprehensive personal finance manuals has become the preserve of female authors"—as if it had not been from the beginning.[113]

The years leading to the publication of *Sylvia Porter's Money Book* were the high point of Porter's career as a financial journalist and marked a propitious moment. Just as the focus of her writing shifted from the global to the individual, the maturing baby boom generation created a vast new market for practical financial advice. By 1979, Porter's column appeared in more than 350 newspapers and was seen by an astounding forty million readers daily.[114] Frequently listed among the most influential women in America, she was also recognized by her peers, receiving the Bob Considine Award for journalism; the William Allen White Award for opinion writing; and the U.S. Treasury's Kate Smith Award for promoting savings bonds.[115] She was admitted to New York's Sigma Delta Chi hall of fame and served on the Pulitzer Prize jury several times (as a nominating judge in 1981, one of eight women and forty-seven men that year).[116] It would be hard to overestimate Porter's popular appeal. The decades she spent proving her expertise and grooming her public image had earned her the trust of a majority of Americans. "Sylvia Porter" truly was a household name—one that had blown apart the stereotype that separated authority from femininity. The next phase of Porter's career was less successful. In a new development, the "matron of money" was about to take her crusade and her influence to the White House.

Photographer Jack Sheaffer captured this portrait of Porter on January 6, 1962, while she was traveling in Tucson, Arizona. It soon became the headshot for her column. Courtesy of University of Arizona Libraries, Special Collections, MS435, 18723.2.

"Anything I am is due to my mother. I am living her life!" Porter said of Rose Maisel Feldman, shown in an undated personal photo. Used with permission of the National Women and Media Collection, State Historical Society of Missouri.

"Our marriage was way ahead of its time," Porter said of her relationship with Sumner Collins, a Hearst newspaper executive. The couple wed in 1943 after meeting on a cruise ship and remained together for thirty-four years. Used with permission of the National Women and Media Collection, State Historical Society of Missouri.

Porter opens one of 100,000 letters she received in 1971 after she wrote a column offering a free unit-price chart to help readers calculate how much they were paying for food and other goods. Used with permission of the National Women and Media Collection, State Historical Society of Missouri.

Sylvia...here's how Baker explained it...the lows come from here...
the highs from here...that's stereo...magnificent sound!

This memorable photo captures Porter visiting President Lyndon Johnson in the Oval Office and offers a funny caption by an unknown friend speculating about their conversation: "Sylvia . . . here's how Baker explained it . . . the lows come from here . . . the highs from here . . . that's stereo . . . magnificent sound!" Johnson approached Porter in 1964 to be president of the Export-Import Bank, an offer she declined. Used with permission of the National Women and Media Collection, State Historical Society of Missouri.

With President Gerald Ford to her right and consumer activist Ralph Nader to her left, Porter discusses anti-inflation efforts at the White House in 1974 as part of the Citizens' Action Committee to Fight Inflation. The failed campaign, which Porter chaired, distributed the infamous "WIN" button she is wearing. Used with permission of the National Women and Media Collection, State Historical Society of Missouri.

Porter found another business partner in James Fox, her third husband, a public relations executive to whom she was married from 1979 until her death in 1991. Used with permission of the National Women and Media Collection, State Historical Society of Missouri.

4

Presidential Adviser

DESPITE PORTER'S VESTED INTEREST in economic policy—and her role in designing and promoting U.S. savings bonds—she had steadfastly maintained her independence as a journalist. She believed she could remain objective even as she advised Treasury secretaries and cultivated sources on Wall Street, but she worried her readers would perceive her as biased if she appeared too cozy with the government or banks. Cultural power had been conferred upon her by the masses, not the elites, and average Americans had to know she was on their side. She also worried that if she ever took a hiatus from her column, the fickle public would quickly shift its allegiance to another economics writer. A shrewd businesswoman, Porter understood the importance of brand loyalty, and she would not risk tarnishing her image or giving readers a reason to shop for another informant. To a publisher who had asked about her involvement in anti-inflation efforts during the 1970s, she replied: "I am going to do my darndest to help, but of course there is the matter of priorities, and the column, as everybody in the White House is surely aware, is Number One."[1]

Porter's role in government expanded when the White House was inhabited by Democrats, whose views on business and the economy more closely matched her own, and contracted when Republicans controlled the executive branch. She was ambivalent when called upon politically because her ambition conflicted with her pragmatism and desire for professional autonomy. In 1962 President John F. Kennedy asked her to serve on his Consumer Advisory Council, which he had created to address growing public indignation over unsafe products and unscrupulous business practices such as planned obsolescence. Porter resigned after one meeting. She had been frustrated by the amount of time wasted on trivial matters, such as what the group's stationery would look like.[2] The group eventually got around to discussing weightier matters, but it was too late for Porter. She had already concluded the council—much like the President's Commission on the Status of Women, which Kennedy had established in 1961—was mostly symbolic, an attempt to control the agitation that was beginning to disturb the calm waters of America's postwar prosperity. The groups gave Kennedy the veneer of a progressive presidency at a time when he lacked the authority to make policy changes. Porter had little interest in committee work that accomplished nothing. As government officials sought her help more frequently in the turbulent years to come, she tried to give it carefully—and on her own terms.

In September 1963, White House aide Ted Sorensen sent Porter a draft of a speech President Kennedy was about to give regarding his proposal to cut taxes. Sorensen wanted to know if she would look it over. Porter, flattered by the White House's confidence in her abilities, cleared her schedule and set to work. She wrote a draft of her own, making a few significant changes, and sent it back to the White House with a note to Sorensen. She suggested Kennedy emphasize this would be the most important legislation of the year and the most significant economic legislation in fifteen years. Reflecting the symbiosis that existed between many politicians and the press in those years, Porter asked to know in advance what night Kennedy was going to address the nation: "I would like to follow up the day after the President speaks with a column mentioning some of the important domestic economic legislation in the last 15 years and by so doing, dramatize the significance of this bill in another way. I must write my column in advance so that it reaches all the newspapers simultaneously, and thus I would like to get to work on this as soon as I have an idea of the timing."[3] Sorensen wrote back in a telegram: "Your contribution was excellent. Talk tentatively scheduled for next Wednesday evening. Reference to 15 years appeared in Tuesday's luncheon speech and likely to be repeated. Many many thanks."[4]

Kennedy spoke to the nation Wednesday, September 18, 1963, in what would be his last major address before his death. He repeated Porter's assertion that the bill would be the most significant economic legislation in fifteen years and laid out his rationale for what was then the largest tax cut in U.S. history. The Revenue Act of 1964 (eventually signed into law by President Lyndon Johnson) slashed personal income taxes about 20 percent and also lowered corporate tax rates. Kennedy argued this would create jobs, free money for investment, and help build new markets for businesses. As promised, Porter published a supportive column the day after Kennedy's speech, without revealing her role. The viewpoint she expressed was not only favorable to Kennedy, however. The entirety of the column was a defense of the very claim Porter, herself, had written about the importance of the tax cut proposal. The assertion that it was the most significant legislation to come before Congress in fifteen years was, she wrote, "a claim which at first glance seems highly exaggerated but which, after study, turns out to have surprising validity."[5]

In January 1964 President Johnson called Porter to Washington to discuss the federal budget before he gave his State of the Union address to Congress and an American public still grieving over Kennedy's assassination. His budget was inflationary, she warned him, especially when coupled with Kennedy's tax cut. Privately, Porter was insistent on this point, but she did not go public with her criticism until Johnson had left office. In fact, after the first federal budget to exceed $100 billion went into effect while Johnson was still president, she wrote in her column: "Does it mean that federal spending is out of control? No!"[6] Years later, she would write that Johnson's attempt to fight the Vietnam War without cutting domestic spending led directly to the economic crisis of the 1970s. But in 1964, as Johnson proposed his budget, Porter expressed her doubts only in private and tried to soften her criticism with a letter praising his speech and a promise to write positively about some of his other proposals. "I have already set the wheels in motion to follow through on the National Education Association report, and I shall try in the weeks to come to explain to the American public your economic program and your war on poverty in the simplest words I can find."[7] She reiterated in a letter to him a month later: "I don't have any doubts about your program. If I seem to be expressing them now and then, it is either because I am not writing as precisely as I should or because I am trying to report another viewpoint so that the American public will not doubt my effort to be objective."[8]

Johnson, who was said to admire women who reminded him of his strong-willed mother, must have been impressed with Porter because he sought her out to fill an executive position no woman had held.[9] In March 1964, Porter had just returned from a vacation in Acapulco, Mexico, when she received a call from the White House. Johnson wanted to appoint her president of the Export-Import Bank. As she recounted the story later, she had sat on the edge of her bed with tears rolling down her cheeks while she said no to the president of the United States.[10] She was simply too afraid of losing the career she had built as a journalist. If she took a break from her column, she feared, a competitor would quickly move in and seize her market share. She also noted that her husband and daughter were in New York, and she had no desire to move to Washington without them. After the conversation, she wrote to thank Johnson for his efforts to appoint women to high positions and again promised to give him positive publicity. She said his actions had demonstrated "how far women still have to go before they reach their potential as constructive contributors to our economy as well as creative members of our society."[11] As Porter well knew, relatively few women had been appointed to federal posts in 1964, and even fewer had been appointed to positions that fell outside departments already perceived as feminine, such as health and education. Finance was considered as masculine a domain within government as it was within journalism, so Johnson had provided Porter with an opportunity to break yet another barrier. However, taking a government position would have jeopardized Porter's financial success and professional independence. She was more comfortable offering ideas from outside the federal bureaucracy than trying to enact change from within—as her next endeavor in government would memorably prove.

Public Enemy No. 1

Of all the decades in the twentieth century, perhaps none was more paradoxical than the 1970s, which pushed Keynesian economic theory beyond its limits. As the decade began, signs of an economic maelstrom were emerging. The nation experienced the highest unemployment rate since the Great Depression—an average of 7 percent from 1973 to 1979—as the gross national product grew 2.5 percent and productivity grew only 0.6

percent.[12] At the same time, prices were growing at an explosive pace. The inflation Porter had predicted during the Johnson administration landed in direct conflict with the Phillips curve of Keynesian theory, which held that unemployment and inflation moved opposite each other. Annual inflation averaged 8.8 percent throughout the decade, compared with the usual 1 or 2 percent, and reached 12.2 percent in 1974.[13]

Senate Majority Leader Mike Mansfield called inflation and recession "social dynamite,"[14] and during the seventies both miserable scenarios played out simultaneously. When Gerald Ford moved into the Oval Office in August 1974, the consumer price index had increased every month since January 1967; previously, prices had never risen for more than six consecutive months. The national unemployment rate was 5.5 percent, and it peaked at 9 percent in May 1975.[15] High unemployment nursed a poisonous despair among those who needed a job and felt unfairly stigmatized. At the same time, as Porter had long warned, high prices rocked the foundation of the economy, creating dangerous resentment among hardworking Americans who were playing by the rules but still falling behind.

Economists have offered many explanations for the devastating inflation of the 1970s, unprecedented for the nation during peacetime. According to one interpretation, the nation was in the throes of "demand-pull" inflation. A massive increase in spending—driven by a combination of the Vietnam War, Johnson's Great Society welfare initiatives, and income tax cuts—forced government and citizens to compete for goods and credit on the private market. The economy became overheated amid high demand. According to another interpretation, the nation was in the grip of "cost-push" inflation as unionized labor demanded higher wages to keep up with the cost of living (in some cases pegging scheduled wage increases directly to the consumer price index). The higher cost of labor, combined with the higher prices businesses were paying for energy and materials, led producers to raise prices. As president, Richard Nixon had sought to contain the damage by imposing wage-price controls from 1971 to 1974. Once the controls were lifted, prices jumped again as businesses tried to recoup money they had lost and the financial markets tried to anticipate future controls.

In the meantime, the Federal Reserve was pursuing an expansive monetary policy to make American exports more competitive. In 1970, the money supply grew 5.1 percent; in 1971, 6.3 percent; and in 1972, 8.5 percent.[16] Coupled with the United States' decision in 1971 to take the dollar off the gold standard, the Fed's monetary policy weakened the dollar and exacerbated inflation.[17] Making the situation worse, in 1973 the Arab members of OPEC embargoed oil exports to the United States, partly to protest American aid to Israel during the Yom Kippur War and partly to protest the devaluation of the dollar. The price of oil in the United States rose 300 percent over five months. Reeling from "supply-shock" inflation, markets across the economy reacted to yet another factor pushing prices upward. The addition of the energy crisis to the problems of inflation, recession, and poor policymaking sent the economy into a tailspin. By that time, President Nixon was mired in the Watergate scandal, which limited his ability to deal with the multifaceted meltdown. When he resigned in August 1974, he left behind a broken economy and a political environment too poisoned to repair it.

When Ford became president after Nixon's exit, the economy was foremost on his mind. During a press conference on August 28, 1974, Ford highlighted three major problems facing the nation: unemployment, energy, and inflation. The last of these was the most menacing, he feared, and he was joined in this belief by millions of Americans struggling to buy groceries or other necessities for their families. Public officials and economists had been warning against inflation since World War II, considering it the Achilles heel of capitalism and the greatest threat to Americans' consumerist way of life. Inflation affected everybody, but it hurt the middle and lower-middle classes the most because higher prices ate up a greater proportion of their income. This made inflation an acute political problem for Ford because Americans encountered it every time they stood at the cash register. Ford had publicly stated his opposition to wage-price controls, which many feared were necessary to solve the problem of inflation. Distancing himself from Nixon, he viewed government regulation as the problem, not the solution, and advocated a shift from collective to individual measures. "I see this as the century of individual freedom," Ford announced as president. "[L]iberty from oppressive, heavy-handed bureaucratic government. . . . That is a goal we must achieve in our third century."[18]

Ford, who had not been elected to executive office, had a mere two years to prove the validity of his vision before voters went to the polls to vote him in or out. Even more pressing, midterm elections were looming, and the Republican Party would likely take a beating for the crimes of Watergate. As Ford took office, he attacked the issue he considered the most clear-cut and nonpartisan. He predicted that if the nation could beat inflation—which he called "Public Enemy No. 1"—the economy would come into alignment.[19] In addition, Ford sought to repair relations between the White House and Capitol Hill, which had been strained during the Nixon administration, and he emphasized openness and transparency in government. He reached out to those who had been on Nixon's long list of enemies and sought divergent opinions from a variety of sources. His approach was the equivalent of throwing open the White House drapes and letting the light shine in.

Setting a new tone for the executive branch, Ford began his presidency by carrying out a commitment Nixon had made before resigning: a series of fourteen economic meetings around the country, to which he invited economic experts, government officials, and representatives of labor, business, banks, and consumers. The participants were given an opportunity to express their concerns and present the president with ideas about how to control inflation. The president then invited a select group of participants to attend a final two-day summit on September 27–28 to discuss the best ideas that had come from the regional meetings.

Porter was invited to attend one of the regional meetings as well as the final summit. At the presummit meeting held in Washington, DC, on September 20, 1974, she identified herself as a representative of the consumer and delivered a passionate statement: "In the inflation fight to date, the consumer has been lectured, exhorted, patronized—but not enlisted. Yet, it is the consumer who is being squeezed by tight and horrendously expensive credit, trapped by soaring prices, battered by crashes in the securities markets. . . . There is an unspoken cry of "WHAT CAN I DO?" in the hearts of millions of Americans that the President can and should answer."[20] She called for the creation of a citizens' anti-inflation campaign and made concrete recommendations for the execution of such an initiative.

Porter insisted that any call for consumers' cooperation should emphasize that they would be acting in their own self-interest. This, she said, would ameliorate the despair that permeated the nation by reminding Americans of their agency and influence in an economy that was two-thirds consumer spending. She also believed anti-inflation initiatives would be the most effective at the local level. She recommended the president lean on mayors and other local officials to establish citizens' committees in their towns and counties. The federal government would then provide educational pamphlets and other resources that could be used to promote community gardens, recycling programs, and energy conservation. The president might make a major statement to endorse and publicize the initiative, she suggested, but the program should be built from the bottom up.

Porter's other recommendations reflected her background in international economics. For example, she recommended the United States work with other oil-consuming nations to pressure OPEC to lower prices and depoliticize its sale of oil. She urged the development of international financial agreements to handle the new, massive flow of funds being exchanged among foreign banks. Finally, she advised the administration to meet with a range of consumer groups, as well as public relations and advertising professionals, to ensure their cooperation. These other suggestions were forgotten as Ford jumped on her idea to put anti-inflation efforts in the hands of individual consumers. Only a week later, at the formal economic summit, Ford used his remarks to applaud Porter's recommendations and declare his intention to establish a citizens' anti-inflation program.

On September 28, 1974, the final day of the summit, the atmosphere was raucous and partisan—one reporter even described it as "scary"[21]— as participants verbally sparred over what ailed the economy and how to fix it. Protesters demonstrated outside, shouting and carrying signs. Ralph Nader, the famous consumer advocate, planned to stage a walkout because of what he considered an underrepresentation of consumers.[22] Other participants railed against the newly tight monetary policies of the

Federal Reserve. Democrats, pointing to a deepening recession, called for more wage-price controls, while the politically conservative Chamber of Commerce confidently predicted the economy would improve within three months. Adding to the confusion, celebrity economists Milton Friedman and Paul Samuelson were in complete—and public—disagreement: Friedman argued that a recession was necessary to stop inflation, while Samuelson argued that restraining the economy in any way would be disastrous.[23] Similarly, Richard Cooper, an economist at Yale, recommended a tax cut, while John Kenneth Galbraith, an economist at Harvard, recommended a tax increase.[24] According to Representative Albert Quie, a Republican from Minnesota, the problem was a victim mentality on the part of all members of society. Nobody was taking responsibility for inflation, which made it difficult to reach an agreement on a solution.[25]

Porter's idea to enlist consumers appealed to the president for several reasons. First, her rhetoric matched his characterization of inflation as a war. She was drawing on the nation's experience during World War II, when Americans at home had eagerly joined the fight by submitting to rationing and wage-price controls, investing in savings bonds, and planning victory gardens. She assumed Americans still felt, as they had thirty years before, like partners of the government, not adversaries. "I believe that consumers are now as eager to help combat inflation as we were eager in World War II to help combat Nazism. The consumer wants to be a participant in this battle, not just a pawn," she said.[26] Journalists, including Porter, had served as press agents for the government during the war, prescribing individual behaviors that would serve the whole.[27] There had been a strong sense of community during World War II that both Porter and Ford believed could be tapped in the current financial crisis.

Porter's focus on the individual also aligned with Ford's conservatism and philosophical aversion to government interference in the markets. It was a simple solution: ask consumers to boycott overpriced products. Businesses, afraid of losing customers, would hold prices steady; the demand-supply curve would reassert itself; and equilibrium would be restored. On the face of it, a program consisting of consumer education and empowerment appeared noncontroversial, which was a further consideration for Ford as he faced a hostile Congress. How could anyone, regardless of his or her politics, take issue with the idea of consumers acting in their own self-interest?

Ford believed the enlistment of consumers in the fight against inflation was politically safe, and he had evidence to support this conclusion. At the summit where Porter had made her statement, the diverse participants had disagreed strongly about where to begin fixing the economy. Porter's idea was the only one that received unanimous approval. And she was not the only person to consider this approach. At least one newspaper had editorialized that inflation was nothing less than a war that must be fought "by the man on the street—you and me."[28] The editorial proposed that a symbol be displayed in the windows of businesses that pledged not to raise prices for six months. In addition, a women's consumer group named "Fight Inflation Together" had organized a boycott of meat to hold down escalating prices the previous year.[29] Porter's ideology of individualism deployed for collective gain was not culturally dissonant. On the contrary, it struck a chord with those who saw personal sacrifice as a key element of the nation's history and culture. One correspondent who approved of Porter's proposal wrote to her that Americans were Puritans at heart, "happiest wearing hair shirts."[30]

Porter had given Ford some measured advice on implementing any campaign that asked consumers for help in the fight against inflation. She recommended the administration proceed slowly, taking the time to meet with key stakeholders and test any proposals before announcing them publicly. Fatefully, this did not happen. Instead, as the economic summit concluded, Ford promised to present a comprehensive anti-inflation program within ten days.[31] He reiterated Porter's suggestions, gave them his public endorsement, and announced that she had agreed to lead a citizens' committee at his request.

Immediately, Porter was inundated by correspondence from public relations agencies and business leaders, congratulating her on Ford's compliments and offering to help with the anti-inflation initiative. The American Association of Advertising Agencies and the Advertising Council each offered to design a campaign to promote the new program. The public relations and advertising industries considered this an opportunity to showcase their skills and win over the government as they had during

World War II. According to a public relations newsletter then in circulation, the anti-inflation plan might "yield far-reaching benefits to PR as well as to the nation."[32]

Hundreds of newspaper articles covered Porter's contribution to Ford's economic initiatives, but they all got one detail wrong: Porter had no desire to serve as the program's coordinator. She had offered to publicize the issue and even serve on a committee to generate ideas, but she had no intention of carrying out the administrative duties. She did not consider herself part of the Ford administration, and she resisted suggestions she was selling out her politics or being manipulated. Even Sumner Collins, in a rare public comment about his wife, tried to dispel the prevailing narrative, telling an interviewer that Porter was not a political appointee and that she was only trying to help generate ideas.[33] The misconception likely originated as a miscommunication between Ford and Porter. Porter told interviewers she had tried to be firm with the White House on the boundaries of her role but found herself at a loss for words when Ford spoke with her personally. He had just visited his wife, Betty, in the hospital, and Porter said she had felt sorry for him. Feeling sympathetic, and no doubt trying to be diplomatic, Porter might have allowed the president to believe she was willing to play a more active role in the campaign. Nevertheless, she worked quickly to relegate herself to a symbolic function. She clarified her position with White House aides and in interviews with reporters. She was happy to chair a committee as a figurehead, she said, but she would not coordinate the program. Admonishing journalists to get their facts straight, she said she had a column to write and was not a member of the Ford administration.[34]

The lack of clarity over Porter's role spoke to a major problem that plagued the initiative from the beginning: a lack of precision and planning. On October 8, 1974, before anyone had agreed to coordinate the effort, Ford introduced his anti-inflation initiative to a national audience in a speech before a joint session of Congress. Again, he credited Porter by name, borrowing her reputation as an advocate of American consumers to soften his perceived aloofness and marshal public support. He offered several vague suggestions and emphasized the program would rely on consumers' spirit and cooperation rather than government bureaucracy.

The president gave the flaccid speech an unfortunate element of spectacle by dramatically revealing a red-and-white button hand-painted with the letters WIN, for "Whip Inflation Now." Looking amateurish and silly, the small pin would become the convenient symbol of a failed idea as journalists and political opponents hung the entirety of Ford's anti-inflation policy on a slogan and a lapel button.

Whip Inflation Now

The idea for a slogan had come from White House speechwriter Paul Theis, whose first suggestion was "IF," which stood for "Inflation Fighter."[35] Under this program, businesses that agreed not to raise prices for six months would be rewarded with "IF" decals and pennants, which they could display in their windows to show customers they were eager warriors against inflation and thus encourage consumers to patronize their stores: "IF you want a better America, patronize stores which display this emblem."[36] The program also called for the government to reserve its own spending for businesses that agreed to the anti-inflation pledge as well as possible tax breaks for workers and businesses. A memo from Paul Theis to William Seidman ended with a major miscalculation: "Since this program is voluntary, it would depend upon the public and local IF committees largely for enforcement. It would require no vast new Federal bureaucracy to administer."[37] Notes on a memo from Porter indicated she approved of the measure directing government spending toward cooperative businesses. However, near the sentence that spoke of local initiatives, she wrote: "*Gotta ask 1st.*" She also wrote a note reemphasizing that the administration should approach the Advertising Council and the Public Relations Society of America.

Porter must have realized it did not make sense to impose a private, grassroots effort from the Oval Office. In fact, this was a fundamental flaw in the program. The administration wanted the anti-inflation initiative to be a citizen-driven effort led by local officials, but the idea, as well as the instructions, had originated at the top of the political hierarchy. Furthermore, rather than take the time to sow the seeds of the program and solicit input from those who would be asked to carry it out, the administration wanted to move quickly with immediate—yet voluntary—implementation by an army of advocates who were not entirely sure what they were supposed to do.

The "IF" slogan was soon abandoned for sounding too tentative, much to the approval of Porter, who had sought input on a new slogan from her contacts in advertising and business.[38] Over the course of five days, a campaign was designed by Benton and Bowles, a New York City advertising firm, which came up with the WIN logo: three white sans-serif letters over a PMS Red No. 185 background.[39] The agency distributed a spec sheet to 6,000 manufacturers of pennants, buttons, and bumper stickers, giving them permission to reproduce the logo as long as they used it tactfully.[40] Out of respect for those who had donated their professional services, the agency also requested suppliers hold down their prices rather than exploit the WIN logo to turn a quick profit.[41]

The week after Ford announced the WIN program in his speech to Congress, his aides requested time on all three television networks. The president would be speaking to the Future Farmers of America in Kansas City, and White House officials assured network executives the speech would include significant policy proposals worthy of an interruption in regular programming. Instead, Ford merely updated the public on the membership of the Citizens Action Committee, emphasizing that Porter, as chair, had demanded he not try to influence the committee. He seemed to be using the appearance to act as the nation's cheerleader-in-chief, rallying Americans to beat inflation and convincing them they had the strength to do it.[42] To that end, he delivered twelve simple recommendations for consumers, business owners, and legislators. To paraphrase, he asked everyone to do the following:

1. Balance their household budgets.
2. Postpone borrowing.
3. Save money.
4. Conserve energy.
5. Shop wisely and look for bargains.
6. Recycle.
7. Make their own household repairs.
8. Avoid raising prices (to retailers).
9. Eliminate unnecessary regulations (to government officials).

10. Improve their productivity (to workers).

11. Clean their plates at dinner.

12. Safeguard their health.

Many of these recommendations matched the "copy points" Porter had been circulating to advertisers and public relations executives as she sought their counsel on how to design an effective campaign.[43] The suggestions for consumers were essentially what she had been telling her readers since World War II about how to manage their personal finances, now presented as a patriotic way to serve the country. It might have been good advice, but it struck the political elite—and the broadcasters who had reluctantly preempted their programming—as absurd coming from the president in a speech carried live on network television. Some commentators described Ford as paternalistic and out of touch. Others, more cynically, viewed the speech as a tactical move to seize airtime before the midterm elections.[44]

As platitudinous as Ford's speech was, it was generally well received by the public. About 167,000 people wrote to the White House offering to help.[45] Businesses, sensing an opportunity, immediately began using WIN rhetoric in their advertising.[46] Other businesses planned to hand out promotional items.[47] Car dealerships, grocery stores, and retailers cut their prices modestly and advertised they had done so.[48] McDonald's even rolled back prices and began airing "McWin" commercials.[49] In the weeks following Ford's speech, Adcraft Manufacturing received orders for more than ten million WIN buttons, including one million for Budget Rental Cars.[50] No less an expert than Robert Slater, the man who had designed the yellow smiley face, predicted the WIN button would exceed that one in popularity.[51]

When the Citizens Action Committee to Fight Inflation was formed, with Sylvia Porter as its chair, it included prominent members from business, nonprofit organizations, the advertising industry, consumer representatives, and political groups. The group immediately adopted a statement of principle that identified its goal as raising public awareness and leading a private volunteer effort to hold down prices and conserve energy: "The Citizens Action Committee to Fight Inflation is a non-partisan, volunteer working committee. The committee will develop public understanding and participation in a nationwide effort to control inflation and save energy. This non-partisan committee dealing with a non-partisan problem will mobilize the nation through all of its people. The committee calls on every American, on Federal, state and local governments, organizations, business and labor to WIN the fight against inflation."[52]

Despite the positive response to the program, major problems were immediately apparent.[53] Russell Freeburg, formerly the managing editor and Washington bureau chief of the *Chicago Tribune*, had been appointed executive director of the committee. He was working out of borrowed space in the Old Executive Office Building in Washington, DC, with two full-time volunteers and no funding when the president went on national television and asked the American people to pledge their assistance.[54] The tiny office was in no way prepared to handle the hundreds of thousands of letters that fell like an avalanche on top of hundreds of phone calls every day. Porter's personal secretary even commented on the office's lack of organization: "I shutter [sic] to think what they are going to do with the mail we send them. If this is a sample of their work, God help us too!"[55]

Freeburg attributed legislators' denial of government funding to their lack of trust in the executive branch following Watergate.[56] In effect, the Citizens Action Committee was reduced to an unfunded federal mandate. "They announced the program and then said, 'Develop it,'" Freeburg said later.[57] Several people involved in the campaign, including Porter, would say they had been given the task of building an airplane while it was in the air.[58] The committee mailed letters to mayors and governors, asking them to set up WIN committees, and encouraged involvement from nonprofit organizations, schools, and labor groups.[59] State and local officials expressed their support but indicated they were confused about what to do. Utah Governor Calvin Rampton wrote to Ford that he was reluctant to ask people to serve on a committee unless their responsibilities were clear.[60] When White House aides met with television producers, such as Norman Lear, to encourage them to work inflation and WIN rhetoric into their scripts, the producers expressed frustration that the WIN program was not more specific. Nevertheless, "the opinion seems to be universally held among these media people whose job it is to judge the desires of their audiences that the American people are ready to sacrifice if the call is clearly explained and loudly sounded," one White House memo stated.[61]

Criticism came from outside as well as inside the government. One of Porter's neighbors sent her a clip of a critical opinion article that had been published in the *New York Times*. The neighbor included a personal note calling the essay a more accurate assessment of the economic situation than the one put forward by Porter and the White House. She also said the piece expressed a view that was more representative of public opinion.[62] The op-ed, written by Betty Jarmusch of Shaker Heights, Ohio, had contested the idea that the average consumer was responsible for inflation and pointed to the problems of Watergate and the Vietnam War. "Somebody up there on the summit felt compelled to place the responsibility—if not the blame—for the economic crisis on us average, pitiful Americans," Jarmusch wrote.[63] Jarmusch found the government's appeal to Americans' patriotism especially cynical, given the self-serving decisions of U.S. banks, corporations, and the military. Other writers thought the committee was a waste of Porter's talent as an economist. One citizen suggested the economy could not be fixed through conservation efforts and pleaded with Ford: "Miss Porter is one of the nation's most erudite and versatile economists. . . . Please don't waste Miss Porter on light bulbs."[64]

Critics were striking at a major flaw in the logic of the Citizens Action Committee (CAC). Porter, Ford, and others had assumed inflation could be handled in a nonpartisan, nonpolitical way. In its one-paragraph statement of principle, the CAC had used the word "non-partisan" three times, and committee members further emphasized it in interviews and other public communication. Porter told one interviewer she was a lifelong Democrat and did not see inflation as a partisan issue. It made her angry when people suggested she had been manipulated by the administration.[65] Supporters of the program believed all parties—Democrats and Republicans, businesses and consumers—would unite around a campaign to encourage individuals to act in their self-interest. In their view, inflation did not carry the same political charge as taxes and government spending. Furthermore, the committee had received no public funding, so it could not be characterized as a new government program. The leaders of the committee thought of their work as a public service rather than a political initiative.

As anger and counterarguments quickly formed in reaction to the committee, its proponents learned that enlisting individuals to control inflation was seen as taking a position on the nation's economic problems—a position that elicited opposition from all sides. The U.S. Chamber of Commerce believed Ford's plan punished businesses, which were asked to lower prices, and favored labor, which was asked to increase productivity but not to hold down wages. The Chamber believed this amounted to unilateral disarmament for businesses in the war against inflation. Others thought the program put the onus on consumers while still encouraging them to part with their money—redirecting it, perhaps, but still spending it.[66] It seemed impossible to separate economics from politics.

On November 11, 1974, members of the committee held a press conference to clarify their mission, neutralize negative publicity, and present a united front to journalists. Freeburg, the executive director, and key members gathered in Room 2008 of the Old Executive Office Building. Porter began the press conference by announcing that a task force led by Mary Katherine Miller, president of the General Federation of Women's Clubs, had reached an agreement on three voluntary anti-inflation pledges to be signed by businesses, workers, and consumers.[67] She primed her audience by confiding the pledges had elicited in her, "an ordinarily quite cynical person, an increasing respect," and directed any follow-up questions to other committee members.[68] The approach might have worked well in an interview but did not charm an antagonistic gaggle of Washington reporters ready to parse words. The first question, after Porter and Miller had announced and read the pledges, went to Porter: If she was so cynical, why did she think the voluntary pledges would help lower inflation? She answered that the response to the committee since its inception had been widespread and positive: "The average citizen is much more serious about this than he or she is being given credit for."[69]

Adept at managing her own public image, Porter was not accustomed to having her words scrutinized by a press corps emboldened by the Watergate scandal. Porter interrupted the next follow-up question by trying to steer the spotlight back to other members of the committee, but not before letting slip a warning about what would happen—by which she meant wage-price controls—if inflation was not brought down. Again, the reporters pounced, wondering whether she had inside information that conflicted with Ford's repeated assurances that under no circumstances would he enact wage-price controls. Porter said no, she had reached that conclusion on her own.

When a reporter asked her to name three specific ideas the committee had received from the public, Porter was finally able to direct the questioning to Miller. What followed, however, was a series of questions that verged on being hostile: How could a small group of citizens possibly solve the problem of inflation? What about government action? This time, several less prominent members of the committee stepped into the fray, arguing that voluntary measures were worth trying in the face of bureaucratic ineffectiveness.[70]

The group was presenting a united front, but that changed with the next question, which was directed to Arch Booth, president of the U.S. Chamber of Commerce. Given the opening, Booth went on the attack. He voiced his vehement disagreement with the committee's conclusions, especially its sympathy with workers.[71] He wanted unions to sign a pledge saying they would not ask for wage increases. In response, Ronald Brown, a lawyer with the National Urban League, interjected to say that members of the committee who had written the pledges were behind them unanimously, and that Booth had not been involved. At this point, members of the committee broke rank and began exchanging heated opinions, goaded by a rapt press corps. Porter defended the decision to ask labor to increase productivity as the ideal way to stabilize prices, invoking her training as an economist.

In response to a wry, penultimate question—"May I ask what keeps this happy family together?"—Porter squarely blamed Booth for the rancor: "I think the task force has achieved a magnificent degree of unanimity. The fact of the matter is that Mr. Booth walked out and came back today only because now we were having our first press conference with substantive results to announce."[72] The whole scene was so uncustomary that journalists dropped their veil of objectivity. One reporter said he hoped Booth would not be kicked out of the committee, and another offered the opinion that government action, not citizen action, would curb inflation. Porter tersely finished by announcing plans to promote community gardens and recycling. She also indicated that the membership of the current task force—"like one happy family"—would remain unchanged.[73]

The press conference badly damaged the Citizens Action Committee by revealing its dysfunction and discord. If there had been any doubt about its future, the answer came the next day, on November 12, 1974, when presidential press secretary Ron Nessen delivered the decisive blow by acknowledging the nation had entered a recession, making the focus on inflation seem moot. Congressional Democrats then demanded the television networks offer their party equal time if they broadcast any WIN-related ads or content. Led by Representative Benjamin Rosenthal of New York, the Democrats accused the Advertising Council of "becoming a propaganda organ for a partisan political point of view."[74] More than thirty representatives signed a letter calling the WIN program controversial and noting that NBC had been worried enough about the Fairness Doctrine that the network allowed Senator Ed Muskie to respond to Ford's speech to the Future Farmers of America.[75] The Ad Council had been involved prior to Ford's speech, they pointed out, which made it complicit in Ford's rhetoric rather than a third party offering help after the WIN campaign was in motion. "We realize that the Ad Council has over the years served increasingly as the federal government's free advertising agency," the letter said. "Many Council campaigns . . . have a tendency to paper over ineffective governmental action in dealing with root social problems."[76] The legislators sent a copy of the letter to the networks and to the Ad Council. In a subsequent press conference, Rosenthal called WIN "a cruel hoax that is not a program but a hollow hope. Consumers need more than pep talks from the coach exhorting everyone to get out there and plant a victory garden, eat everything on their plates and pay higher taxes."[77]

Members of the committee—especially those, like Porter, who considered themselves Democrats or independents—resented the political attacks and thought the House Democrats were overreaching. Robert Keim of the Ad Council responded forcefully to the legislators with a letter defending his industry and the integrity of the committee.[78] Keim pointed

out the Ad Council had never designed any television spots for the committee because there was no money to do so. Even if it had, he said, the
ads would have been comparable to antidrug public service announce-
ments, donated to the government to save taxpayers money and serve
the public interest. The founding principle of the Ad Council, he wrote,
was the idea that individual Americans could be mobilized to act in ways
that could help ameliorate socioeconomic problems.[79] This was not an
endorsement of any political view about the government's role in creating
or solving those problems, he argued, but simply an attempt to persuade
individuals to engage in productive, healthy behaviors. A television sta-
tion in northeastern Pennsylvania lent its support, airing an editorial that
wondered aloud why anyone would have a problem with the committee's
work. "We are all so desirous of hearing that side of the story that WDAU
here and now announces its editorial endorsement of the WIN program
and—under the Fairness Doctrine—invites Mr. Rosenthal and his bunch
of losers to reply."[80]

A Comic Opera

Realizing she had become more enmeshed in government than she ever
wanted to be—and trying to stay above partisan politics—Porter had
been slowly backing away from the committee's work since it began. She
had asked Mary Katherine Miller to take the lead. "It is my deep feeling
that I have grabbed enough, if not too much, in fact, of the spotlight. . . .
I, therefore, am determined to move into the background and to turn the
spotlight over to you and what you do. I will back you up," she wrote to
Miller.[81] Porter was more comfortable playing a symbolic or a promotional
role, as she had for many government initiatives. It was a way to stay in the
public eye and attract publicity for her column and books. In fact, the timing of the Citizens Action Committee coincided neatly with the upcoming
publication of *Sylvia Porter's Money Book*. The attention might boost sales,
as long as Porter could find a way out of the political jungle.

   In November 1974, as the recession looked more menacing, Porter
received a letter from Freeburg, the CAC's executive director, advising
her to get out. The committee faced opposition from Democrats and was
getting little support from the White House. "Everything is adding up

to some very rough times politically. I don't see any way you can come out a winner. Your career and personal political beliefs must receive first consideration," Freeburg wrote to Porter.[82] He reported getting bleak feedback from companies that had once supported the program. The textile industry, he said, could no longer cooperate because they expected a third of their production capacity to be shut down by December 15. The automotive industry, also, was facing a slump. No more orders were being placed for WIN buttons. Freeburg advised Porter to look for a graceful exit even as he continued to seek ways to make the CAC more effective.

Freeburg eventually left the post of executive director while Donald Sheehan, a volunteer consultant, proposed setting up the CAC as a nonprofit group that would educate the public about capitalism. "If business needs anything it needs to be understood," he wrote.[83] If fulfilled, the memo would have marked a departure from the CAC's focus on the needs of consumers. The memo openly conflated the roles of citizen and consumer, implying the government needed to socialize Americans into capitalism just as it socialized children into democracy—a philosophical position that lent some validity to the accusations of politicization in the CAC's work. Edward Block, who replaced Freeburg as executive director of the committee, acknowledged WIN had been a failure.[84] Under his leadership, the CAC's mission was updated to focus on energy and food conservation.[85] However, the viability of the committee remained a concern, as an intense meeting at the White House would soon make painfully clear.[86]

On January 18, 1975, Porter presided over a nearly three-hour-long meeting of the newly incorporated and tax-exempt Citizens Action Committee. The meeting, originally to be held at the Old Executive Office Building, was given a more impressive venue: the Cabinet Room of the White House. The meeting was designed to set a new agenda for the committee and shore up embattled members with a show of administrative support. It failed on both measures. President Ford's economic advisers gave the committee an economic briefing, which was followed by a visit from the president himself, who thanked the committee for its hard work and emphasized the administration would be focusing its efforts on unemployment, not inflation. Committee members were little more than a captive audience for these monologues; their input was not solicited, and they were not invited to ask questions. Porter would later tell an interviewer she was mortified by the officials' behavior and had tried to interrupt but was not successful.[87] After the officials left the room, Porter told the committee she believed that it finally had a mission, but that she still believed inflation was the bigger problem: "If we are to avoid the straitjacket of wage-price controls, rationing in any area and the other restraints which are repugnant to a free society, we will have to do it on our own. I hope I spoke for the committee."[88]

With this single statement, Porter exposed the assumption in her logic, and also a conflict within the committee, that would never be resolved: although she had doggedly insisted the committee's work was not political, she had just disavowed government intervention in the economy. It might have seemed like common sense to her, but others heard it as a frank, ideological statement about the proper role of government. Carol Foreman of the Consumer Federation interjected to say that Porter did not speak for her. Foreman and Clarence Mitchell of the National Association for the Advancement of Colored People (NAACP) had been distressed they had not been allowed to ask questions of the president or other officials when they were in the room. Foreman was also angry that the pledges she and others had developed were not used. "I think that the committee got under way without a great deal of planning and that it hasn't functioned very well as a result of that and then it has reneged on some of the things I thought we agreed to in the first few minutes when we were here the first time around. I think it is a horse running on three crippled legs and it is about time to dispose of the committee against inflation," she said.[89]

Ronald Brown of the Urban League agreed, pointing to how much time committee members had spent writing the discarded pledges. Furthermore, he took issue with Porter's statement that the committee was nonpartisan. "I think when our chairwoman makes sweeping statements, we all find repugnant any kind of rationing or any kind of program with government intervention, it rankles a few of us. I think that tends to make it a partisan kind of thing, which it isn't," he said.[90] Porter accepted the reprimand, but the damage was done. The schism that had threatened the committee since its inception finally had broken open, revealing the miscalculation made by Porter, Ford, and others. They had believed there were certain truths in economics that were unassailable, that it was possible for people with different political perspectives to reach a consensus on a common problem. They were wrong. Foreman resigned in disgust immediately after the meeting and would later tell an interviewer: "Is there any bigger joke in the country than the WIN button?"[91]

The WIN slogan was dropped in March, and the committee limped along, looking for money and a mission.[92] In addition to changing its focus to energy, the CAC had also decided at meetings in February and March that government funding should be sought and private donations used to supplement public revenue. A young activist named Valerie Ransone took over the administrative duties as national coordinator and tried to redirect the current of bad publicity, even self-referentially poking fun at the committee's mistakes by appearing in a news photo with the large slogan hung upside-down in the office. There was no slowing the river of bad press, however. News headlines delivered easy puns, such as "Win-Less Volunteer Program to Press Energy Conservation"; "WIN Motto Is Loser as Ford Committee Drops Theme"; and "WIN, the Anti-Inflation Slogan, Scrapped after a Losing Season."[93] Ransone, who remained in contact with Porter, was hoping for $150,000 from the Federal Energy Administration to fund conservation efforts but never received it. Ironically, her salary was being paid with a $10,000 check from an anonymous Dallas oil executive. The check had been mailed to the WIN program on November 11 but lay in a pile of unopened letters for months because there had been no one to open it.[94]

Porter finally resigned from the committee. In a letter to President Ford, she cited the challenges the committee had faced and suggested it would be better served by someone with more time to devote to it.[95] "We were unable to exploit the success of your WIN symbol because we had no programs for voluntary action and virtually no staff or funding," she wrote, echoing what she would tell reporters.[96] Nevertheless, she wrote, the committee remained intact and held promise as a mechanism to encourage energy conservation. She recommended Tom McCall, the former governor of Oregon, to replace her as chairman. McCall announced publicly that he would accept the position if asked by the president him-self, but the call never came.[97] Without champions or a chairman, the CAC ceased to function. A year later, Leo Perlis of the AFL-CIO called for its dissolution.[98]

Some members of the committee sensed a loss far greater than an ill-conceived program that had been created too hastily and then misman-aged. In the scorn that had been heaped upon their initiative, they sensed a poisonous cynicism that promised to taint any effort to unify Ameri-cans. Thinking the nation's problems were too dire for such antipathy, the NAACP's Clarence Mitchell told a reporter he had no desire to be part of a "comic opera."[99] To idealists, it appeared the nation had entered an era in which volunteer public servants were unfairly ridiculed—not for mis-managing an attempt to improve social conditions, but for making any attempt at all.

But the focus on the individual that had been so marketable as a per-sonal finance column simply did not work as public policy, especially after the disillusionment caused by the Vietnam War and Watergate. In addition, Ford's metaphor of a "war" against inflation never took hold in the way he had hoped. An anonymous memo in Porter's personal papers summed up the failure:

> This is not the day after Pearl Harbor. There is no Axis whose target coordinates are known. There are no beaches to hit or ships to sink or ports to capture by which we may know, week by week, whether we are winning.
>
> This is the day after Hugh Hefner and instant credit and barbecue grills and two cars in every garage and great acquisitive expectations. . . . You cannot talk your way out of inflation. You cannot talk your way into prosperity. . . . You also dare not dismiss the fact that Americans no lon-ger buy the quick scare.[100]

The government—through its appointed citizens—had essentially prescribed an individualistic solution to a systemic problem. The ensu-ing debacle showed there were some economic issues Americans would not allow to be depoliticized. Given the events of the sixties and seven-ties, voters were reluctant to embrace paternalistic lectures about personal responsibility. The red-and-white WIN buttons foisted on the public became a joke and led younger journalists to question Porter's credentials. Noting the media's frequent references to Porter as a "trained economist," *Washington Post* reporter Nicholas Von Hoffman, clearly ignorant of her career or expertise, wrote: "Where Porter received her training wasn't mentioned in the dispatches. . . . Maybe what Porter really said was that she was a trained *home* economist" (emphasis in original).[101] Von Hoffman's condescending suggestion was that Porter take her WIN buttons and dump them on the threshold of the Federal Reserve.

Porter had put herself at the center of the nation's news agenda. The visibility may have helped propel her to the top of the bestseller lists when *Sylvia Porter's Money Book* came out in 1975, but the misadventure had hurt her reputation. She had gambled some of her cultural capital and lost. Although she was still a powerful player, she had shown she was not infallible. After the *Money Book*—and the devastating death of her second husband in 1977—Porter began strategizing her endgame. There was still one goal she had not pursued but soon would: her own magazine.

5

Brand Name

AS THE ECONOMIC TUMULT of the seventies continued, Porter's career gathered steam and increased in volatility. Now a legendary columnist and bestselling author, Porter received at least 2,000 letters a week from readers and received more requests for television and radio bookings than she could possibly accept.[1] She was invited to host a radio program three times a week on NBC (an offer she declined),[2] and was frequently invited to appear on *Wall Street Week* with Louis Rukeyser.[3] It seemed that lending her name and reputation to President Ford's failed anti-inflation campaign might have cost her the approval of some colleagues but had cemented her status as a national figure. Simply put, Sylvia Porter was an icon: financial adviser to the masses. In 1972 the New York Financial Writers Association finally saw fit to accept her as a member, a year after women had been admitted to the National Press Club and the same year women at the *New York Times, Time,* and NBC sued their employers for sex discrimination.[4] Activists around the country were demanding equal rights for women under the law and more recognition of women's contributions to society. The second wave of the feminist movement—nothing short of a social revolution—inspired a younger generation of journalists to take a special interest in Porter's career.

From Glamour Girl to Wonder Woman

The feminism of the late sixties and early seventies gave the public a new framework for appreciating Porter's achievements. Proponents of women's rights celebrated her as a pioneer and a role model for smart, career-oriented women.[5] Whereas journalists had once portrayed Porter as an anomaly, they now covered her as part of a large cultural movement.

144

Headline writers were still prone to sexist statements, such as "Femininity and Wit Mask Sylvia's Money Expertise," which implied that money was not a naturally feminine (or humorous) pursuit, but media coverage of Porter in the seventies generally was more Wonder Woman than Glamour Girl.[6]

Porter welcomed these portrayals as a strong, feisty, unapologetic career woman, but she told one writer she was beyond feminism. "I've lived it!" she said, pointing to her overwhelming success despite forty years of discrimination in a male-dominated field. She told a student in 1974 that she had overcome sexism by making herself attractive—but not available—to men: "If I had played around or did anything wrong, they would have found any excuse to get rid of me. I dressed carefully and conducted myself with dignity. Had I been fat or sloppy, I might not have had a chance."[7] Porter's popularity among men was, indeed, an important factor in her success, a fact recognized by the gender-conscious younger generation. One writer described the attention heaped on her by the opposite sex, who doted on her at meetings and press conferences. The admiration was reciprocated by Porter, who enjoyed the company of men and charmed her high-status sources with easy repartee.[8] The same writer also noted Porter's support of female colleagues, which was a common observation in the feminist-framed media portrayals. However, positioning Porter as an eager member of the sisterhood obscured the contradictions in Porter's relationships with women and with the women's movement.

Porter supported feminism as a public endeavor but not always a private one, eliding one of the key tenets of second-wave feminism. For example, despite her encouragement of women's equal participation in political and professional spheres, she upheld a conventional narrative about domestic gender roles. She told one interviewer women would emasculate their husbands if they were too aggressive and, at times, should "back up and be the little female" if they wanted to preserve their marriages.[9] She also spoke openly of her initial discomfort with the publicity-seeking tactics of second-wave feminists but said she had arrived at the realization that some amount of spectacle was necessary for the movement to gain traction.[10] While Porter eventually bestowed her approval on the 1970s archetype of the passionate women's-libber, she continued to assert her belief that, as a practical matter, women should defer to men in personal relationships if they wanted things to go smoothly.

Porter never wavered in her position that women should be given the same professional opportunities as men but shifted her rhetoric over the years to align with the dominant ideology regarding social roles. In the thirties and forties, she argued for women's presence in the workplace in terms of individual rights and the needs of a nation at war. After World War II, she tempered her passion and simply argued the issue was moot because women already were working for wages and were not going to quit. In the sixties, she emphasized that women worked outside the home because their families needed the money, and she further argued that if they stopped, the American economy would collapse.[11] It was not until the seventies, safely within the cultural context of the second-wave women's movement, that Porter would express an emotional, deeply felt reaction to male chauvinism. She used spoken commentary on a feminist television program to respond to an unnamed male political columnist who had said women's jobs were secondary to men's: "By what standard does any man determine that his right to work in a paying occupation is greater than a woman's right, and by what yardstick does that columnist decide that his loss of a job would be a catastrophe, but my loss? Hunh, it'd be a loss of an extra job."[12]

Porter believed more in the freedom of individuals than in the power of sisterhood, but she did advocate women's recognition of one another. In 1981 she received a Headliner Award from the Association for Women in Communications. In her acceptance speech, she mentioned that a few years prior, a female scientist had declined a Woman of the Year award on the premise that men and women should be considered equally for the same awards. Porter took a different view. "As long as women still do not have equal rights, equal recognition, or even the chance to compete on an equal basis within the establishment, I would continue to uphold awards to women as women, to women as role models to spur other millions of women on the way upward," she said.[13] Porter also said she despised women who made it to the top but did not reach their hand back to help others. "These 'Aunt Toms.' I have as much hatred for these women as any young woman," she sputtered to an interviewer. "Successful women who don't share what they have learned are beneath contempt. These women suffer from youth envy and simple jealousy. I do not know how to spell the word jealousy."[14]

Women could not afford to wait for men to grant them equal status, Porter said. They had to demand it by educating themselves, refusing to work for companies that did not promote women, and acting in solidarity with one another. She began to define women's success not only by individual attainment but also by collective impact. For example, mentioning a woman who had sued her employer for sex discrimination, Porter told an interviewer in 1972 the woman would lose her job but the company was now scrambling to hire other women to improve its image. Despite the personal sacrifice this woman had made, Porter spoke glowingly of what she had accomplished.[15] Porter's approval was evident, but she spoke only in general terms; she did not name the woman or the lawsuit. Tellingly, a number of women journalists had filed lawsuits against their employers in New York and Washington, DC, that very year. Porter might have voiced her support for their cause, but she never commented publicly on those lawsuits or on any specific instances of professional discrimination against women. What Porter espoused in theory she did not always put into practice. Asked by a reporter whether it was men's or women's fault that women held so few executive positions in business, she said it was the fault of both.[16]

Nevertheless, women who followed Porter into financial journalism were mindful of her impact on their careers. Jane Bryant Quinn, who entered the field in direct competition with Porter, said: "Finance was a man's job, and then Sylvia proved that it was the job of anybody who understood it. She fought a lot of battles that I didn't have to."[17] Ellen Hermanson, a researcher, told an interviewer that everyone in financial journalism—especially women—owed many of their opportunities to her.[18] In 1971, acknowledging the arrival of Quinn and others into the field, Porter told an interviewer she was delighted women were being sought for jobs in financial journalism, noting that had not been the case several decades ago.[19] Ignoring Lydia Ratcliff, Porter would claim Brooke Shearer had been her first full-time writer and said she had chosen Shearer over a long list of male applicants. She admitted practicing a kind of reverse sexism but said she wanted to support other women in the field.[20]

One such woman who worked for Porter in the eighties was grateful for the opportunity that led to her own success in financial journalism. Beth Kobliner graduated from Brown University in 1986 and wrote to Brown alumnus Joel Davis, president of the company that was then publishing *Sylvia Porter's Personal Finance Magazine*, to ask about a job. Davis put her in touch with Pat Estess, the magazine's editor, who introduced her to Porter.[21] Kobliner was just twenty-one years old and did not have a professional portfolio. She was surprised when Porter hired her and stunned when she realized she would be writing the columns herself, especially because she had no background in finance. Porter's driver picked up Kobliner once or twice a week and transported her to Pound Ridge, where she delivered the work she had been doing. The two women went over it together, with Porter making light—but precise—edits. Eventually, Porter agreed to allow Kobliner to insert internal credit in a column every other week. One time, when an editor had deleted the credit, Porter even typed a letter to the syndicate's president, protesting the omission.[22] After working for Porter, Kobliner wrote for *Money* magazine as the youngest person ever to be hired as a writer at Time, Inc., and went on to publish her own book and website on personal finance. She was grateful to Porter, who had served as her inspiration and mentor.

Other women writers perceived Porter's role in their careers to be more symbolic. According to Shearer, who wrote for Porter in the seventies, the kind of intimate guidance required to groom a successor was simply not her style. "I don't think anybody did that for her, and therefore she was not going to do it for us. It just didn't even occur to her. She grew up in a rough-and-tumble world, where you didn't have things given to you."[23] Financial writer Carol Mathews echoed that perception, saying Porter could be generous with other women, but that she had "felt that discrimination very, very keenly."[24] Eileen Shanahan, who was a well-known economics writer for the *Journal of Commerce* in the fifties and the *New York Times* in the sixties and seventies, told an interviewer: "I was the only woman in daily newspapers in Washington doing national economic policy for a long, long time. And Sylvia Porter was in New York and that was about it. I never knew her very well because we only met a few times because she hardly ever came to Washington or I to New York, but she was always cordial. Didn't help me, really, but she was cordial and friendly and supportive and go-get-'em, and so forth."[25] Warren Boroson, who wrote for Porter late in her career, said she was threatened by younger writers and thus incapable of sustaining long-term associations.[26] Even Kobliner, who had enjoyed a positive relationship with Porter, earned her contempt when she left to work for *Money* magazine. In a memo to the syndicate, Porter's husband sniffed that he and Porter had not been satisfied with Kobliner's output and claimed her contract would have been terminated had she not resigned.[27]

Although Porter was theoretically supportive of other women in the field, she was fiercely protective of her turf. She responded to questions about possible successors with haughty defensiveness. In 1974, she told Shearer, who was writing a profile about her, "Let's face it. There's no other game in town. No one has come up with my particular touch. And I have no intention of giving up my column until the day I die."[28] Almost ten years later, she would continue to claim she had no competition, despite the arrival of many other women—and men—into the field. None of them could match her skill and knowledge, she said. Once there appeared a successor "good enough to give me a push is the day—I trust with grace and gracefulness—I'll perform a deep curtsy and step aside. That day has not yet come," she said.[29]

In practice, Porter tried to thwart potential competitors. In 1982 her lawyers wrote to her syndicate, expressing concern that another column it carried, "Smart Shopping" by Lori Gray, competed with Porter's and thus constituted a conflict of interests. The vice president of the syndicate, seemingly surprised someone of Porter's stature would feel threatened by a startup columnist such as Gray, responded: "[W]hen a writer has the scope of a Sylvia Porter (and so far as I know, no one else does) she may touch occasionally on almost any area—from IRAs to buying stereos to garage sales to life insurance. Lori Gray will never wander into any of these other areas. Hers is a column of very modest scope and, I must admit, modest distribution. No one will ever approach Sylvia Porter in breadth, authority, integrity, and reportorial scoops, and I can't imagine encouraging anyone to try."[30]

Porter's apparent insecurity caused many difficulties in her professional relationships. "She was a very, very hard-driving person, very pushy. I realized early that if I let her, she'd walk all over me," said Lee Cohn, who cowrote Porter's newsletter, *Reporting on Governments*.[31] In fact, Porter once tried to renege on a compensation agreement with Cohn and his coauthor, Ben Weberman, who each wrote twenty-six newsletters a year. Under their work agreement, each was paid $18,000 and given five shares of the business every year. In 1973 Sumner Collins, Porter's second husband and the newsletter's publisher, did not transfer shares to the writers because, he wrote to his attorney, he was afraid of losing control of the enterprise.[32] Cohn wrote to ask why they had not received their shares. Porter's attorney—just as he had during the conflict with Ratcliff over *Sylvia Porter's Money Book*—responded that whatever the original agreement was, the writers had gotten their due and were selfish for demanding more.[33] However, there was no legal way out of the deal, and Collins resumed the proper transfer of shares. Weberman later assumed full ownership of the newsletter and bought Cohn's portion before selling the enterprise to a competitor.

The Last Dance

When Sumner Collins died of cancer in January 1977, the loss affected Porter not only personally but also professionally. Collins had lent the full weight of his business expertise to his wife's career. He encouraged her to think of herself as a brand, but he treated her journalistic success carefully and seemed to understand the roots of her authority. Collins had grounded Porter, anchoring her to the life and goals they shared. With Collins gone, Porter's inner circle and outer behavior changed dramatically. Collins's death and the instability that followed marked the start of the final stretch in Porter's career, a period when old relationships ended and new ones began. Porter's daughter bought land in Maine and moved there, by Porter's account, to escape the trappings of her mother's life.[34] Lydia Ratcliff, Porter's chief ghostwriter, had retired to her farm in

Vermont. About two years after Collins passed away, Porter married James Fox. A public relations executive, Fox set about corporatizing and sustaining Porter's brand through third-party business ventures and products. These were significant changes, which immediately became apparent in Porter's appearance and demeanor.

In September 1979 Porter sat before Tom Brokaw on NBC's *Today*. Porter was promoting her newest book of practical financial advice for middle-class Americans, which updated the material in her *Money Book* for the decade about to begin. Brokaw noted frightening facts about the economy—sky-high energy prices, repressive interest rates, slow job growth, stagnating wages—and wondered how people could cope. Porter agreed with Brokaw that it was a scary time and said her mailbox was full of letters from Americans wondering how to keep up with inflation. She warned viewers in search of a safe investment not to buy gold. For everybody else, she had only one word: chicken. "Chicken is a bargain. Chicken's a real bargain. So is turkey," she said.[35] Porter said she had always served veal to guests because it was versatile, but she would do so no longer. She would buy chicken in bulk and store it in her freezer. "This is the time of year to stock up," she said. A bemused Brokaw pointed out that most people did not eat veal; they had relied on chicken and many could not afford even that. The interview was strained, as Porter exhibited her first public signs of detachment, both from middle-income consumers, whom she had been advising for decades, and from the sharp, articulate persona she had developed during her career. The modern, Pauline Trigère–wearing, wisecracking Porter of just a few years prior appeared to be gone, replaced by a woman who looked remarkably older and out of touch.

Two months after the *Today* interview, Porter appeared on *The Merv Griffin Show*. For this appearance, she wore a blue gown with a ruffled collar and a massive diamond necklace. Her hair was bleached blond. She spoke loudly and frequently mugged to the audience. Griffin asked her thoughts about the economic crisis. She acknowledged Americans were facing an economic squeeze but exclaimed that some stores on Fifth Avenue were doing quite well because "the Arabs are in here buying, the Japanese are in here buying, the Dutch are in here buying, the Germans are in here buying. Everybody's buying except us!" Again, she advised the public not to buy gold, which she called a "barbaric metal."[36] The other guest that day, broadcast journalist Barbara Walters, appeared amused by her old acquaintance, whose behavior differed markedly from the controlled professionalism she had displayed only a few years earlier.

Trying to project an image that would appeal to whatever audience was in front of her, Porter betrayed the formidable discipline she had long exercised in her interviews with journalists. For example, asked by a reporter for the *Miami Herald* whether she had trouble balancing her checkbook, "like most women do," Porter answered, "Sure."[37] But she would soon tell *People* magazine, "That old bromide about women not being able to balance their checkbooks is ridiculous."[38] She also told *People* that she preferred stocks to bonds, even though she had built her career as a bond expert and still published a bond-trading newsletter.[39] To another interviewer, she claimed not to care about money at all, saying that if she had set out to be rich, she probably would have failed.[40] This last assertion—that she had never cared about money—seemed incongruous with her contractual conflicts and immoderate lifestyle, not to mention her publication of a veritable encyclopedia on the subject. Addressing the question of what had motivated her for so many years, but failing to offer a clear answer, she wrote to a friend: "What drives people like me? Not money, though I scarcely can say anyone can feel secure in a world as shaky and threatened as ours is now; not fame, for I've tasted that quite deeply and feel no striving for more and more; not frustration, for I am not in any way frustrated; not any of the obvious answers—and certainly not any of the who's-kidding-whom grandiose stuff that the big-wigs try to feed a gullible public."[41] Everyone who knew Porter recognized her internal drive, but few—perhaps not even Porter herself—understood it.

As Porter became more forward-thinking about her career, she sought ways to establish a legacy, something that would forever link her name with the journalistic genre she had originated. This was an objective her third husband encouraged and was committed to orchestrating. In the early eighties, Porter and Fox formed the Sylvia Porter Personal Finance Magazine Company and the Sylvia Porter Organization with a third party, publishing executive Carole Sinclair, to oversee and expand Porter's

empire. They produced books, videotapes, audiotapes, a retirement newsletter, computer software, and even a board game. But their primary product was a personal finance magazine that would carry Porter's brand and
continue her tradition of providing wide-ranging financial advice to the
middle class even after her death.

Starting a magazine with Porter had long been a goal of Sinclair's. The
two first collaborated in 1975 when Sinclair was working in the marketing
department of Doubleday and designed the brilliantly successful publicity campaign for *Sylvia Porter's Money Book*. "I could see what was happening in the area of business and finance. It was booming," Sinclair told
an interviewer.[42] She began looking for a magazine publisher and eventually pitched the idea for a personal finance magazine to Davis Publications, which published *Ellery Queen's Mystery Magazine, Alfred Hitchcock's
Mystery Magazine*, and *Isaac Asimov's Science Fiction Magazine*: digest-sized
genre magazines that licensed the names of famous figures. Joel Davis,
president of the company, hired Sinclair in 1979 with the sole purpose of
starting a magazine and retirement newsletter bearing Porter's name.

Sylvia Porter's Personal Finance Magazine launched in November 1983
with a party in the Drawing Room of the Helmsley Palace Hotel in New
York City.[43] Designed to be less sophisticated than *Money* but more ambitious than Kiplinger's *Changing Times*, the magazine had an initial circulation of 250,000 and was aimed at baby boomers with a median annual
income of $45,300 and a median age of forty-seven.[44] Each issue focused
on educating the upper middle class about investing its money, making
capital and large-scale purchases, and protecting itself against contingencies. The masthead listed Porter as editor-in-chief, Sinclair as publisher,
Pat Estess as editor, and Elana Lore as managing editor. It was produced
by the Sylvia Porter Personal Finance Magazine Company, which was
majority-owned by Davis Publications but also included Bear Stearns and
actor Burt Lancaster as investors.[45]

The industry considered the magazine, published six times a year,
an enormous success—perhaps even one of the most successful magazine launches ever.[46] *Advertising Age* credited Porter's "golden touch" for
the large amount of advertising sold in the first several issues, unusual
for a new magazine.[47] Porter had appeared on the cover of the first issue,

drawing attention to her trusted reputation, but her work would serve as a guide, not a focus, of the content. Sinclair and Davis told journalists that Porter edited every article that appeared in the magazine, but her declining health would make that level of involvement impossible.[48] Although she read every issue and called the magazine's offices if something did not meet her standards, she left most of the decisions to Fox, Sinclair, and the magazine's staff.[49]

In the early years of the magazine, its founders had difficulty agreeing on the scope of the content. Fox wanted to see exclusive, in-depth interviews with important people, like those that appeared in *Playboy*, which he believed would command publicity.[50] Porter suggested an efficient question-and-answer format for many articles, which she had used in her newspaper and *Ladies' Home Journal* columns.[51] She did not want to establish an advisory committee for the magazine because she thought it would be a mistake to give outsiders that much influence. The managing editor, Pat Estess, simply wanted a clear mission that was not driven by advertising or fickle cultural trends.[52] Gradually, the editors arrived at an effective formula, more technical than initially planned, which went beyond the basic principles of money management to provide in-depth analysis of financial issues. The ads strongly favored mutual funds and other investment vehicles driven by exploding interest and participation in the equity markets.

It took the magazine several years to achieve the right look and balance of editorial content, but its future looked promising. It was nominated for numerous industry awards, and it made *Ad Week*'s list of the top ten magazines in advertising revenue and page growth from 1984 to 1986.[53] It eventually led its competitors *Changing Times, Forbes, Business Week,* and *Inc.* in newsstand sales, coming in second only to *Money*.[54] Its circulation nearly doubled in six years.[55] By 1987 the publication had gained its footing and was publishing ten issues a year instead of six.[56]

Structural problems plagued the magazine, however, and despite its success it never became profitable. The titles Davis Publications had previously brought to market were fan-based digests that relied on submissions by readers. The overhead of the digests was low, which made profitability easier to achieve and, by comparison, made Porter's magazine seem like a money pit because it required original, commissioned reporting by staff writers and freelancers. Greg Daugherty, who was hired as managing editor in 1985 and eventually served as executive editor, found the company to be a strange fit for a magazine like Porter's. He wrote later: "On my first day at the magazine, the president of the company had taken me aside and said with frightening sincerity, 'We put out *Queen* with just two editors— and one of them isn't even full-time. I want you to find out why it takes eight people to put out *Porter.*' Somehow I knew we were in trouble."[57] James Fox thought Joel Davis, the company's president, was being disingenuous in his characterization of the other magazines' finances. Fox believed the company was paying the salaries of people working on other magazines with revenue from *Sylvia Porter's Personal Finance Magazine* (often referred to as SPPFM in memos).[58] In addition, Davis had borrowed the startup money for SPPFM and lent it to the subsidiary created to publish the magazine, charging the subsidiary a premium interest rate.[59] Fox believed Davis was ensuring the magazine would never be profitable since his contract with Porter required him to pay her $5,000 a month plus a share of the magazine's profits in order to license her name.[60]

Ultimately, though, it would be the economy—not poor management—that killed *Sylvia Porter's Personal Finance Magazine*. On October 19, 1987, the Dow Jones Industrial Average dropped 22 percent, damaging many mutual funds and annihilating their advertising budgets. Unfortunately, the November 1987 issue of SPPFM was already on newsstands; in it, the magazine exuded optimism about the financial markets and, seemingly, its own future. The magazine clung to life for a year as circulation rose without a solid advertising base to support it. According to the Audit Bureau of Circulation, *Sylvia Porter's Personal Finance Magazine* had 459,549 readers as of June 30, 1988; however, ads were down 36.67 percent in the January–February 1989 issue.[61] Lacking a diverse family of magazines with which to bundle advertising—a tactic other publishers, such as Time, Inc., could use to ride out the recession—Davis Publications began looking for a buyer for SPPFM.[62] Fox and Carole Sinclair were hoping Davis would sell to a company that would continue the magazine rather than fold it, but Davis's priority was getting the highest possible price in order to satisfy his debt.[63] What interested buyers wanted, however, was the one thing Davis could not offer: Porter's name. She, alone, owned the rights to her name and was only licensing it to the magazine and other products affiliated with SPPFM.[64] Without a buyer willing to continue under that arrangement, Davis sold the list of subscribers to *Changing Times* (eventually renamed *Kiplinger's Personal Finance*) for $2.2 million, and *Sylvia Porter's Personal Finance Magazine* folded.[65]

Fading Flame

Porter considered the magazine the first failure of her life,[66] but its demise was more emblematic of this stage of her career than perhaps she cared to admit. As a brand, Sylvia Porter was still top shelf. Public relations executives rated her name as one of the most marketable seals of approval that could be given to a product or service.[67] But as a journalist, she was in shaky territory after trading authority and authenticity for superstardom, and she suffered some discrediting of her work. By the eighties, Porter's use of ghostwriters was no secret to anyone working in financial journalism. A joke began to circulate: "Half of America reads Sylvia Porter's column. The other half writes it."[68] Furthermore, subscribing newspapers were noticing mistakes they might have overlooked before. A letter to Porter from the business editor of the *Rochester (NY) Times-Union* pointed out errors in her recent columns about used cars, insurance premiums, and patent law, which readers had called to his attention. He said he understood why Porter relied on researchers but suggested they had been turning in sloppy work.[69] The business editor of the *Green Bay Press-Gazette* complained about an eighty-four-word sentence in Porter's column in a letter cleverly composed as a run-on sentence of exactly eighty-four words. He pointedly addressed his letter about the column to "anonymous," although the letter reached Porter and she responded personally.[70]

Publishers-Hall Syndicate had moved Porter's column from the *New York Post* to the *New York Daily News* in 1978, two years after Dorothy Schiff had sold her then-faltering enterprise to Australian businessman Rupert Murdoch. The *Daily News* was, by then, the nation's largest-circulation metropolitan newspaper, and its liberal editorial page was more in line with Porter's consumerism than the *Post* would have been under the politically conservative Murdoch. Porter later said she had switched newspapers after the *Post*'s new management renegotiated its contract for Porter's column without notifying Porter that it was doing so. "Since they unilaterally renewed my contract, I unilaterally quit theirs," she said. "I had become part of the furniture there. Well dammit, the furniture got up and walked out."[71] Nevertheless, leaving the *Post* was painful for Porter. She told another interviewer: "I had been wooed by every paper in New York, but I turned them all down. An old newspaperman taught me to always go home with 'the man who brung you to the party.' For me that was the *Post*. They gave me my chance. But there was nothing there left to be loyal to."[72]

During the eighties, Porter doused old relationships and pursued new ones. She fired the literary agency that had represented her since the 1940s, believing her longtime friend and agent Carol Brandt had not suitably promoted her new book, *Sylvia Porter's Your Own Money*.[73] Porter asked her attorney to notify Brandt that in the future Porter would be arranging her own promotions with Avon, the book's publisher.[74] Three years later, however, Porter was similarly unhappy with Avon over promotional efforts for her income tax guide. Her attorney wrote another letter, again complaining about a lack of promotion and distribution.[75] In 1986, Porter gave sole power to Carole Sinclair to negotiate literary matters on her behalf.[76] In response, Porter received a letter from Carol Brandt's husband and business partner that acknowledged the severance of their association. However, he also reminded Porter of the length of their personal and professional relationship and noted that his wife had been especially proud of Porter's achievements.[77]

Porter, Sinclair, and Fox had formed the Sylvia Porter Organization (SPO) around the time they started *Sylvia Porter's Personal Finance Magazine* in order to consolidate and manage Porter's professional properties, including the newspaper column. Porter owned a majority of SPO, Sinclair owned a large minority, and Fox owned a smaller minority.[78] In 1989 the group started *Sylvia Porter's Active Retirement Newsletter* with Davis Publications and took over the newsletter after Davis sold the magazine.[79] Fox tried to help manage the newsletter but lacked the journalism background necessary to fully understand what was required. In one memo, he suggested the newsletter needed more original reporting but indicated he did not know how to hire a Washington stringer or what to require of someone in that position.[80] He also assumed the audience was politically conservative—"otherwise, they would not be concerned about finances"—and complained the newsletter had devoted too much space to discussion of social issues, which, he believed, were mainly of interest to lower-income people.[81]

Fox and Sinclair tried to keep SPO solvent after *Sylvia Porter's Personal Finance Magazine* folded, but they frequently disagreed. Sinclair eventually became the sole president in an arrangement that stipulated she would own all Sylvia Porter–branded properties in full after the deaths of Porter and Fox.[82] She was determined to make the company a success and tried to drum up enough work to stay afloat while receiving a decent salary. She had a vision for Porter's legacy that included a family of newsletters, multimedia projects, the newspaper column, and a resurrected tax series published by a different company.[83] She had approached Simon & Schuster about copublishing the retirement newsletter, which she hoped would provide the operating funds necessary to lease office space in New York. In the meantime, she and an employee planned to work out of Porter's Fifth Avenue apartment. The deal never came to fruition, however, and a full newsletter was simply too expensive to produce.[84] Sinclair asked Porter to make a personal loan to SPO in order to sustain operations until the business became profitable.[85] It is not clear whether Porter made such a loan, but within a year and half Fox would declare SPO insolvent and try to dissolve the company.[86]

As Porter, ill with emphysema, neared the end of her life, Sinclair and Fox competed for control of her remaining business properties. Fox did not want Sinclair to own more of the company than he did after Porter's death—a battle that quickly became personal as both parties claimed to have Porter's endorsement.[87] In August 1990, Fox called Sinclair to a meeting at Porter's house in Pound Ridge and told her that he and Porter agreed SPO should be dissolved. He said they wanted Sinclair to continue working for Porter as a literary agent. According to a memo Fox wrote for his files, Sinclair refused to accept the proposal and demanded to speak with Porter at her bedside. Fox's perception was that Sinclair was play-ing to Porter's ego and using their warm personal relationship to con-vince Porter that SPO should continue.[88] Sinclair, for her part, had hired an attorney, who apparently accused Fox of embezzlement and threatened to file a lawsuit.[89]

The company's arrangements with writers and researchers soured amid the confusion. Some writers believed they had not been paid their due; others ended up doing more work on a collaborative effort than the initial agreement had stipulated. According to one news report, a free-lancer who had written more than five hundred newspaper columns for Porter over seven years was paid $150 for each column but received internal credit only once.[90] Another frustrated freelancer, who had been commissioned to write *Sylvia Porter's Your Finances in the 1990s*, wrote to Sinclair in exasperation, complaining he had not been given access to Por-ter and had received little guidance on the project. He said he had already completed more work than required by his $35,000 contract, yet had only been paid half of what he was owed.[91] Now the publisher was calling for extensive rewrites, which he could not afford to do since he had moved on to other projects. This writer indicated that Fox had told him he should not worry about the book's thoroughness because it would be submitted to a panel of experts who would make necessary changes. In addition, the writer said, he had been given stacks of material to condense for the book but later learned SPO did not own the rights to any of that material, which resulted in weeks of wasted effort. He was able to use only back copies of Porter's retirement newsletter and previous newspaper columns, which required him to undertake hundreds more hours of research than he had originally agreed to do.[92]

Porter was reluctant to acknowledge how much work others did for her and was defensive about the issue until the end of her life. She told an interviewer in 1989: "I don't have any staff. I've tried it, and I just don't trust research unless I've done it myself. I have it all in my head anyway. That's all I really need."[93] Responding to an acquaintance who had written to say he understood she was no longer active in writing her column or magazine, Porter replied:

Dear Bill:

You've been around long enough not to believe those stock market rumors! What do you mean by less active?

Are you talking about the column which I still do 156 times a year, the magazine which I do not write although every word is reviewed and approved by me? Or you were thinking of the Bantam audio tape series? The Tax Book? The Grolier serial book series? The IBM/SEARS computer data service? The Sylvia Porter Money Game? The best-selling computer software? The *Money Book* for teen-agers? The Avon series of paperbacks? Bill, I may not write every word of every project, but that meets my definition of "active."[94]

Meanwhile, Porter's newspaper column, represented by Universal Press Syndicate, was bleeding subscribers; subscriptions and revenue had dropped 35 percent in five years.[95] The decline in subscriptions was due, in part, to consolidation in the newspaper industry as advances in electronic media pressured the business models of print outlets. Newspapers closed or merged in cities where there once had been competing daily newspapers. (In 1945, 117 cities had more than one newspaper; in 1990, 34 cities did.)[96] Furthermore, Porter's column had been a favorite of afternoon newspapers, which were closing at a much higher rate than morning papers.

A second reason for the cancellations, according to John McMeel, president of Universal Press, was that the field of journalists covering finance had expanded. In a memo to Porter, he wrote: "The cancellations are as gut-wrenching to me as they are to you. . . . By far the overriding reason for termination is not unhappiness with the editorial quality, but the desire to try something else. We are not only competing with individual columnists but also the wire services. This type of competition did not exist in the 60s and 70s."[97] It is possible the syndicate also felt a bit misled by Porter, who launched a personal finance magazine just as Universal Press acquired her column. McMeel believed the magazine competed with the column, and he was reluctant to allow cross-promotion between the two products. For her part, Porter complained that Universal's publishing division had released a paperback with material from *Money* magazine.

"It would seem to me there is plenty in my columns which could be made into a paperback and this conflict does not fill me with joy," she wrote.[98]

Sinclair tried to improve the relationships among executives in the Sylvia Porter Organization, the magazine, and Universal Press. In 1987 she met with Bob Duffy, the marketing director of Universal Press, on Porter's behalf.[99] Sinclair and Porter believed the dwindling column subscriptions were the result of poor support and promotion by Universal Press, while the syndicate believed the drop in circulation was due to attrition by small newspapers.[100] Duffy pointed out that editors who had subscribed to Porter's column twenty or thirty years ago were no longer at the newspapers, which meant Porter needed to appeal to a new generation of editors. To do this, Duffy believed, Porter's column should be distributed with a chart or graphic (reflecting the industry's new emphasis on visual presentation). He also believed Porter should make the column more sophisticated. Perhaps without realizing it, Duffy was prescribing a return to the style of writing Porter had used to build her career: vivid, wide-lens economic analysis boiled down for average readers.

Despite these discussions, SPO sold the column to the Los Angeles Times Syndicate later that year. The new syndicate distributed it to 150 newspapers three times a week for a circulation of twenty-five million readers.[101] It would be the column's last home. As Porter's health deteriorated, the syndicate urged her to name someone to carry on the column in the event of her death or incapacitation. She refused. On May 14, 1991, Fox finally gave the syndicate permission to name a successor. Porter did not care who it was, Fox told her attorney, and she did not care whether the new columnist was a man or a woman.[102] After receiving dozens of unsolicited applications from people wanting to be the next Sylvia Porter, the Los Angeles Times Syndicate announced the honor would go to Kathy Kristof, who would become its new personal finance columnist.

On June 5, 1991, Sylvia Porter died of emphysema. For years she had suffered from the illness that resulted from a lifelong addiction to cigarettes. Her obituary, formidable in scope, ran in hundreds of newspapers around the country—but it was the last time most people would read her name. Despite the final efforts of Fox and Sinclair to institutionalize her legacy, Porter would go largely unrecognized by historians and younger generations of journalists. She had spent nearly six decades in the public eye, championing the economic rights of millions of people, forging a path for women in journalism, and dramatically changing the way financial journalism was practiced. Yet, in the end, Porter was simply forgotten. She was snuffed from the field as inauspiciously as she had crept into it, leaving a pervasive legacy that disguised her influence as surely as those signature initials had hidden her gender when she started. "Had I known what I was doing I might have been afraid," she once reminisced about her trailblazing career. "All I knew was this was an absolutely wide-open field of journalism which no one had entered. So I did."[103]

Conclusion

WHEN I BEGAN THIS PROJECT years ago, I had a working theory about Sylvia Porter's development of personal finance journalism. My theory was that in order to gain public acceptance as a woman writing about money, Porter had played into traditional gender norms by focusing her writing on homes and families after World War II. I thought she had carved a space for women within financial journalism the same way other professionals had done in nursing, family law, and social work. Historians have written extensively about women who invoked their authority in the domestic sphere to exert influence in the public sphere. I had conceptualized personal finance journalism as another chapter of that long tradition.

Porter was early to recognize the nation's women as an untapped market for information about money. Millions of young women encountered her advice for the first time in her *Ladies' Home Journal* columns, which took women's financial concerns seriously and highlighted their potential power as consumers. She served as an inspirational model of what women could accomplish as professionals and competent money managers. The daughter of a woman who believed in women's advancement, she championed women's professional and political rights and challenged middle-class women to pursue an education and a career. Porter was a feminist when feminism was out of fashion. She shrewdly tailored her arguments for women's rights to prevailing gender norms as they changed over the course of the twentieth century. At times in direct contrast with her writing, Porter used interviews with other journalists to construct a mythical public image that conformed to the prevailing gender ideology. She promoted a strong, can-do attitude during World War II; a fashion-obsessed domesticity during the postwar period; and a pioneering independence during the second wave of feminism. Her collusion with conventional media narratives fed her public popularity and gave her cultural license to advance a new form of journalism. The genre she originated opened doors for women in a specialty dominated by men.

However, the development of personal finance journalism did not unfold quite the way I had theorized. Porter did not confine herself to writing about home economics; she did not restrict her claims of authority to "feminine" issues; and she did not limit herself to writing for women. Like many Americans of the 1940s and 1950s, she was looking outward at the rest of the world, fitting together the pieces of the emerging global economy and assessing the postwar status of the United States. In her newspaper column and magazine articles, Porter masterfully linked what was happening in the larger economy to what was happening in her readers' homes. She made issues such as inflation, monetary policy, and the economic boom come alive. She was committed to spreading financial literacy so middle-class Americans would not be caught unaware, as they had been in 1929. She explained to them—in terms they could readily understand—why they *should* care about the price of tea in China. She even made her cause a patriotic one by linking economic literacy with the fight against communism. Her style was personal, but her perspective was global. She did not use domestic matters in her column to soften the edges of her authority; she used them because they made finance understandable to average readers. My research has shown that while gender was an important factor in Porter's public persona, it was not the decisive factor in her journalism.

Gender influenced the *how* of Porter's career more than the *what*. Motivated by the economic crisis of the Depression, she promoted the rights and responsibilities of the middle class and pioneered a form of journalism that respected the consumer's growing role in the economy. What drove Porter's development of personal finance journalism—with its depoliticized focus on individuals rather than nations—were business decisions. She offered Americans practical advice that appealed to a large plurality of her potential audience, whatever their politics or occupation. The rise of the middle class and the postwar economic expansion created an appetite for digestible financial advice that grew into a full-fledged hunger once the baby boom generation started reaching adulthood. White middle-class baby boomers had not experienced the financial straits their parents suffered during the Depression. Instead, they had grown up in relative affluence. They were able to plan their financial futures from a young age and were encouraged to do so. By the time of their maturation, Porter was in a position to capitalize on her reputation as a financial expert.

Gender might not have determined the content of Porter's journalism, but it is a leading factor in her legacy. She proved women could write about finance, creating opportunities for women in a field where they had once been unwelcome. A large number of personal finance journalists today are women—so many, in fact, that one has to wonder whether personal finance has become a pink ghetto. Are women in financial news given an equal opportunity to cover the stock market, for example, or corporate mergers? Or, because personal finance fits so neatly with the stereotype of women as household managers, have journalists come to think of personal finance as a feminine domain? Porter's legacy, like so much of history, is complicated.

In the most general sense, Porter's story is that of a journalist who became a brand, demonstrating the natural, qualitative shifts that accompany such a change. Porter's decision to appeal to a mass market forced her to commoditize her journalism, which ultimately made it less memorable and cost her credibility. To keep up her multitudinous media appearances, Porter hired others to write her column. Because the column accommodated multiple styles and voices, it necessarily became more formulaic and lost Porter's global perspective as an economist. Unfortunately, the baby boomers who would form the bulk of her audience never knew the crusading journalist who had established a mass-circulation syndicated column about a subject few others covered. The mass-media exposure Porter sought also forced her to maintain a nonthreatening public image, which meant conforming to prevailing gender norms and not pressing too hard for political change. Porter was a cultural force, but she played it safe—and that has made it easy to take her work for granted. The now-ubiquitous nature of the genre she created, which serves as evidence of her impact, might be the very reason her important role in journalism history has been overlooked.

Porter's career reinforces the usefulness of gender as a category for historical analysis and reminds us that women's history not only restores women to their rightful place in the record—it *completes* the record. Most young journalists today do not know who Sylvia Porter was, yet one cannot fully understand the history of financial journalism without knowing her story. It is not difficult to grasp her importance. One only has to visit the personal finance section of a bookstore and imagine that, in the beginning, there was only Sylvia.

Abbreviations

* * *

Notes

* * *

Bibliography

* * *

Index

Abbreviations

DSP	Dorothy Schiff Papers
LHJ	*Ladies' Home Journal*
NYP	*New York Post*
NYPL	New York Public Library
SPP	Sylvia Porter Papers
WHMC	Western Historical Manuscript Collection

Notes

Introduction

1. Elsa Maxwell, "Portias of the Press—One Is S. F. Porter," *NYP*, Dec. 22, 1942, folder 119, SPP, WHMC, Ellis Library, University of Missouri, Columbia, MO.

2. John Quirt, *The Press and the World of Money* (Byron, Calif.: Anton and California Courier, 1993), 252.

3. "Housewife's View," *Time*, June 16, 1958, 61.

4. Sylvia Porter to Harry Nason, July 2, 1974, folder 216, SPP, WHMC.

5. Warren Boroson, telephone interview by the author, July 26, 2006, Vienna, VA.

6. Robert Vanderpoel, "How High Can We Pile Up the Debt, Asks Glamour Girl," n.p., Oct. 3, 1942, folder 118, SPP, WHMC.

7. Trudy Lieberman, "What Ever Happened to Consumer Reporting?" *Columbia Journalism Review* (Sept.–Oct. 1994): 34.

8. Knight Kiplinger, "Chat with the Editor in Chief," *Changing Times: The Kiplinger Magazine* (July 1985): 5.

9. Lee Cohn, interview by the author, Washington, DC, July 31, 2006.

10. Gerda Lerner, "Placing Women in History: Definitions and Challenges," *Feminist Studies* 3, nos. 1–2 (fall 1975): 5–14; reprinted in *Major Problems in American Women's History*, ed. Mary Beth Norton and Ruth M. Alexander, 3rd ed. (Boston: Houghton Mifflin, 2003), 2.

11. Based on news reports and correspondence, Porter's circulation was an estimated forty million in 1970. The entire U.S. population was about 203 million that year, according to the U.S. Census (available from http://www.censusscope.org/us/chart_popl.html, accessed May 29, 2011).

12. Judith Cramer and Pamela Creedon, eds., introduction to *Women in Mass Communication*, 3rd ed. (Thousand Oaks, CA: Sage, 2007), 6; American Society of Newspaper Editors, Newsroom Employment Census (2010) (available from http://asne.org/key_initiatives /diversity/newsroom_census.aspx, accessed Sept. 28, 2011); Lee Becker, Tudor Vlad, Jisu Huh, and Nancy Mace, "Annual Enrollment Report: Graduate and Undergraduate Enrollments Increase Sharply," *Journalism and Mass Communication Educator* 58, no. 3 (fall 2003): 273–90.

13. June O. Nicholson, "Women in Newspaper Journalism (since the 1990s)," in Pamela Creedon and Judith Cramer, eds., *Women in Mass Communication*, 3rd ed. (Thousand Oaks, CA: Sage, 2007), 5, 38–40.

14. Nicholson, "Women in Newspaper Journalism," 39.

15. Shayla Thiel Stern, "Increased Legitimacy, Fewer Women? Analyzing Editorial Leadership and Gender in Online Journalism," in Creedon and Cramer, *Women in Mass Communication*, 135–37.

16. Randall Poe, "How Porter Translates 'Bafflegab,'" *Across the Board*, July 1978, folder 139, SPP, WHMC, 46.

17. Carl Brandt to Sylvia Porter, Dec. 8, 1948, folder 216, SPP, WHMC.

18. Ted O. Thackrey to Paul Tierney, July 15, 1942, folder 117, SPP, WHMC.

19. Elizabeth Whitney, "Sylvia Porter: A Living Legend Becomes an Institution," *St. Petersburg Times*, Feb. 2, 1989, sec. I, 1.

20. Porter, "The Automobile Dealer's Stake in the Consumer" (speech, 1954), folder 48, SPP, WHMC; Porter, "A Charter of Economic Human Rights" (speech given in Cleveland, Sept. 28, 1956; at the Colgate University Foreign Policy Conference in Hamilton, NY, July 3, 1957; in Rochester, NY, Jan. 28, 1959; and in Louisville, KY, Feb. 13, 1959), folder 51, SPP, WHMC. A refined version was printed in *Vital Speeches of the Day*, Sept. 1, 1957, 678–81.

21. Warren Boroson, "A Worthy Showing from New Jersey," *Morris County (NJ) Daily Record*, Oct. 1, 1996, sec. B, 1.

22. William Galeota, "Miss Porter's School: A Columnist's Advice Wields Wide Influence from Coast to Coast," *Wall Street Journal*, March 24, 1972, folder 137, SPP, WHMC.

1. Wall Street Crusader

1. "Sylvia & You," *Time*, Nov. 28, 1960, 48.

2. Ibid.

3. James Madison High School, a public school in Brooklyn, graduated an eclectic list of luminaries in the twentieth century, including Supreme Court Justice Ruth Bader Ginsburg, education entrepreneur Stanley Kaplan, *Mad* magazine publisher William Gaines, and multiple Nobel Prize winners (Hobart Rowen, "The Past and Future of Financial Reporting," *Washington Post*, Sept. 12, 1993, sec. H, 1).

4. Interestingly, Porter's upbringing stands in direct contrast to that of Eileen Shanahan, another prominent financial journalist, who described herself as fitting the archetype of a successful businesswoman articulated in the book *The Managerial Woman*, published in 1977. Shanahan, who was eleven years younger than Porter, told an interviewer: "I fit right into the pattern that they described, though the women they focused on were about ten years older than I am—about the father who said, 'Dare anything, do it,' and the mother who was more cautious. But I always got the message, usually from my father in particular, that: 'You can do anything; do it!'" (Mary Marshall Clark, oral history interview with Eileen

Shanahan, May 30, 1992, Washington Press Club Foundation, Washington, DC, available from http://beta.wpcf.org/oralhistory/shan1.html, accessed Jan. 16, 2013, 1).

5. Jean Baer, *The Self-Chosen: "Our Crowd" Is Dead, Long Live Our Crowd* (New York: Arbor House, 1982), 259.

6. Baer, *Self-Chosen*, 259.

7. Kathleen D. Fury, "Super-Sylvia," *LHJ*, Jan. 1976, 26.

8. Baer, *Self-Chosen*, 258.

9. Nearly all of the women profiled in Madelon Golden Schilpp and Sharon Murphy's anthology of women journalists, *Great Women of the Press* (Carbondale: Southern Illinois University Press, 1983), coped with missing fathers, husbands, or brothers because of death, incapacity, or absence. The pattern was also noted by Maurine Beasley and Sheila Gibbons in *Taking Their Place: A Documentary History of Women and Journalism*, 2nd ed. (State College, PA: Strata, 2003); and by Barbara Belford in *Brilliant Bylines: A Biographical Anthology of Notable Newspaperwomen in America* (New York: Columbia University Press, 1986). Belford speculated that the loss of a male provider made it necessary—or provided a reasonable excuse—for women to violate traditional gender norms by embarking on a public career such as journalism.

10. Porter adopted "Field" as her maiden name and used it throughout her life, although her brother, John, eventually reclaimed Feldman as his family name.

11. See John Kenneth Galbraith, *The Great Crash*, 3rd ed. (Boston: Houghton Mifflin, 1972), 75–80; and Jerry R. Rosenberg, *Inside the Wall Street Journal* (New York: Macmillan, 1982), 46.

12. Galbraith, *Great Crash*, 75. Throughout the book, Galbraith cited the following factors in the crash: self-delusion, investment trusts (the precursor to mutual funds), margin buying, and a lack of political will. He cited the following factors in the subsequent depression: economic ignorance, the lopsided distribution of income (the richest 5 percent of Americans received one-third of the nation's income), and a lack of political will.

13. Quirt, *Press and the World of Money*, 32.

14. Ibid.

15. Rosenberg, *Inside the Wall Street Journal*, 57–58.

16. For a discussion of the newspaper during the Depression, World War II, and postwar periods, see Rosenberg, *Inside the Wall Street Journal*, 45–72.

17. Chris Roush, *Show Me the Money: Writing Business and Economics Stories for Mass Communication* (Mahwah, NJ: Lawrence Erlbaum Associates, 2004), 7. Roush provides a brief overview of the history of business reporting on 5–8.

18. Wayne Parsons, *The Power of the Financial Press: Journalism and Economic Opinion in Britain and America* (New Brunswick, NJ: Rutgers University Press, 1990), 81–112. Parsons cited a study of the *Times* of London, the *New Statesman*, the *New York Times*, *Time* magazine, and the *Economist*, which had found the term "the economy" did not come into general use

in the press until the 1930s. Parsons also cited a study by political scientist Richard Rubin that found economic stories made up 26 percent of the articles on the front pages of major newspapers in 1935, an all-time high. Parsons also found that financial journalism swings between emphasizing the macro and the micro, depending on current events.

19. Frank Luther Mott, *American Journalism: A History, 1690–1960*, 3rd ed. (New York: Macmillan, 1962), 688–94.

20. Maurine Beasley, "The Emergence of Modern Media, 1900–1945," in *The Media in America: A History*, 5th ed., ed. Wm. David Sloan (Northport, AL: Vision Press, 2002), 299.

21. Michael Emery and Edwin Emery, with Nancy L. Roberts, *The Press and America: An Interpretive History of the Mass Media*, 8th ed. (Needham Heights, MA: Allyn and Bacon, 1996), 314–15.

See, also, Michael Schudson, *Discovering the News: A Social History of American Newspapers* (New York: Basic Books, 1978), 88–159, for a discussion of objectivity in the thirties. The professional ideal of objectivity—which Schudson distinguished from the naïve empiricism of the *New York Times* at the turn of the century—was a reaction to the disillusionment that followed World War I propaganda and the rise of public relations. The *New York Times* model of factual reporting at the end of the nineteenth century was rooted in the belief (or, rather, the lack of doubt) that journalists could report the facts as truth; values and facts were not viewed as separate. In contrast, the ideal of objectivity in the twentieth century was rooted in a belief in reporters' inherent subjectivity, which they were expected to overcome in their professional capacity as truth-tellers. Thus, the zeal for an objective way of seeing arose at the very time it was recognized there was no objective reality. Schudson believed journalistic trends of the thirties—the increasing use of bylines, the rise of the columnist, the specialization of reporters, and the interest in interpretive reporting—were reactions to propaganda disseminated by the government and corporations, as journalists tried to cope with their disillusionment and growing belief in relativism. That would explain why newspapers started putting reporters' names on stories at the very time it was assumed reporters should all be telling the same story, he argued.

22. Galbraith, *Great Crash*, 106.

23. Drew Pearson and Robert Allen cowrote the anonymous "Washington Merry-Go-Round."

The trend in interpretive reporting culminated in 1940 with the founding of the liberal newspaper *PM*, which lasted nine years. *PM* did not aim for objectivity and instead presented a politically liberal account and analysis of the day's news. The newspaper did not accept paid advertising on principle.

24. Mildred Lewis and Milton Lewis, *Famous Modern Newspaper Writers* (New York: Dodd, Mead, 1962), 97. In their chapter on Porter, the authors say she had a photographic memory, although this assertion is not repeated in any other articles or primary sources about Porter.

25. Baer, *Self-Chosen*, 260.

26. Alice Kessler-Harris, *Out to Work: A History of Wage-Earning Women in the United States* (New York: Oxford University Press, 1982), 250–72; the quotation from Norman Cousins is cited on 256.

27. Robyn Muncy, *Creating a Female Dominion in American Reform: 1890–1935* (New York: Oxford University Press, 1991). Muncy showed how a network of women activists and government appointees sustained a reform agenda between the Progressive Era and the New Deal.

28. Maurine Beasley, "Eleanor Roosevelt's Press Conferences: Case Study in Class, Gender, and Race," *Social Science Journal* 37, no. 4 (2000): 517–28.

29. Sara M. Evans, *Born for Liberty: A History of Women in America*, Free Press Paperbacks ed. (New York: Simon & Schuster, 1989; 1997), 218.

30. Ishbel Ross, *Ladies of the Press: The Story of Women in Journalism by an Insider* (New York: Harper, 1936), 2.

31. Stanley Walker, foreword to Ross, *Ladies of the Press*, xi.

32. Ida Tarbell, *All in the Day's Work: An Autobiography* (New York: Macmillan, 1939; Chicago: University of Illinois Press, 2003), 22–26 and 83–84. Tarbell's work fits neatly with historians' findings that women journalists frequently have been reform-minded, on a mission to "clean up" government or to expose unfair business practices.

33. Marian R. Glenn, "Woman in Business," *Forbes*, Sept. 15, 1917, 30.

34. Bill Saporito, "How the Economy Became Hot News in the Last 100 Years," *Columbia Journalism Review* (March–Apr. 1999): 47; Bea Garcia, "Two S. Floridians Who Made Journalism History," *Miami Herald*, Dec. 28, 1999, sec. C, 1.

35. "The Business News Luminaries," TJFR Group, 1999 (available from http://news bios.com/newslum/notables.htm, accessed Aug. 5, 2007). With the exception of Tarbell, the women who made this list are missing from the historical literature on women in journalism. The only mention of Porter is in the introduction to Maria Braden, *She Said What? Interviews with Women Newspaper Columnists* (Lexington: University Press of Kentucky, 1993), 1–22.

36. Braden, *She Said What?*, 280.

37. Ibid.

38. Clara Germani, "Women and Money: Making It Means Managing It," *Christian Science Monitor*, March 15, 1982, 12.

39. "Pre-Script," *American*, July 1939, folder 117, SPP, WHMC. July 8, 1932, was the day that stock market prices hit bottom before starting their slow climb back to where they had been before the crash.

40. "Sylvia & You," 48; Baer, *Self-Chosen*, 260.

41. Lewis and Lewis, *Modern Newspaper Writers*, 99.

42. Ibid., 99–100.

43. Randall Poe, "How Porter Translates 'Bafflegab,'" *Across the Board*, July 1978, folder 139, SPP, WHMC, 46.

44. At the time, the strategy of using initials in place of a first name was common among professional women seeking careers in male-dominated fields. Clare Reckert, the *New York Times'* first woman financial reporter, used the byline "C. M. Reckert" when she began writing for the paper during World War II. Porter herself described the practice as commonplace in a series of articles she wrote about women in finance in 1936. Jane Bryant Quinn used her initials when she edited a financial newsletter for McGraw-Hill before becoming a *Newsweek* columnist and bestselling author. Some professional women went even further. Historian Julie Matthaei has described the experience of Ruth Weyand, who graduated from the University of Chicago Law School in the 1930s. She could not get hired, so she approached her former dean and requested that all her records be changed to "R. Weyand" and omit any reference to her sex. Her plan was to move to another state and masquerade as a man (Julie A. Matthaei, *An Economic History of Women in America: Women's Work, the Sexual Division of Labor, and the Development of Capitalism* [New York: Schocken, 1982], 287–88).

45. "Sylvia & You"; Lewis and Lewis, *Modern Newspaper Writers*; "The Story of the Personality behind the By-Line," n.p., June 1, 1948, folder 122, SPP, WHMC.

46. Elizabeth Whitney, "Sylvia Porter: A Living Legend Becomes an Institution," *St. Petersburg Times*, Feb. 2, 1989, sec. I, 1.

47. Sylvia Porter to Harry Nason, July 2, 1974, folder 216, SPP, WHMC. The ellipses appear in the original; they do not signify content that has been omitted.

48. The ownership of the *Post* is discussed in Mott's *American Journalism* on 654–55, and tabloids in general are discussed on 666–73. There is a discussion of the newspaper landscape in New York City in 1932 in Emery and Emery, *Press and America*, 293. The *Post* is only nominally mentioned in the book, whose discussion of tabloids focuses on the instigators of "yellow journalism," Joseph Pulitzer and William Randolph Hearst.

49. Sylvia Porter, speech apparently given at the annual convention of the American Bankers Association (May 1975), folder 75, SPP, WHMC, 1.

50. Mott, *American Journalism*, 655. P. L. Trussell was the business editor.

51. Sylvia Porter, "Canada's Bond Offer 'Feeler' in U.S. Market," *NYP*, Aug. 6, 1935.

52. Sylvia Porter, "Mismanaged Issues Clog Capital Mart," *NYP*, Aug. 8, 1935.

53. Porter, American Bankers Association speech, 2.

54. Porter, American Bankers Association speech, 1.

55. "Stock Market Trading for December," *New York Times*, Jan. 1, 1936.

56. Cohn, interview by the author.

57. "Pre-Script," 1.

58. Walter E. Schneider, "Wall Street 'Joan of Arc' Crusades in N.Y. Post," *Editor & Publisher Answers: "Who Is Sylvia?"* [pamphlet], Jan. 3, 1942, folder 117, SPP, WHMC.

59. Quirt, *Press and the World of Money*, 254.

60. According to Beth Kobliner, an assistant to Porter in the 1980s, Porter described her politics as socially liberal and fiscally conservative (telephone interview by the author, Vienna, VA, July 27, 2006). Porter told an interviewer that she had voted Democratic in every

presidential election except 1972, which she sat out because she did not like Richard Nixon or George McGovern (Whitney, "Living Legend").

61. Quirt, *Press and the World of Money*, 255.

62. Maxwell, "Portias of the Press."

63. Sylvia Porter, "Women in Finance . . . Louise Watson, Partner in Investment Firm, Finds Market Thrilling and Gives a Bit of Advice on Trading Risks," *NYP*, June 16, 1936, 21. The emphasis in the quotation is mine.

64. Sylvia Porter, "To the Women: Some Hints on Developing War Trends and the Policies to Adopt," *NYP*, Dec. 12, 1941.

65. Sylvia Porter, "To the Women: You Can Get Jobs in the Financial Fields; Banks to Employ Thousands," *NYP*, July 6, 1942.

66. Sheila M. Rothman, *Woman's Proper Place: A History of Changing Ideals and Practices, 1870 to the Present* (New York: Basic Books, 1978), 6, 177–218.

67. Matthaei, *Economic History of Women*, 251.

68. Ibid., 235–55.

69. Ibid., 256–77.

70. Patricia M. Hummer, *The Decade of Elusive Promise: Professional Women in the United States, 1920–1930* (Ann Arbor: UMI Research Press, 1979), 1–19.

71. Kessler-Harris, *Out to Work*, 257–59.

72. Sylvia Porter, "Dorcas Campbell—Pioneer in Banking," *NYP*, Sept. 25, 1959, folder 411, SPP, WHMC.

73. Sylvia Porter, "Women in Finance . . . Miss Andress Knows All the Answers, and Questions, Too: She's a Collector of 'Firsts' in Business and in Books," *NYP*, June 25, 1936.

74. Sylvia Porter, "Lady, Take a Bow," *NYP*, Feb. 21, 1936.

75. Porter told a journalist the lead of her story had been: "The company whose customers are all women held its annual report meeting in a building which does not permit women" (Whitney, "Living Legend").

76. Porter, "Annual Reports a Puzzle Due to Tax Law Delays," *NYP*, Aug. 4, 1942. Porter reported that women owned 23 percent of General Mills' common stock and 50 percent of its preferred stock.

77. James Bell to Sylvia Porter, Aug. 12, 1942, folder 117, SPP, WHMC.

78. "Guest List for Dinner Last Night to Emil Schram," *Wall Street Journal*, June 26, 1941; "Wall Street Whispers," *Finance*, Feb. 1972, folder 137, SPP, WHMC.

79. Baer, *Self-Chosen*, 262.

80. Hummer, *Decade of Elusive Promise*, 7–8.

81. Porter, "Women in Finance . . . Louise Watson."

82. Porter, "Women in Finance . . . Miss Eggleston 'Needed the Money'; She Speculated and Won; So Another Woman Financier Began a Career in Wall Street," *NYP*, July 7, 1936, 21.

83. Porter, "Women in Finance . . . Mina Bruere Left the Concert Stage for Banking Career; Don't Imitate Men, Be Original, Is Her Advice to Women," *NYP*, June 18, 1936, 35.

84. Porter, "Women in Finance . . . Miss Taylor, World's First Woman Investment Counsel, Is Changing the 'Men Only' Psychology of Wall Street," *NYP*, June 30, 1936.

85. Sylvia Porter, "Women in Finance . . . Mrs. Foster, Who Writes Books and Plays the Market, Believes a Career and Marriage Simply Do Not Mix," *NYP*, July 2, 1936.

86. Porter, "Women in Finance . . . Mrs. Foster."

87. Porter, "Women in Finance . . . Mina Bruere," 35.

88. Porter, "Women in Finance . . . Louise Watson," 21.

89. Porter, "Women in Finance . . . Ethel Mercereau, Partner in E.A. Pierce and Company, Rose from Stenographer to Dominant Place in Business," *NYP*, June 20, 1936.

90. Sylvia Porter, "Women in Finance . . . Miss Cook Has Keen Appetite for Food and Selling, So the World Lost a Lawyer and Gained a Financier," *NYP*, June 27, 1936.

91. Sylvia Porter, "Women in Finance . . . Miss Fuchs Believes Good Housekeeper Makes Good Banker; Finds Greatest Human Interest in the Trust Department," *NYP*, July 9, 1936, 28.

92. Porter, "Women in Finance . . . Miss Eggleston," 21.

93. Porter, "Women in Finance . . . Miss Andress.'"

94. Sylvia Porter, "Women in Finance . . . Mrs. Jacob [Mary] Riis Finds Romance in the Ticker Tape; 'Being in Wall Street Keeps you Alive to World,'" *NYP*, June 23, 1936.

95. Sylvia Porter, "The Brain Has No Sex" (speech given in Philadelphia on Jan. 9, 1950; Atlanta on Oct. 18, 1950; Toledo, Ohio, on Jan. 15, 1953; Stamford, CT, on Sept. 28, 1955; and Tucson, AZ, on Oct. 23, 1955), folder 40, SPP, WHMC.

96. Baer, *Self-Chosen*, 261. Harry Saylor was then editor-in-chief.

97. The top of the section identified the business section's focus as "Business & Finance" and "Markets, Economic Trends." Over the next several years, the section would shrink and expand several times, reflecting indecision about how much space the paper should devote to financial news. In 1941, under new management, it would once again have its own section front and identify its contents as "Industry, Business, Finance, Labor Relations." In 1942, however, it would again shrink to less than a page and lose its page heading.

98. Sylvia Porter, "Arbitraging Back in Profitable Play," *NYP*, Jan. 16, 1936; "Treasury Ban on Free Riding Being Violated," *NYP*, June 2, 1936; "State 'Legal' Bond Lists Face Revision," *NYP*, Jan. 9, 1936; "U.S. Fund to Freeze Gold en Route Here," *NYP*, March 21, 1938.

99. Galeota, "Miss Porter's School," 1.

100. Sylvia Porter, "Treasury Ban on Free Riding Being Violated," *NYP*, June 2, 1936; "Chiselers Defy U.S., Profit on New Bonds at Expense of Public," *NYP*, Dec. 10, 1936 (published with an accompanying editorial decrying the practice); "Speculators Slapped by U.S. Treasury's Financing, Which Wipes Out Opportunity for Safe, Easy Money Deals," *NYP*, June 5, 1939.

101. Quirt, *Press and the World of Money*, 256.

102. Sylvia Porter, "Capital Flees to U.S. on Austrian Crisis," *NYP*, March 12, 1938; "U.S. Fund to Freeze Gold en Route Here," *NYP*, March 21, 1938; "Foreign Governments Leave

Americans Holding the Bag through Repatriation," *NYP*, June 22, 1939; "Foreign Countries' War Chests Kept in U.S.," *NYP*, June 26, 1939.

103. For example, the War Production Board decided what the nation's factories would produce, how much of it, and who would receive it. The Office of Defense Transportation regulated the use of cars and gas. The Office of Price Administration set price ceilings and rationed food and other consumer goods to offset inflation and reduce hoarding. The National Housing Agency constructed housing in areas where workers were needed and established rent controls in boom areas where demand for housing would exceed the supply. The Office of War Information controlled the release of information and disseminated propaganda designed to support the allies' cause. The National War Labor Board limited wages and mediated labor disputes to ensure production would continue. See Jordan Braverman, *To Hasten the Homecoming: How Americans Fought World War II through the Media* (Lanham, MD: Madison Books, 1996), esp. 11–20.

104. Mark H. Leff, "The Politics of Sacrifice on the American Home Front in World War II," *Journal of American History* 77, no. 4 (March 1991): 1296–1318, 1314.

105. It should be noted that newspapers were not uniformly supportive of President Roosevelt during the war. The *New York Daily News*, *Chicago Tribune*, and *Washington Times-Herald* were critical of the president. The *Daily News* raised the specter of totalitarianism at home because of the explosion in government control over people's lives. The *Tribune* even suggested the administration might have been complicit in the attack on Pearl Harbor, an idea echoed in the *Times-Herald* (Braverman, *To Hasten the Homecoming*, 31–32).

106. Leff, "Politics of Sacrifice," 1309.

107. The only other woman to be recognized by the Headliners Club in 1943 was Virginia Scott of the *Great Falls (Mont.) Leader*, whose article about a dog and a fire hydrant won the award for best domestic feature ("2 Women Will Get Headliners' Prizes," *New York Times*, May 28, 1943, 42).

108. Sylvia Porter, "Twelve Men against the Nation," *Reader's Digest* 41, no. 247 (Nov. 1942): 1–4.

109. Porter, "Twelve Men Against the Nation," 2.

110. Ibid., 2–4.

111. Edith C. Olshin, "Princess Charming of Wall Street," *Magazine Digest*, Nov. 1948, 113.

112. Sen. D. Worth Clark to editor, *Reader's Digest*, telegram, 1942, folder 119, SPP, WHMC.

113. Marc Rosen to Sylvia Porter, Jan. 14, 1943, folder 119, SPP, WHMC; John Graham to Sylvia Porter, Nov. 30, 1942, folder 119, SPP, WHMC.

114. Sylvia Porter, "U.S. to Trace Aniline Link," *NYP*, Nov. 27, 1941; "Aniline Men Related to High Nazis," *NYP*, Nov. 28, 1941. The company's name was General Aniline & Film Corp.

115. Sylvia Porter, "I. G. Farben Still Here—and Still Helping Germany—Dissolution Is Only Started," *NYP*, March 19, 1942, 15.

116. Sylvia Porter, "Farben Officials Placed Kin in Key Jobs in U.S. as Plotters against Us," *NYP*, March 23, 1942; "The Nazi Chemical Trust, a State within a State, Created Hitler and the War," *NYP*, March 20, 1942; "Farben Agents Wed U.S. Girls and Became American Citizens," *NYP*, March 25, 1942; "Farben Got Secrets from U.S. by Joining Its Large Firms," *NYP*, March 26, 1942; "If Farben Comes, War Follows," *NYP*, March 27, 1942, Apartment Guide, 6; "Farben Agents Use S. America as Base for Plots against U.S.," *NYP*, March 30, 1942.

117. Sylvia Porter, "Farben Is the State and Hitler Its Puppet in the Nazi New Order," *NYP*, March 24, 1942.

118. When the Fed wants to raise long-term interest rates, it sells U.S. bonds, reducing the money supply and thus making it more expensive to borrow; when it wants to lower rates, it buys bonds, putting money into the supply and making it cheaper to borrow.

119. Sylvia Porter, "Direct Sale of U.S. Bonds to Reserve Banks is Logical; Disaster Cries Unjustified," *NYP*, Jan. 30, 1942.

120. Sylvia Porter, "Stop Withdrawing Savings to Buy Bonds and Hoard; You're Hurting the Country," *NYP*, Feb. 4, 1942.

121. Sylvia Porter, "Food Costs Cheaper Today Than Ever for Working Man; It's All in the Statistics," *NYP*, Feb. 16, 1942.

122. Braverman, *To Hasten the Homecoming*, 35.

123. Schneider, "Wall Street 'Joan of Arc,'" 1.

124. Sylvia Porter, "To the Women: Some Hints for Holiday Gift Shopping; Start Now and Buy Staples," *NYP*, Nov. 21, 1941.

125. Sylvia Porter, speech given to the Republican Women's Clubs of New York State, printed in *Republican Defense Bulletin* 1, no. 1 (Feb. 1942), folder 117, SPP, WHMC.

126. See, for example, Sylvia Porter, "To Women Who Overbuy: You're Forcing Scarcities, Rigid Control, Rising Costs," *NYP*, Dec. 19, 1941; and "To the Women: Your Buying on Time Plans Must Be Cut or More Curbs Will Come," *NYP*, Dec. 26, 1941.

127. Of course, advertisers and businesses had long recognized women's power as consumers and monitors of the household budget; the government and financial services industry were slower to catch on.

128. Mei-ling Yang, "Creating the Kitchen Patriot: Media Promotion of Food Rationing and Nutrition Campaigns on the American Home Front during World War II," *American Journalism* 22, no. 3 (summer 2005): 56.

129. Mei-ling Yang, "Creating the Kitchen Patriot," 64–65.

130. Sylvia Porter, "Pioneer Three-Day Forum on Women's Responsibility Opens at Stephens College," *NYP*, Nov. 6, 1941; "Woman's Place in Future Will Be Outside the Home, Experts at Forum Agree," *NYP*, Nov. 7, 1941.

131. Sylvia Porter, "Forum Agrees on Coming of New Phase for Women and Need for Education," *NYP*, Nov. 10, 1941, 20.

132. Sylvia Porter, "A Wider 'Community Life,' More Equality in Marriage for Women in War Tasks," *NYP*, Jan. 16, 1942, 12.

133. Sylvia Porter, "Women Entering New Era of Financial Independence; Social Revolution Coming," *NYP*, Jan. 7, 1942, 18; Porter, "A Wider 'Community Life.'"

134. Porter, "Women Entering New Era."

135. Ibid., 18.

136. Sylvia Porter, "13,500,000 Women in Jobs in Virtually Every Field; All Records Being Broken," *NYP*, Jan. 8, 1942, 8; "Women Find Job Equality in Big Machines that Need Little Strength to Operate," *NYP*, Jan. 9, 1942, 12; "Women Workers Excel Men in Thousands of War Jobs; Good at Light, Detail Tasks," *NYP*, Jan. 12, 1942, 10.

137. Sylvia Porter, "Big Percentage of Women Will Hold Industrial Jobs When Peace Releases Men," *NYP*, Jan. 13, 1942, 14.

138. Sylvia Porter, "50% of American Women to be Wage Earners by 1950; A New Freedom Is Emerging," *NYP*, Jan. 20, 1942, 8.

139. Sylvia Porter, "Loneliness Is the Price Facing Girls in War Jobs; Are Less Likely to Wed," *NYP*, Jan. 15, 1942, 8.

140. Claudia D. Goldin, "The Role of World War II in the Rise of Women's Employment," *American Economic Review* 81, no. 4 (Sept. 1991): 741–56.

141. Kessler-Harris, *Out to Work*, 273–77.

142. Nancy Walker, *Shaping Our Mothers' World: American Women's Magazines* (Jackson: University Press of Mississippi, 2000), 81–82.

143. Kessler-Harris, *Out to Work*, 274.

144. "War Work Is Put Ahead of Politics," *New York Times*, Jan. 17, 1942, 20.

145. Display Ad 37, *New York Times*, Dec. 14, 1944, 39.

146. Ted O. Thackrey to Paul Tierney, July 15, 1942, folder 117, SPP, WHMC.

147. Sylvia Porter, "Success of Price Control Depends on Self-Control," *NYP*, July 20, 1942.

148. The anecdote regarding the reader's new greeting appears in several articles, including "Sylvia Porter: One in 10,000," *Editor & Publisher*, Feb. 5, 1949, folder 123, SPP, WHMC.

Reflecting its focus on the individual, the standing title of Porter's newspaper column became "Your Pocketbook and the War." A month later, it became "Your Dollar and the War." After the war, it was simply "Your Dollar."

2. Glamour Girl of Finance

1. The speech recounted was Porter, "War—and Government Control of the Bond Markets" (given at a meeting of the Wisconsin Bankers Association, June 1940), folder 38, SPP, WHMC. The anecdote appears in Porter's speech "The Brain Has No Sex" (given in Philadelphia on Jan. 9, 1950; Atlanta on Oct. 18, 1950; Toledo, OH, on Jan. 15, 1953; Stamford, CT, on Sept. 28, 1955; and Tucson, AZ, on Oct. 23, 1955), folder 40, SPP, WHMC.

2. Edith C. Olshin, "Princess Charming of Wall Street," *Magazine Digest*, Nov. 1948, 113.

3. Robert Vanderpoel, "How High Can We Pile Up the Debt, Asks Glamour Girl," n.p., Oct. 3, 1942, folder 118, SPP, WHMC.

4. Walter E. Schneider, "Wall Street 'Joan of Arc' Crusades in N.Y. Post," *Editor & Publisher Answers: "Who Is Sylvia?"* [pamphlet], Jan. 3, 1942, folder 117, SPP, WHMC.

5. Cliff Millen, "A Financial Editor Can Be Beautiful!" *Des Moines Tribune*, Oct. 18, 1949, folder 125, SPP, WHMC.

6. Millen, "A Financial Editor Can Be Beautiful!"

7. "A Most Helpful Brunette," *Newsweek*, March 18, 1957, 82–83.

8. John Denson, introduction to Mildred Lewis and Milton Lewis, *Famous Modern Newspaper Writers* (New York: Dodd, Mead, 1962), 14.

9. "Personality Behind the By-Line."

10. Margaret Turner, "From 'Mister' to Darling: People Stop to Look at Sylvia Porter, Then Stay to Listen," *Atlanta Journal and Constitution*, Oct. 1, 1950, folder 128, SPP, WHMC.

11. Sylvia Porter to Lester Merkel [copy to Carl Brandt], July 20, 1951, folder 4, SPP, WHMC.

12. Jean Baer, *The Self-Chosen: "Our Crowd" Is Dead, Long Live Our Crowd* (New York: Arbor House, 1982), 264.

13. Olga Curtis, "Sylvia Porter, and How to Make Money Though Married," *Denver Sunday Post*, July 21, 1963, sec. *Empire Magazine*, folder 129, SPP, WHMC, 16–17.

14. Curtis, "How to Make Money," 264.

15. Randall Poe, "How Porter Translates 'Bafflegab,'" *Across the Board*, July 1978, folder 139, SPP, WHMC.

16. Ruth Hawthorne Fay, "Women at the Top: Sylvia F. Porter" [photocopy], *Cue*, Nov. 19, 1949, folder 126, SPP, WHMC.

17. Sylvia Porter to Carl Brandt, Dec. 14, 1949, folder 2, SPP, WHMC.

18. *Reporting on Governments* was published under Porter's initials until the 1970s, about thirty years after the *New York Post* had started using her full name.

19. Curtis, "How to Make Money Though Married."

20. Sylvia Porter to Carl Brandt, Dec. 14, 1949.

21. The focus of Porter's newsletter differed from that of W. M. Kiplinger's *Washington Letter*, founded in 1923, which was aimed at small business owners.

22. Display Ad 264, *New York Times*, Sept. 20, 1953, sec. BR, 14.

23. Maxwell, "Portias of the Press."

24. Leonard Lyons, "The Lyons Den," *Broadway Gazette*, 1943, folder 119, SPP, WHMC.

25. Whitney, "Living Legend."

26. Turner, "From 'Mister' to Darling."

27. Display Ad 23, *New York Times*, Nov. 17, 1947, sec. A, 25.

28. *Meet the Press*, NBC, Nov. 9, 1952 (accession no. T: 29909, media no. 022401), preserved television recording, Museum of Television and Radio, New York City.

29. Bernice Baumgarten to Carl Brandt, March 21, 1944, folder 1, SPP, WHMC.

30. Sylvia Porter to Leon Shimkin, Oct. 18, 1947, folder 1, SPP, WHMC.

31. *Mary Margaret McBride Show*, ABC, March 2, 1953 (LWO 15577, reel 231B), preserved audio recording, Motion Picture, Broadcasting, and Recorded Sound Division, Library of Congress.

32. Sylvia Porter to Carl Brandt [copy of letter from Porter to J. K. Lasser], Jan. 21, 1953, folder 7, SPP, WHMC.

33. Carol Brandt to William Tug, Aug. 28, 1968, folder 12, SPP, WHMC.

34. *Mary Margaret McBride*, March 2, 1953.

35. *Ibid.*

36. Bernard B. Perry to Carl Brandt, July 6, 1945, folder 1, SPP, WHMC.

37. Sylvia Porter to Carl Brandt, July 29, 1949, folder 2, SPP, WHMC.

38. Judy McCluskey, "A Visit with Sylvia Porter," *Providence Sunday Journal*, Dec. 8, 1963, folder 130, SPP, WHMC, 8–10.

39. Doris Lockerman, "Women and the Dollar Sign," *Atlanta Constitution*, Sept. 27, 1950, folder 127, SPP, WHMC.

40. Olshin, "Princess Charming of Wall Street," 113.

41. Curtis, "How to Make Money Though Married," 16.

42. "Personality Behind the By-Line," 3.

43. Ibid.

44. Curtis, "How to Make Money Though Married," 17.

45. Allene Talmey, "4 Unique Columnists," *Vogue*, Nov. 1, 1958, 112. Porter told her agent that Talmey had helped her in the beginning of her career by giving her an assignment for *Vogue* (Carol Brandt to Sylvia Porter, Feb. 16, 1961, folder 10, SPP, WHMC).

46. McCluskey, "A Visit with Sylvia Porter," 9.

47. Curtis, "How to Make Money Though Married," 16.

48. Ferman Wilson, "The Lady Squawks?," *Miami Herald*, Apr. 25, 1948, folder 122, SPP, WHMC.

49. "City Desk," *St. Petersburg Times*, n.d. Apr. 1948, folder 122, SPP, WHMC.

50. A transcript of this program appears in the pamphlet *Town Meeting: Bulletin of America's Town Meeting of the Air*, ABC, Nov. 7, 1950, folder 128, SPP, WHMC.

51. Porter, "How Far Can We Go Safely in Piling Up the War Debt?," speech printed in *Executives' Club News*, Oct. 2, 1942, folder 118, SPP, WHMC, 3.

52. Nancy F. Cott, *The Grounding of Modern Feminism* (New Haven, CT: Yale University Press, 1987), 271.

53. Daniel Horowitz, *Betty Friedan and the Making of the Feminine Mystique: The American Left, the Cold War, and Modern Feminism* (Amherst: University of Massachusetts Press, 1998). See 1–15 for a more expansive discussion of his argument.

54. Curtis, "How to Make Money Though Married," 16.

55. McCluskey, "A Visit with Sylvia Porter"; Katherine T. Hill, "Finance Editor Has Money Trouble Too: Like Other Women, Sylvia Porter Gets Balled Up over Paltry 10's and

20's," Oct. 13, 1949, *Louisville (KY) Courier-Journal*, folder 125, SPP, WHMC. Porter also told Hill that at a Washington party, she had asked Dean Acheson and John Snyder how they explained convertible currency or the devaluation of the British pound to their wives. Both said, in effect, "Heaven forbid trying."

56. "Housewife's View," 61.

57. Porter, "The Automobile Dealer's Stake in the Consumer" (speech, 1954), folder 48, SPP, WHMC.

58. Porter, "How Far Can We Go Safely in Piling Up the War Debt?," 3.

59. Leonard Lyons, "Broadway Gazette," *Washington Post*, May 1, 1946, 5.

60. Elaine Tyler May, *Homeward Bound: American Families in the Cold War Era* (New York: Basic Books, 1988), 27–36, 51–57, 73–91.

61. Joanne Meyerowitz, introduction to *Not June Cleaver: Women and Gender in Postwar America, 1945–1960* (Philadelphia: Temple University Press, 1994), 2.

62. Nancy Walker, *Shaping Our Mothers' World*, vii–xvii.

63. Debra Osburn Pozega, "Invisible Women in Transitional Times: The Untold Stories of Working Women in the 1950s" (Ph.D. diss., Michigan State University, 2001), 143–44.

64. William Chafe, *The American Woman: Her Changing Social, Economic, and Political Roles, 1920–1970* (New York: Oxford University Press, 1972), 218–19.

65. "Women in Journalism Program Scores Success with Lectures, Luncheons," *50th Anniversary Times* 1, no. 11 (University of Missouri: Feb. 1959), box 29, folder 897, Sara Lockwood Williams Papers, WHMC.

66. Porter, "Woman's Place in the Business World" (speech, March 1948), folder 39, SPP, WHMC.

67. Susan M. Hartmann, "Women's Employment and the Domestic Ideal in the Early Cold War Years," in *Not June Cleaver: Women and Gender in Postwar America: 1945–1960*, ed. Joanne Meyerowitz (Philadelphia: Temple University Press, 1994), 86.

68. Susan J. Douglas, *Where the Girls Are: Growing Up Female with the Mass Media* (New York: Random House, 1994), 49.

69. Betty Friedan, *The Feminine Mystique* (New York: W. W. Norton, 1963, 2001), 15. Horowitz located the origins of Friedan's feminist arguments in her labor journalism after the war. See Horowitz, *Making of the Feminine Mystique*, esp. 121–96, which traces Friedan's path from being a writer for the *UE News*, a union newspaper, to being a freelance journalist for women's magazines.

70. Sylvia Porter to Carl Brandt, June 2, 1950, folder 3, SPP, WHMC.

71. Sylvia Porter to Brooks Roberts, June 11, 1952, folder 5, SPP, WHMC.

72. Schneider, "Wall Street Joan of Arc."

73. Porter, "Women Are No Longer News" (speech given at the Tobe-Coburn School commencement in New York City on June 4, 1957; at Hood College in Frederick, MD, on June 8, 1958; and at the University of Missouri in Columbia, MO, on Feb. 12, 1959), folder 52, SPP, WHMC, 6.

74. Porter, "Women Are No Longer News," 6.

75. Porter, "Woman's Place in the Business World."

76. Ibid.

77. Porter, "Brain Has No Sex," 2.

78. Sylvia Porter, "Sex and Savings," *New York Post*, Aug. 9, 1949, folder 349, SPP, WHMC.

79. Sylvia Porter, "Sex in Finance," *New York Post*, Nov. 11, 1949, folder 352, SPP, WHMC.

80. Sylvia Porter, "We Are a Nation of Working Wives," *New York Post*, May 2, 1950, folder 355, SPP, WHMC.

81. Porter, "We Are a Nation of Working Wives."

82. Porter, "Working Wives Open New Fields," *New York Post*, May 10, 1950, folder 355, SPP, WHMC.

83. Sylvia Porter, "'Ideal' Corporate Wife," *New York Post*, Oct. 25, 1954, folder 381, SPP, WHMC.

84. Sylvia Porter, "Women's Wealth," *New York Post*, Sept. 20, 1950, folder 356, SPP, WHMC.

85. Sylvia Porter, "1958's Girl Graduate Goes to Work," *New York Post*, May 29, 1958, folder 403, SPP, WHMC.

86. Sylvia Porter, "Equal Pay? Not Yet," *New York Post*, March 17, 1953, folder 372, SPP, WHMC.

87. Sylvia Porter, "Kitty Foyle in 1954," *New York Post*, July 8, 1954, folder 380, SPP, WHMC.

88. Susan Ware, *It's One o'Clock and Here Is Mary Margaret McBride: A Radio Biography* (New York: New York University, 2005), 191.

89. Ware, *Radio Biography*, 191.

90. Porter sent a message to a rally in Oklahoma supporting the drive for the Equal Rights Amendment in the seventies (Porter to Carol Tucker, Sept. 26, 1977, folder 21, SPP, WHMC). But there is no evidence she joined the National Organization for Women or participated in other collective efforts. And she was careful to laud domesticity as a vocation for women. Responding with a form letter to a sorority president asking for advice in 1975, Porter wrote: "Discipline, dedication and drive—these are the basic ingredients of any formula for success. And do not by any means restrict your questions to a 'successful woman.' The Three 'D's' would be at the core of any success, I would think, even including marriage" (Porter to Juliath Gilmore, Sept. 30, 1975, folder 19, SPP, WHMC).

91. Porter, "To Tillie and Rosie," *New York Post*, Nov. 17, 1950, folder 358, SPP, WHMC. The male sources for this column were not named "for obvious reasons," Porter wrote. It is probable that the frequent anonymous quotations that appeared in Porter's newspaper column were composite quotations, expressing a point of view she believed to be widespread but not actually spoken as part of an interview. The tone of the anonymous quotations is similar to the fabricated "reader" questions that Porter later answered in her *Ladies' Home*

Journal column. Porter's newspaper columns contained many anonymous sources until the late fifties, when she hired an assistant to help with her reporting. After that, her column used more named sources.

92. N. Walker, *Shaping Our Mothers' World*, xiii.

93. Sylvia Porter, "What Every Woman Should Know about Her Husband," *Good Housekeeping*, Aug. 9, 1944, 39.

94. Porter, "What Every Woman Should Know About Her Husband," 164.

95. Sylvia Porter, "Your Money or Your Life: Here's How You Can Make Your Money Grow," *Ladies' Home Journal*, May 1947, 61; Louise Paine Benjamin, "Your Money or Your Life: Here's How You Can Make Yourself Grow," *Ladies' Home Journal*, May 1947, 65.

96. Sylvia Porter, "Sylvia Porter's Advice to Young Wives about Money," *Redbook*, Nov. 1964, 63.

97. Porter, "Sylvia Porter's Advice to Young Wives about Money," 119.

98. Sylvia Porter to William Lowe, ca. 1951, folder 3, SPP, WHMC.

99. Ibid.

100. Sylvia Porter to Carl Brandt, May 1, 1951, folder 4, SPP, WHMC.

101. Carl Brandt to Porter, Feb. 9, 1954, folder 8, SPP, WHMC.

102. Porter told an audience in 1953 that consumer spending made up about two-thirds of the economy, a proportion that remained sixty years later (Porter, "The Consumer's Stake in Distribution," speech to the Boston Conference of Distribution [Boston, Oct. 30, 1953], folder 45, SPP, WHMC, 1).

103. David Abrahamson, *Magazine-Made America: The Cultural Transformation of the Postwar Periodical* (Cresskill, NJ: Hampton Press, 1996). Abrahamson wrote that in the fifteen years after World War II, gross national product rose 250 percent, payment for personal services rose 300 percent, and new construction jumped 900 percent. By 1960, per-capita income was 30 percent higher than it was in 1946.

104. According to historian James Gilbert, from 1945 to 1970, manufacturing and construction jobs increased 35 percent while jobs in government, retailing, finance, and insurance rose 200 percent. He also noted that short-term consumer debt in 1970 was twenty-two times larger than it had been in 1945. See James Gilbert, *Another Chance: Postwar America, 1945–1968* (Philadelphia: Temple University Press, 1981), 178, 189.

105. Journalist David Halberstam offered a colorful description of postwar marketing developments in his book *The Fifties* (New York: Fawcett Columbine, 1993), 155–87.

106. Sylvia Porter, "A Charter of Economic Human Rights" (speech given in Cleveland, Sept. 28, 1956; at the Colgate University Foreign Policy Conference in Hamilton, NY, July 3, 1957; in Rochester, NY, Jan. 28, 1959; and in Louisville, KY, Feb. 13, 1959), folder 51, SPP, WHMC. A refined version is printed in *Vital Speeches of the Day*, Sept. 1, 1957, 678–81.

107. Sylvia Porter, speech given at the Hunter College commencement (New York City, Jan. 31, 1951), folder 41, SPP, WHMC, 4.

108. Sylvia Porter, "The Importance of Economics in Our World Today," speech given to the New York Financial Advertisers (New York City, Nov. 28, 1951) and to the New York Newspaper Women's Club (New York City, Oct. 27, 1954), folder 43, SPP, WHMC, 1.

109. Sylvia Porter, "Menus—'44 and '47" New York Post, Sept. 11, 1947, folder 339, SPP, WHMC.

110. Sylvia Porter, "Who Gets Hurt?" New York Post, Apr. 14, 1947, folder 336, SPP, WHMC, 5.

111. Sylvia Porter, "Who Gets Hurt?"

112. Sylvia Porter to George Humphrey [copy], June 6, 1956, folder 9, SPP, WHMC.

113. George Humphrey to Sylvia Porter, June 12, 1956, folder 9, SPP, WHMC.

114. Sylvia Porter to George Humphrey, June 25, 1956 [copy], folder 9, SPP, WHMC. Demonstrating her talent for changing her tune depending on who was listening, Porter gave a totally different opinion of the auto industry when she spoke to car dealers in 1954: "With so much of the American market untouched even during the peak year of prosperity, it is ridiculous to talk of 'overproduction,' to worry about the 'saturation' of the markets" (Porter, "Automobile Dealer's Stake in the Consumer," 7).

115. Sylvia Porter, "Stock Forecasts," New York Post, March 4, 1946, 30.

116. Sylvia Porter, "Policy Alters U.S.," New York Post, March 14, 1947, folder 336, SPP, WHMC.

117. Sylvia Porter, "Peoria and Prague," New York Post, March 1, 1948, folder 342, SPP, WHMC.

118. Porter, "The Importance of Economics in Our World Today," 1.

119. "Pantepec Raises Shorts Interest: Flurry Following Stock Tip Moves American Exchange Total Up 79,748 Shares," New York Times, Jan. 21, 1955, sec. A, p. 29.

120. Burton Crane, "Winchell Scored for Market Tips at Senate Inquiry," New York Times, March 5, 1955, sec. A., p. 1.

121. Sylvia Porter, "Bare 'Killing' on WW Oil Tip," New York Post, March 7, 1955, folder 383, SPP, WHMC.

122. Quirt, Press and the World of Money, 256.

123. Sylvia Porter, "Cockeyed Wages," New York Post, July 3, 1951, folder 362, SPP, WHMC.

124. Sylvia Porter, "A Tax Plan for the Rich," New York Post, Feb. 11, 1947, folder 335, SPP, WHMC.

125. Porter, "Tax Plan for the Rich."

126. Sylvia Porter, "Finance Courses," New York Post, Feb. 16, 1951, folder 359, SPP, WHMC.

127. Janet Goetze, "Journalist Pioneers Financial Column," Oregonian, May 11, 1971, folder 137, SPP, WHMC.

128. Galeota, "Miss Porter's School."

129. William H. Ewing to Sylvia Porter, June 17, 1954, folder 8, SPP, WHMC.

130. "AP Newsfeatures Going on Tape-Wire," *Editor & Publisher*, Feb. 13, 1971, folder 137, SPP, WHMC.

131. Display Ad 25, *Wall Street Journal*, Apr. 21, 1959, 19.

132. Bernard Baruch to Sylvia Porter, Dec. 12, 1953, folder 7, SPP, WHMC.

3. Expert with an Empire

1. "Sylvia & You." The magazine had an extensive fact-checking department composed almost entirely of women, whom *Time* and other news magazines would not hire as writers.

2. "Sylvia & You," 46.

3. Ibid.

4. Sylvia Porter press kit, box 55, DSP, Manuscripts and Archives Division, Humanities & Social Sciences Library, NYPL.

5. "Sylvia & You," 47.

6. Ibid., 46.

7. Ibid., 47.

8. Ibid.

9. Ibid., 48.

10. Jeffrey Potter, *Men, Money and Magic: The Story of Dorothy Schiff* (New York: Coward, McCann & Geoghegan, 1996), 274. This authorized biography of Schiff is based largely on interviews with her and includes extensive quotations. See 161–213 for an overview of Schiff's takeover and editorial approach at the *New York Post*.

11. Potter, *Men, Money and Magic*, 266.

12. Sylvia Porter to Dorothy Schiff, Jan. 14, 1955, box 55, DSP, NYPL.

13. Sylvia Porter to Dorothy Schiff, Dec. 26, 1961, box 55, DSP, NYPL.

14. Dorothy Schiff, memorandum for her files, July 16, 1956, box 55, DSP, NYPL.

15. Richard Manson to Dorothy Schiff, Feb. 17, 1954, box 55, DSP, NYPL; Harry Rosen to Dorothy Schiff, Oct. 13, 1954, box 55, DSP, NYPL.

16. Sylvia Porter to Schiff, Dec. 13, 1949, folder 2, SPP, WHMC.

17. Carl Brandt to Irwin Margulies, Dec. 19, 1949, folder 2, SPP, WHMC.

18. Sylvia Porter to Carl Brandt, Dec. 14, 1949, folder 216, SPP, WHMC.

19. Schiff, memorandum, July 16, 1956, 1.

20. Ibid., 1–2.

21. Ibid., 2–4.

22. Porter to Schiff, Dec. 26, 1961, 1.

23. Ibid., 2.

24. Ibid.

25. Ibid.

26. Dorothy Schiff to Sylvia Porter [copy], Jan. 2, 1962, box 55, DSP, NYPL, 1.

27. Sylvia Porter to Dorothy Schiff, Feb. 10, 1961, box 55, DSP, NYPL.

28. Schiff to Porter, Jan. 2, 1962, 2.

29. Dorothy Schiff to Marvin Berger, Feb. 26, 1962, box 55, DSP, NYPL; Jean Gillette to Lee Cook, Feb. 27, 1962, box 55, DSP, NYPL.

30. Paul Sann to Dorothy Schiff, March 26, 1962, box 55, DSP, NYPL.

31. Paul Sann to Dorothy Schiff, Feb. 13, 1964, box 55, DSP, NYPL.

32. Sann to Schiff, Feb. 13, 1964.

33. Dorothy Schiff to Paul Sann, Feb. 13, 1964, box 55, DSP, NYPL.

34. Paul Sann to Robert Hall [copy], May 3, 1968, box 55, DSP, NYPL.

35. Dorothy Schiff to Paul Sann, Feb. 18, 1969, box 55, DSP, NYPL.

36. Dorothy Schiff to Paul Sann, Nov. 12, 1974, box 55, DSP, NYPL.

37. Dorothy McCardle, "Feminist 60s Urged by Saluted Sextet," *Washington Post and Times-Herald*, June 14, 1960, sec. B, 6.

38. Display Ad 125, *Wall Street Journal*, May 16, 1960, 28. Porter spoke at the Third National Congress on Better Living, a meeting of one hundred homemakers in Washington, DC, sponsored by *McCall's* magazine, in 1960. In 1967 she won another award from the National Federation of Business and Professional Women's Clubs, this one for advancing the status of wage-earning women ("BPW Gives Top Hat Awards," *Washington Post and Times-Herald*, July 26, 1967, sec. C, 1).

39. In 1971 the group of ninety-seven members in SABW still included just five women ("Business Editor Named to Head Writers' Group," *Washington Post and Times-Herald*, May 10, 1971, sec. D, 12; "They Just Have More Money," *St. Petersburg Times*, May 25, 1987, sec. E, 2). The group later was renamed the Society of Business Editors and Writers (SABEW).

Among Porter's other honors during this period: In 1964 she received a Meritorious Public Service Award from the Internal Revenue Service; in 1966 she received a Spirit of Achievement Award from the Albert Einstein College of Medicine and was named an honorary member of Phi Chi Theta, a fraternity of women in business and economics; in 1967 she was named one of the one hundred most accomplished women by *Harper's Bazaar*; in 1970 she was given the Hunter College Centennial Medal for Noteworthy Achievement; in 1973 she was named to the Hunter College Hall of Fame; in 1970 she was named Woman of the Year in Communications by the Advertising Club of New York; and in 1975 she was named one of the fifty most influential women by the Newspaper Enterprise Association.

40. Carol Brandt to Sylvia Porter, Aug. 19, 1965, folder 4, SPP, WHMC. According to Brandt's obituary in the *New York Times*, she also represented Thornton Wilder, John Dos Passos, Vincent Sheehan, and Marcia Davenport.

41. Lydia Ratcliff, telephone interview by the author, July 22, 2006, Vienna, VA.

42. Sylvia Porter, "Spending Your Money," *LHJ*, Oct. 1965, 52; Sept. 1966, 24; Oct. 1967, 52.

43. Sylvia Porter, "Spending Your Money," *LHJ*, June 1966, 54.

44. Sylvia Porter, "Spending Your Money," *LHJ*, March 1966, 32.

45. Sylvia Porter, "Spending Your Money," *LHJ*, Feb. 1966, 54.

46. Sylvia Porter, "Spending Your Money," *LHJ*, Apr. 1967, 58–59.

47. Sylvia Porter, "Spending Your Money," *LHJ*, July 1971.

48. Sylvia Porter, "Spending Your Money," *LHJ*, Dec. 1966, 56.

49. Sylvia Porter, "Spending Your Money," *LHJ*, June 1970, 20. Porter spoke frequently about the different treatment of men and women under the social security system. The system treated women primarily as dependents, not providers, even though women made up almost half of the paid workforce by 1977. See Sylvia Porter, "The Inequitable Treatment of Women in Our Social Security System" (speech, n.p, 1977), folder 78, SPP, WHMC. The system now allows both men and women to collect benefits as workers or dependents.

50. Sylvia Porter, "Spending Your Money," *LHJ*, Aug. 1966, 38; Feb. 1969.

51. "The VIP Line: Columnist Asks Creation of Wage-Price Controls," *Miami Herald*, Aug. 16, 1971, folder 137, SPP, WHMC.

52. Sylvia Porter, "What's a Wife Worth?," *NYP*, July 13, 1966, folder 452, SPP, WHMC.

53. Sylvia Porter, "Women and U.S. Jobs," *NYP*, May 6, 1964, folder 439, SPP, WHMC.

54. N. Walker, *Shaping Our Mothers' World*. In chap. 4, 101–44, Walker expands on the notions of class and consumerism propagated by women's magazines after World War II until the mid-1960s. She writes: "In the context of the Cold War, consumption was a patriotic activity, reinforcing capitalism as an ideology in opposition to the evils of communism" (130).

55. Ruth Rosen, *The World Split Open: How the Modern Women's Movement Changed America* (New York: Penguin Books, 2000), 300–301.

56. Cott, *Grounding of Modern Feminism*, 4–5.

57. Sylvia Porter, "Housewives Face New Pension Tax," *NYP*, May 17, 1950, folder 355, SPP, WHMC; "Have You a Maid?" *NYP*, Jan. 10, 1951, folder 359, SPP, WHMC.

58. Chafe, *American Woman*, 234.

59. Cynthia Harrison, *On Account of Sex: The Politics of Women's Issues, 1945–1968* (Berkeley and Los Angeles: University of California Press, 1988), 171.

60. Sara Evans, *Born for Liberty*, 265; Rosen, *World Split Open*, 79.

61. Rosen, *World Split Open*, 79.

62. Ibid.

63. Sara Evans identified competing strains of feminism during this "decade of discovery": (1) the liberal feminism of older professional women who focused on securing the rights of individuals through legal challenges and political action; and (2) the more radical feminism of younger women who questioned the entire social order, starting at home, and engaged in a separatist politics based on the idea that "sisterhood is powerful." The professional feminists sought institutional change through organizations such as the National Organization for Women, founded in 1966, and the Women's Equity Action League, founded in 1968. The younger members of the women's liberation movement sought cultural change through consciousness-raising groups, elaborate protests, and a feminine-centered counterculture. See Evans, *Born for Liberty*, 274–85. Ruth Rosen also discusses the tensions between these groups of feminists in *World Split Open*, 81–88.

64. Sylvia Porter, "No Women Allowed," *NYP*, May 3, 1962, folder 427, SPP, WHMC.

65. Sylvia Porter, "Sylvia Porter 'Invades' the Exchange," *NYP*, June 20, 1962, folder 427, SPP, WHMC.

66. Sylvia Porter, "A Woman on the Exchange?," *NYP*, Sept. 17, 1965, folder 447, SPP, WHMC.

67. Sylvia Porter to Carl Brandt, Sept. 18, 1951, folder 4, SPP, WHMC.

68. Sylvia Porter to Carl Brandt, July 24, 1951, folder 4, SPP, WHMC.

69. Sylvia Porter, "Good News," *NYP*, Jan. 18, 1952, folder 365, SPP, WHMC.

70. Sylvia Porter, "Mac Loses His Job," *NYP*, Feb. 28, 1949, folder 347, SPP, WHMC.

71. Sylvia Porter, "Successful Wives," NYP, March 15, 1956, folder 390, SPP, WHMC.

72. Lydia Ratcliff, telephone interview by the author, July 22, 2006, Vienna, VA; Warren Boroson, telephone interview by the author, July 26, 2006, Vienna, VA; Beth Kobliner, telephone interview by the author, Sept. 18, 2006, Vienna, VA; Brooke Shearer, interview by the author, Aug. 11, 2006, Washington, DC.

73. Ratcliff, interview by author.

74. Ibid.

75. Shearer, interview by author.

76. Ratcliff, interview by author.

77. Shearer, interview by author.

78. Ibid.

79. Sylvia Porter, "Sick-Sick Movies," *NYP*, July 11, 1952, box 55, DSP, NYPL.

80. Richard Manson to Dorothy Schiff, July 16, 1952, box 55, DSP, NYPL.

81. Dorothy Schiff to Richard Manson, July 16, 1952, box 55, DSP, NYPL.

82. The column was Porter, "'Bright' Movie Story," *NYP*, July 23, 1952, box 55, DSP, NYPL. The letter was Alfred Corwin to Sylvia Porter [copy], July 23, 1952, box 55, DSP, NYPL.

83. Porter told an editor in 1973 that her column was published in 350 newspapers, the same number reported two years later on the dust jacket of *Sylvia Porter's Money Book*. Sylvia Porter to Bobbi Ann Ossip, March 28, 1973, folder 14, SPP, WHMC.

84. Sylvia Porter to Ferris Mack, Apr. 2, 1975, folder 17, SPP, WHMC.

85. Sylvia Porter to Edwin D. Hunter, Feb. 14, 1974, folder 15, SPP, WHMC.

86. Shearer, interview by author.

87. Ibid.

88. Ibid.

89. Sylvia Porter, "The Blue Chip," *NYP*, May 2, 1967, folder 457, SPP, WHMC.

90. Sylvia Porter, "Business News Coverage," *NYP*, May 9, 1967, folder 457, SPP, WHMC.

91. For example, see Sylvia Porter, "Consumer Gyps and How to Avoid Them," *NYP*, March 26, 1962, folder 426, SPP, WHMC; "Borrow—or Save?" *NYP*, March 21, 1966, folder 450, SPP, WHMC; "How to Bargain-Hunt," *NYP*, March 30, 1966, folder 450, SPP, WHMC; "10 Steps to a Summer Job," *NYP*, March 31, 1966, folder 450, SPP, WHMC; "'Chain' Selling Schemes," *NYP*, Apr. 1, 1966, folder 450, SPP, WHMC.

92. *Mary Margaret McBride*, March 2, 1953.

93. Sylvia Porter, *Sylvia Porter's Money Book: How to Earn It, Spend It, Save It, Invest It, Borrow It—and Use It to Better Your Life* (Garden City, New York: Doubleday, 1975).

94. Glenn Fowler, "Sylvia Porter, Financial Columnist, Is Dead at 77," *New York Times*, June 7, 1991, sec. B, 6.

95. Cohn, interview by author.

96. Carol Brandt to William Tug, Aug. 28, 1968.

97. Robert Hall to Sylvia Porter, Dec. 22, 1964, folder 11, SPP, WHMC.

98. Sylvia Porter to Robert Hall, Jan. 12, 1965, folder 11, SPP, WHMC.

99. Sylvia Porter to Carol Brandt, Oct. 15, 1968, folder 216, SPP, WHMC.

100. Sylvia Porter to Carol Brandt, Oct. 15, 1968.

101. Tom Congdon to Sylvia Porter, Oct. 15, 1973, folder 14, SPP, WHMC.

102. Acknowledgments to *Sylvia Porter's Money Book*.

103. Shearer, interview by author.

104. Carol Brandt to Sylvia Porter, Aug. 4, 1975, folder 216, SPP, WHMC.

105. Hal Meyerson to Sylvia Porter, Aug. 6, 1986, folder 29, SPP, WHMC.

106. Hal Meyerson to A. L. Campbell [copy], Apr. 17, 1981, folder 23, SPP, WHMC.

107. A. L. Campbell to Hal Meyerson, [copy], Apr. 27, 1981, folder 23, SPP, WHMC.

108. Stephen Cogil, "Booksellers Bullish on Christmas Prospects," *Publisher's Weekly*, Nov. 10, 1975, 35–36.

109. Goetze, "Journalist Pioneers Financial Column."

110. Kenneth W. James to Sylvia Porter, July 5, 1975, folder 19, SPP, WHMC.

111. Porter to Sterling Noel [copy], June 23, 1973, folder 14, SPP, WHMC.

112. The title of Quinn's book—*Everyone's Money Book*—could be seen as a stab at the eponymous title of Porter's book.

113. David R. Francis, "A 'Life-Cycle' View of Financial Planning," *Christian Science Monitor*, Feb. 17, 1984, sec. B, 12.

114. Melissa Davis, "Personalities," *Washington Post*, Jan. 4, 1979, sec. B, 3.

115. Clyde Haberman and Albin Krebs [n.t., Information Bank Abstracts via Lexis-Nexis], *New York Times*, Oct. 19, 1979, sec. B, 4. She was named one of eleven Women of the Decade by *Ladies' Home Journal*, alongside Margaret Mead, Katharine Hepburn, Beverly Sills, Marian Anderson, Betty Ford, Helen Hayes, Barbara Walters, Joan Ganz Cooney, Barbara Jordan, and Elisabeth Kubler-Ross. She was also placed on the *World Almanac*'s list of the twenty-five most influential women in the United States ("Katharine Graham Named Most Influential," Associated Press [via LexisNexis], New York, Nov. 11, 1979).

116. John Hohenberg to Sylvia Porter, May 5, 1971, folder 137, SPP, WHMC; John Hohenberg to Sylvia Porter, March 12, 1973, folder 138, SPP, WHMC; "Nominating Judges Are Chosen for Pulitzer Prizes in Journalism," *New York Times*, Jan. 5, 1981, sec. B, 5; "55 Journalists Named to Pulitzer Jury," Associated Press [via LexisNexis], New York, Jan. 5, 1981.

4. Presidential Adviser

1. Sylvia Porter to Mack Williams [copy], Oct. 11, 1974, folder 167, SPP, WHMC.

2. Connecticut Walker [Brooke Shearer], "Columnist Sylvia Porter—She Cares about Your Money," *Parade*, Apr. 7, 1974, folder 138, SPP, WHMC. Connecticut Walker was a pseudonym for Brooke Shearer, one of Porter's assistants.

3. Sylvia Porter to Ted Sorensen, telegram [copy], Sept. 10, 1963, folder 129, SPP, WHMC.

4. Ted Sorensen to Sylvia Porter, telegram, Sept. 12, 1963, folder 129, SPP, WHMC.

5. Porter, "Historic Bill," *New York Post*, Sept. 19, 1963, folder 129, SPP, WHMC.

6. Sylvia Porter, "Big and Healthy," *New York Post*, Sept. 30, 1965, folder 447, SPP, WHMC.

7. Sylvia Porter to Lyndon Johnson [copy], Jan. 10, 1964, folder 130, SPP, WHMC.

8. Sylvia Porter to Lyndon Johnson [copy], Feb. 10, 1964, folder 131, SPP, WHMC.

9. David Halberstam, *The Best and the Brightest*, Twentieth Anniversary ed. (New York: Random House, 1972; Ballantine Books, 1992), 443.

10. C. Walker, "Columnist Sylvia Porter."

11. Sylvia Porter to Lyndon Johnson [copy], March 26, 1964, folder 131, SPP, WHMC.

12. Yanek Mieczkowski, *Gerald Ford and the Challenges of the 1970s* (Lexington: University Press of Kentucky, 2005), 98. Mieczkowski's biography of Ford provides a sympathetic but comprehensive overview of Ford's experience in the White House as well as his economic and political perspective.

13. Mieczkowski, *Gerald Ford and the Challenges of the 1970s*, 99.

14. Quoted in Gene Carlson, wire report, United Press International, Sept. 27, 1974, folder 166, SPP, WHMC.

15. "Civilian Unemployment Rate," Bureau of Labor Statistics, U.S. Department of Labor (available from http://research.stlouisfed.org/fred2/data/UNRATE.txt, accessed May 31, 2011).

16. Mieczkowski, *Gerald Ford and the Challenges of the 1970s*, 101.

17. Ibid., 101–2.

18. Quoted in Ibid., 76.

19. Hermann G. Stelzner, "Ford's War on Inflation: A Metaphor That Did Not Cross," *Communication Monographs 44* (Nov. 1977): 284–297.

20. Statement by Sylvia Porter, prepared for pre–summit conference on inflation, Sept. 20, 1974, Washington, DC, folder 166, SPP, WHMC.

21. David Barnett, n.t., n.p., Sept. 28, 1974, folder 166, SPP, WHMC.

22. Carlson, wire report.

23. Robert Reno, n.t., *Newsday*, Sept. 29, 1974, folder 166, SPP, WHMC.

24. Mieczkowski, *Gerald Ford and the Challenges of the 1970s*, 115.

25. Quoted in Barnett, n.t.

26. Sylvia Porter, remarks given at President Gerald Ford's Pre–Summit Conference on Inflation (Washington, DC, Sept. 20, 1974), folder 72, SPP, WHMC.

27. See, for example, Thomas Howell, "The Writers' War Board: U.S. Domestic Propaganda in World War II," *Historian* 59, no. 4 (1997): 795–812; and Yang, "Creating the Kitchen Patriot: Media Promotion of Food Rationing and Nutrition Campaigns on the American Home Front during World War II."

28. Mack Williams, "As the News-Tribune Sees It," *Tarrant County (Texas) News-Tribune*, Sept. 13, 1974, folder 166, SPP, WHMC.

29. Williams, "As the News-Tribune Sees It."

30. Tom Wolf to Sylvia Porter, Oct. 10, 1974, folder 167, SPP, WHMC.

31. The rush to execute the Citizens Action Committee to Fight Inflation appears to have been a recommendation by presidential aide Robert Hartmann (Mieczkowski, *Gerald Ford and the Challenges of the 1970s*, 121).

32. Denny Griswold, n.t., *Public Relations News*, Oct. 7, 1974, folder 167, SPP, WHMC.

33. Fern Marja Eckman, "Woman in the News: Inflation Tips for Ford," *New York Post Magazine*, Oct. 5, 1974, folder 109, SPP, WHMC, 1.

34. Quoted in Myron Kandel, n.t., *Review of the Financial Press* 2, no. 40, Oct. 10, 1974, folder 167, SPP, WHMC.

35. Paul Theis to William Seidman [copy], Sept. 26, 1974, folder 166, SPP, WHMC.

36. Mieczkowski, *Gerald Ford and the Challenges of the 1970s*, 134.

37. Paul Theis to William Seidman [copy], Sept. 26, 1974, folder 166, SPP, WHMC.

38. Some suggestions for an anti-inflation slogan that Porter received were: "Slow down, dial down, and calm down" (from the automotive industry); "Anything we can do . . . we can do better" (from the steel industry); and, "We must all work a little harder, so we can produce a little more; we must consume a little less, so we can save a little more" (R. C. Gerstenberg to Sylvia Porter, Oct. 4, 1974, folder 167, SPP, WHMC).

39. Robert Keim to Sylvia Porter, Nov. 20, 1974, folder 172, SPP, WHMC.

40. "B&B Unit Creates WIN Campaign in Five Busy Days," *Advertising Age*, Oct. 21, 1974, folder 169, SPP, WHMC.

41. Ibid. One advertising executive wanted Porter to get a new headshot while wearing the button. Another suggested they ask all newspaper columnists do the same. These ideas never came to fruition.

42. President Gerald Ford, speech, "10/15/74—Future Farmers of America," Oct. 15, 1974, box 2, President's Speeches and Statements, Gerald R. Ford Presidential Library (available from http://www.fordlibrarymuseum.gov/library/document/0122/1252096.pdf, accessed May 31, 2013).

43. Robert Keim, memo to Advertising Council staff, Oct. 11, 1974, folder 167, SPP, WHMC.

44. Philip Shabecoff, "Ford Urges Steps to Curb Inflation," *New York Times*, Oct. 16, 1974, folder 168, SPP, WHMC; Rep. Benjamin Rosenthal, memo to Democrats in the U.S. House of Representatives, Nov. 14, 1974, folder 171, SPP, WHMC.

45. Citizens Action Committee, Communications and Public Awareness Subcommittee, minutes from meeting held Nov. 13, 1974, Washington, DC, folder 171, SPP, WHMC.

46. Russell Freeburg, memorandum to Citizens Action Committee, Oct. 30, 1974, folder 170, SPP, WHMC.

47. Russell Freeburg, memorandum to President Gerald Ford [copy], Oct. 18, 1974, folder 168, SPP, WHMC. The security firm Guardsmark put WIN patches on 3,900 uniforms, and Mayflower Van Lines wrote to say it would paint the WIN logo on its moving trucks. The Gannett newspaper chain promoted and distributed 20,000 WIN buttons and planned a special advertising section around the initiative.

48. James P. Sterba, "New 'Advice' to Curb Inflation: Buy Now, Buy More—Spend!" *New York Times*, Nov. 17, 1974, 67, folder 171, SPP, WHMC. Virginia National Bank announced a program to steady the price of its consumer services, maintain current interest rates, and encourage its customers to save. NU Look Fashions in Columbus, Ohio, wrote to say it was lowering its prices.

49. Ibid.

50. "Few Losers (or Winners) in WIN Campaign," *New York Times*, March 23, 1975, 165.

51. Freeburg, memo to Ford, Oct. 18, 1974.

52. "Statement of Principle," Citizens Action Committee to Fight Inflation, adopted Oct. 12, 1974, folder 170, SPP, WHMC. It quickly became apparent which participants would take the most vocal and active roles on the committee. They were Arch Booth, president of the U.S. Chamber of Commerce; Carol Foreman, president of the Consumer Federation of America; Robert Keim, president of the Advertising Council; Leo Perlis, president of the AFL-CIO; Joseph Alioto, chairman of the U.S. Conference of Mayors; Ronald Brown, a lawyer with the National Urban League; and Frank Stanton, chairman of the American National Red Cross. The committee included many others, such as consumer advocate Ralph Nader, who did not actively participate.

53. CAC meeting minutes, Nov. 13, 1974.

54. Ibid.

55. Sally Rosen to Porter, n.d., Oct. 1974, folder 170, SPP, WHMC.

56. CAC meeting minutes, Nov. 13, 1974.

57. Quoted in Mieczkowski, *Gerald Ford and the Challenges of the 1970s*, 139.

58. CAC meeting minutes, Nov. 13, 1974. This metaphor—building an airplane in the air—appeared in frequent interviews with Freeburg, Porter, and others after the dissolution of the CAC.

59. Freeburg, memo to CAC, Oct. 30, 1974.

60. Calvin Rampton to President Gerald Ford [copy], Oct. 19, 1974, folder 169, SPP, WHMC.

61. Dick Krolik, memorandum to William Baroody Jr., William Seidman, Russell Freeburg [copy], Nov. 15, 1974, folder 172, SPP, WHMC.

62. Mary Jane Lomas to Sylvia Porter, Oct. 16, 1974, folder 168, SPP, WHMC.

63. Betty Jarmusch, "The Summit, from the Valley," *New York Times*, Oct. 13, 1974, 251.

64. Robert Shaw to President Gerald Ford [copy], Oct. 21, 1974, folder 168, SPP, WHMC.

65. Sidney Rutberg, "Sylvia Porter and the Will to WIN," *W* magazine, Nov. 29, 1974, folder 110, SPP, WHMC, 10.

66. Sterba, "New 'Advice' to Curb Inflation."

67. Typed transcript, press conference of the Citizens' Action Committee to Fight Inflation, Room 2008, Old Executive Office Building, Washington, DC, Nov. 11, 1974, folder 172, SPP, WHMC, 1.

68. Transcript, CAC press conference, Nov. 11, 1974, 1.

69. Ibid., 4.

70. Ibid., 6.

71. Ibid., 12–13.

72. Ibid., 16.

73. Ibid., 19.

74. Rosenthal, memo to Democrats.

75. Press release from office of Rep. Ben Rosenthal, U.S. House of Representatives, "30 Lawmakers Seek Halt to WIN Campaign's Partisan Free Ad Blitz," Nov. 27, 1974, folder 171, SPP, WHMC.

76. Press release from office of Rep. Ben Rosenthal, 2.

77. Ibid., 1.

78. Robert Keim to Rep. Ben Rosenthal [copy], Dec. 17, 1974, folder 171, SPP, WHMC.

79. Ibid., 1.

80. WDAU-TV editorial No. 1257, Dec. 11, 1974, folder 171, SPP, WHMC, 1.

81. Sylvia Porter to Mary Katherine Miller [copy], Oct. 17, 1974, folder 173, SPP, WHMC, 1.

82. Russell Freeburg to Sylvia Porter, Nov. 23, 1974, folder 173, SPP, WHMC.

83. Donald Sheehan, "The WIN Program: A Look Ahead," Dec. 11, 1974, folder 174, SPP, WHMC, 1.

84. William Chapman, "President's 'WIN' Program Faltering," Dec. 20, 1974, folder 175, SPP, WHMC. Edward Block was on loan to the government from his position at Illinois Bell Telephone.

85. Sylvia Porter, memorandum to CAC, Jan. 3, 1975, folder 176, SPP, WHMC.

86. Donald Sheehan, memorandum to CAC, Jan. 16, 1975, folder 176, SPP, WHMC.

87. Fred Barnes, "The White House Campaign That Became a Wry Joke," *Washington Star-Times*, Feb. 12, 1975, folder 179, SPP, WHMC.

88. CAC meeting transcript, Jan. 18, 1975, 35.

89. Ibid.

90. Ibid.

91. Barnes, "White House Campaign That Became a Wry Joke."

92. Memorandum to CAC, n.a., March 4, 1975, folder 179, SPP, WHMC.

93. See, for example, Douglas Watson, "Win-Less Volunteer Program to Press Energy Conservation," *Washington Post*, March 12, 1975, 3; Linda Charlton, "WIN, the Anti-Inflation Slogan, Scrapped after a Losing Season," *New York Times*, March 9, 1975, 32; "WIN Motto Is Loser as Ford Committee Drops Theme," *Detroit Sunday News*, March 9, 1975, 4-E.

94. Watson, "Win-Less Volunteer Program to Press Energy Conservation."

95. Sylvia Porter to President Gerald Ford, March 1975, folder 179, SPP, WHMC.

96. Porter to Ford, March 1975, 1.

97. Tom McCall to Sylvia Porter, June 12, 1975, folder 179, SPP, WHMC; Jerald terHorst, "WIN Program Creeping Back," *Chicago Tribune*, May 16, 1975, folder 179, SPP, WHMC.

98. Leo Perlis to members of the CAC, Jan. 6, 1976, folder 179, SPP, WHMC.

99. "WIN Motto Is Loser as Ford Committee Drops Theme."

100. "A Dispassionate Evaluation Passionately Argued," Dec. 1974, folder 175, SPP, WHMC.

101. Nicholas Von Hoffman, "The Fumbling Feds: WIN with Anti-Saloon Tactics," *Washington Post*, Nov. 22, 1974, sec. B, 8.

5. Brand Name

1. Goetze, "Journalist Pioneers Financial Column."

2. Sally Rosen to Sylvia Porter, March 2, 1973, folder 14, SPP, WHMC.

3. Sally Rosen to Sylvia Porter, March 15, 1973, folder 14, SPP, WHMC.

4. "Wall Street Whispers." According to the article, she had been barred from the group "not because she was a glamorous gal, which she is, but because she made so much money it was embarrassing for the fellas. . . . There were 29 holdouts. Male chauvinists, no doubt."

5. For example, Goetze, "Journalist Pioneers Financial Column"; and Fury, "Super-Sylvia."

6. Betty Jaycox, "Femininity and Wit Mask Sylvia's Money Expertise," *Akron (Ohio) Beacon Journal*, May 25, 1972, folder 138, SPP, WHMC.

7. Quoted in Donna Lee Goldberg's academic paper for a journalism course at Syracuse University, Apr. 29, 1974, 5.

8. Eckman, "Woman in the News: Inflation Tips for Ford."

9. Phyllis Battelle, "Sylvia Porter: A Friend's View," *Seattle Post-Intelligencer*, Feb. 9, 1975, sec. D, 3.

10. Ibid. See also Ginny Ade, "Sylvia Porter, Successful Business Columnist, Invites Others to Cash In," *Progressive Woman* (Nov. 1971): 20-22.

11. Sylvia Porter, "Mrs. America Has It—a Job," *New York Post*, June 14, 1962, folder 427, SPP, WHMC.

12. *Woman Alive!* PBS, Nov. 26, 1975 (accession no. T:15371, media no. 022020), preserved television recording, Museum of Television and Radio, New York City.

13. Sylvia Porter, acceptance speech for the Women in Communications Headliner Award (1981), folder 93, SPP, WHMC.

14. Poe, "How Porter Translates 'Bafflegab.'"

15. Jaycox, "Femininity and Wit."

16. Ibid.

17. Moore, "From Columnist to Publisher."

18. Richard Eisenberg, "Matron of Money Markets Her Name," *USA Today*, Dec. 5, 1983, folder 141, SPP, WHMC.

19. Goetze, "Journalist Pioneers Financial Column."

20. Poe, "How Porter Translates 'Bafflegab,'" 47.

21. Beth Kobliner, telephone interview by the author, July 27, 2006, Vienna, VA.

22. Beth Kobliner, telephone interview by the author, Sept. 18, 2006, Vienna, VA.

23. Shearer, interview by author.

24. Martha T. Moore, "Sylvia Porter: From Columnist to Publisher," Feb. 20, 1989, Gannett Westchester Newspapers, folder 146, SPP, WHMC.

25. Shanahan, oral history interview, 30.

26. Boroson, interview by author.

27. James Fox to Steve Christensen, June 13, 1988, folder 31, SPP, WHMC.

28. C. Walker, "Columnist Sylvia Porter."

29. Eisenberg, "Matron of Money Markets Her Name."

30. Donna Martin to Hal Meyerson [copy], Aug. 18, 1982, folder 24, SPP, WHMC.

31. Cohn, interview by author.

32. Sumner Collins to Hal Meyerson, May 16, 1974, folder 216, SPP, WHMC.

33. Hal Meyerson to Sumner Collins, May 17, 1974, folder 216, SPP, WHMC.

34. In her interview with Jean Baer, Porter said her daughter had "repudiated" her way of life (Baer, *Self-Chosen*, 264). According to Lydia Ratcliff, Porter and her daughter had a complicated relationship, and Cris often did not approve of the way Porter conducted her business (Ratcliff, interview by author).

35. *Today*, NBC, Sept. 27, 1979, v.c.1, SPP, WHMC. The book was *Sylvia Porter's New Money Book for the 1980s*, a follow-up to *Sylvia Porter's Money Book*.

36. *The Merv Griffin Show*, Nov. 21, 1979 (accession no. B:51266, media no. 045159), preserved television recording, Museum of Television and Radio, New York City.

37. "Columnist Asks Creation of Wage-Price Controls," *Miami Herald*, Aug. 16, 1971, folder 137, SPP, WHMC.

38. "Mr. and Mrs. Sylvia Porter: It's a Title He Doesn't Mind," *People*, Nov. 18, 1974, folder 138, SPP, WHMC.

39. "Mr. and Mrs. Sylvia Porter"; Moore, "From Columnist to Publisher."

40. Fury, "Super-Sylvia," 30, 125.

41. Sylvia Porter to Sterling Noel [copy], June 28, 1974, folder 15, SPP, WHMC.

42. "Sylvia Porter 'Edits Every Word' in Her Magazine," *Advertising Age*, Feb. 6, 1984, folder 113, SSP, WHMC, 33.

43. Sylvia Porter to Donna Martin, invitation, Nov. 4, 1983, folder 272, SPP, WHMC.

44. "Sylvia Porter Has Golden Touch," *Advertising Age*, Oct. 18, 1984, folder 113, SPP, WHMC.

45. "Advising the Masses," *Mutual Fund Sourcebook* (spring 1985): 11–12, 20, folder 113, SPP, WHMC. Shares sold for $81,000 each.

46. Philip H. Dougherty, "Sylvia Porter Magazine Off to Ambitious Start," *New York Times*, Nov. 15, 1983, sec. D, 34.

47. "Sylvia Porter Has Golden Touch."

48. "Sylvia Porter 'Edits Every Word' in Her Magazine."

49. Boroson, interview by author.

50. Sylvia Porter, memo to Carole Sinclair and Pat Estess, Feb. 6, 1984, folder 273, SPP, WHMC.

51. Porter, memo, Feb. 6, 1984.

52. Pat Estess to Joel Davis and Carole Sinclair [copy], Jan. 18, 1985, folder 273, SPP, WHMC, 2.

53. Carol Sinclair, memorandum for *Sylvia Porter's Personal Finance Magazine* [copy], Jan. 11, 1989, folder 273, SPP, WHMC.

54. Ibid.

55. Ibid.

56. "Wall Street's Black Monday Claims First Magazine Victim," *Media Industry Newsletter*, Jan. 11, 1989, folder 115, SPP, WHMC.

57. Greg Daugherty, "Where Were the Germans and the Times When Sylvia Porter's Needed Them Most?" *Business Journalism Review* (fall 1989): 28–29, 42, folder 115, SPP, WHMC.

58. James Fox, memorandum for his files, Feb. 28, 1989, folder 273, SPP, WHMC.

59. Fox, memo, Feb. 28, 1989.

60. Ibid.

61. "Wall Street's Black Monday Claims First Magazine Victim."

62. Ibid. Carole Sinclair took issue with the correlation drawn in the press between advertising losses and the possible sale of *Sylvia Porter's Personal Finance Magazine*, and it is possible Joel Davis had been looking for a reason to sell the magazine even before the recession. However, the magazine's advertising and circulation figures—as well as its reliance on mutual funds and inability to bundle advertising packages—lend credibility to the characterization of the magazine as a victim of the market crash.

63. Fox, memo, Feb. 28, 1989.

64. Sinclair, memo, Jan. 11, 1989; Fox, memo, Feb. 28, 1989.

65. Corbin Wilkes to Joel Davis, Apr. 6, 1989, folder 29, SPP, WHMC.

66. Boroson, interview by author.

67. Jack Bernstein, "PR Faves Include 'Time,' 'Journal,'" *Advertising Age*, Nov. 2, 1987, 59; Jack Bernstein, "PR Execs Pick Favored Media," *Advertising Age*, Oct. 31, 1988, 12.

68. Warren Boroson, "A Worthy Showing from New Jersey," *Morris County (NJ) Daily Record*, Oct. 1, 1996, sec. B, 1.

69. John Rumsey to Sylvia Porter, Sept. 20, 1977, folder 21, SPP, WHMC.

70. Harry Maier to Field Newspaper Syndicate, Jan. 25, 1975, folder 17, SPP, WHMC.

71. Poe, "How Porter Translates 'Bafflegab,'" 41–42.

72. Ibid., 41.

73. Carole Sinclair, memorandum, Jan. 28, 1987, folder 29, SPP, WHMC.

74. Hal Meyerson to Carol Brandt [copy], Apr. 4, 1983, folder 25, SPP, WHMC.

75. Hal Meyerson to Laverne Berry [copy], Jan. 30, 1986, folder 25, SPP, WHMC.

76. Sylvia Porter to Carole Sinclair, May 27, 1986, folder 276, SPP, WHMC.

77. Carl Brandt to Sylvia Porter, Oct. 14, 1986, folder 29, SPP, WHMC.

78. Fox, memo, Feb. 28, 1989.

79. Joel Davis to John Meneough, March 17, 1989, folder 233, SPP, WHMC.

80. James Fox to Carole Sinclair, March 4, 1989, folder 233, SPP, WHMC.

81. James Fox to Carole Sinclair, June 5, 1989, folder 234, SPP, WHMC, 1.

82. Fox, memo, Feb. 28, 1989.

83. Ibid.; Sinclair, memo, Jan. 11, 1989; James Fox to Carole Sinclair, Jan. 15, 1990, folder 273, SPP, WHMC.

84. Fox to Sinclair, Jan. 15, 1990; Fox, memo, June 5, 1989.

85. Fox, memo, Feb. 28, 1989.

86. James Fox, memorandum for his files, Sept. 19, 1990, folder 234, SPP, WHMC.

87. Carole Sinclair to James Fox, Oct. 3, 1990, folder 234, SPP, WHMC.

88. Fox, memo, Sept. 19, 1990, 1.

89. Ibid.; Sinclair to Fox, Oct. 3, 1990.

90. Eisenberg, "Matron of Money Markets Her Name."

91. Dennis E. Powell to Carole Sinclair [copy], March 5, 1990, folder 35, SPP, WHMC.

92. Ibid.

93. Whitney, "Living Legend."

94. Sylvia Porter to William Freund [copy], June 23, 1987, folder 30, SPP, WHMC.

95. Sinclair, memo, Jan. 28, 1987.

96. Michael D. Murray, "The Contemporary Media: 1974–Present," in *The Media in America: A History*, 5th ed., ed. Wm. David Sloan (Northport, AL: Vision Press, 2002), 471.

97. John McMeel to Sylvia Porter, Feb. 9, 1984, folder 25, SPP, WHMC.

98. Sylvia Porter to John McMeel [copy], Feb. 13, 1986, folder 28, SPP, WHMC.

99. Sinclair, memo, Jan. 28, 1987.

100. Ibid.

101. "Sylvia Porter; Widely Read Financial Columnist and Author," *Los Angeles Times*, June 7, 1991, sec. A, 24.

102. James Fox to Hal Meyerson [copy], May 14, 1991, folder 37, SPP, WHMC.

103. Goetze, "Journalist Pioneers Financial Column."

Bibliography

Primary Sources

Magazine Articles and Newspaper Columns: Sylvia Porter as Author

"'Bright' Movie Story." *NYP*, July 23, 1952. Box 55. DSP. NYPL.

"'Chain' Selling Schemes." *NYP*, Apr. 1, 1966. Folder 450. SPP. WHMC.

"'Ideal' Corporate Wife." *NYP*, Oct. 25, 1954. Folder 381. SPP. WHMC.

"10 Steps to a Summer Job." *NYP*, March 31, 1966. Folder 450. SPP. WHMC.

"13,500,000 Women in Jobs in Virtually Every Field; All Records Being Broken." *NYP*, Jan. 8, 1942.

"1958's Girl Graduate Goes to Work." *NYP*, May 29, 1958. Folder 403. SPP. WHMC.

"50% of American Women to Be Wage Earners by 1950; A New Freedom Is Emerging." *NYP*, Jan. 20, 1942.

"A Tax Plan for the Rich." *NYP*, Feb. 11, 1947. Folder 335. SPP. WHMC.

"A Wider 'Community Life,' More Equality in Marriage for Women in War Tasks." *NYP*, Jan. 16, 1942.

"A Woman on the Exchange?" *NYP*, Sept. 17, 1965. Folder 447. SPP. WHMC.

"Aniline Men Related to High Nazis." *NYP*, Nov. 28, 1941.

"Annual Reports a Puzzle Due to Tax Law Delays." *NYP*, Aug. 4, 1942.

"Arbitraging Back in Profitable Play." *NYP*, Jan. 16, 1936.

"Baby Costs." *NYP*, Sept. 6, 1963. Folder 435. SPP. WHMC.

"Bare 'Killing' on WW Oil Tip." *NYP*, March 7, 1955. Folder 383. SPP. WHMC.

"Big and Healthy." *NYP*, Sept. 30, 1965. Folder 447. SPP. WHMC.

"Big Percentage of Women Will Hold Industrial Jobs When Peace Releases Men." *NYP*, Jan. 13, 1942.

"Borrow—or Save?" *NYP*, March 21, 1966. Folder 450. SPP. WHMC.

"Business News Coverage." *NYP*, May 9, 1967. Folder 457. SPP. WHMC.

"Buying & Using Mutual Funds." *NYP*, Jan. 13, 1970. Folder 473. SPP. WHMC.

"Canada's Bond Offer 'Feeler' in U.S. Market." *NYP*, Aug. 6, 1935.

"Capital Flees to U.S. on Austrian Crisis." *NYP*, March 12, 1938.

"Chiselers Defy U.S., Profit on New Bonds at Expense of Public." *NYP*, Dec. 10, 1936.

"Cockeyed Wages." *NYP*, July 3, 1951. Folder 362. SPP. WHMC.

"Consumer Gyps and How to Avoid Them." *NYP*, March 26, 1962. Folder 426.

"Direct Sale of U.S. Bonds to Reserve Banks Is Logical; Disaster Cries Unjustified." *NYP*, Jan. 30, 1942.

"Dorcas Campbell—Pioneer in Banking." *NYP*, Sept. 25, 1959. Folder 411. SPP. WHMC.

"Economic News." *NYP*, Jan. 17, 1949. Folder 347. SPP. WHMC.

"Economic War." *NYP*, May 27, 1947. Folder 337. SPP. WHMC.

"Equal Pay? Not Yet." *NYP*, March 17, 1953. Folder 372. SPP. WHMC.

"Eyeglasses vs. Contacts." *NYP*, Dec. 13, 1974. Folder 502. SPP. WHMC.

"Farben Agents Use S. America as Base for Plots against U.S." *NYP*, March 30, 1942.

"Farben Agents Wed U.S. Girls and became American Citizens." *NYP*, March 25, 1942.

"Farben Got Secrets from U.S. by Joining Its Large Firms." *NYP*, March 26, 1942.

"Farben Is the State and Hitler Its Puppet in the Nazi New Order." *NYP*, March 24, 1942.

"Farben Officials Placed Kin in Key Jobs in U.S. as Plotters against Us." *NYP*, March 23, 1942.

"Finance Courses." *NYP*, Feb. 16, 1951. Folder 359. SPP. WHMC.

"Food Costs Cheaper Today Than Ever for Working Man; It's All in the Statistics." *NYP*, Feb. 16, 1942.

"Foreign Countries' War Chests Kept in U.S." *NYP*, June 26, 1939.

"Foreign Governments Leave Americans Holding the Bag through Repatriation." *NYP*, June 22, 1939.

"Forum Agrees on Coming of New Phase for Women and Need for Education." *NYP*, Nov. 10, 1941.

"Gobbledygook!" *NYP*, Feb. 20, 1952. Folder 365. SPP. WHMC.

"Good News." *NYP*, Jan. 18, 1952. Folder 365. SPP. WHMC.

"Have You a Maid?" *NYP*, Jan. 10, 1951. Folder 359. SPP. WHMC.

"Historic Bill." *NYP*, Sept. 19, 1963. Folder 129. SPP. WHMC.

"Housewives Face New Pension Tax." *NYP*, May 17, 1950. Folder 355. SPP. WHMC.

"How to Bargain-Hunt." *NYP*, March 30, 1966. Folder 450. SPP. WHMC.

"How You Meet It." *NYP*, Oct. 10, 1947. Folder 339. SPP. WHMC.

"If Farben Comes, War Follows." *NYP*, March 27, 1942. Apartment Guide, 6.

"I. G. Farben Still Here—and Still Helping Germany—Dissolution Is Only Started." *NYP*, March 19, 1942.

"Kitty Foyle in 1954." *NYP*, July 8, 1954. Folder 380. SPP. WHMC.

"Lady, Take a Bow." *NYP*, Feb. 21, 1936.

"Loneliness Is the Price Facing Girls in War Jobs; Are Less Likely to Wed." *NYP*, Jan. 15, 1942.

"Mac Loses His Job." *NYP*, Feb. 28, 1949. Folder 347. SPP. WHMC.

"Menus—'44 and '47." *NYP*, Sept. 11, 1947. Folder 339. SPP. WHMC.

"Mismanaged Issues Clog Capital Mart." *NYP*, Aug. 8, 1935.

"Mrs. America Has It—a Job." *NYP*, June 14, 1962. Folder 427. SPP. WHMC.

"No Women Allowed." *NYP*, May 3, 1962. Folder 427. SPP. WHMC.

"Peoria and Prague." *NYP*, March 1, 1948. Folder 342. SPP. WHMC.

"Pioneer Three-Day Forum on Women's Responsibility Opens at Stephens College." *NYP*, Nov. 6, 1941.

"Policy Alters U.S." *NYP*, March 14, 1947. Folder 336. SPP. WHMC.

"Sex and Savings." *NYP*, Aug. 9, 1949. Folder 349. SPP. WHMC.

"Sex in Finance." *NYP*, Nov. 11, 1949. Folder 352. SPP. WHMC.

"Sick-Sick Movies." *NYP*, July 11, 1952. Box 55. DSP. NYPL.

"Since Suffrage." *NYP*, Aug. 23, 1950. Folder 356. DSP. NYPL.

"Speculators Slapped by U.S. Treasury's Financing, Which Wipes Out Opportunity for Safe, Easy Money Deals." *NYP*, June 5, 1939.

"Spending Your Money." *LHJ*. Oct. 1965–Dec. 1974.

"State 'Legal' Bond Lists Face Revision." *NYP*, Jan. 9, 1936.

"Stock Forecasts." *NYP*, March 4, 1946.

"Stop Withdrawing Savings to Buy Bonds and Hoard; You're Hurting the Country." *NYP*, Feb. 4, 1942.

"Success of Price Control Depends on Self-Control." *NYP*, July 20, 1942.

"Successful Wives," *NYP*, March 15, 1956. Folder 390. SPP. WHMC.

"Sylvia Porter 'Invades' the Exchange." *NYP*, June 20, 1962. Folder 427. SPP. WHMC.

"Sylvia Porter's Advice to Young Wives about Money." *Redbook*, Nov. 1964, 63.

"The Blue Chip." *NYP*, May 2, 1967. Folder 457. SPP. WHMC.

"The Nazi Chemical Trust, a State within a State, Created Hitler and the War." *NYP*, March 20, 1942.

"The President's Letter—Translated." *NYP*, Jan. 21, 1958. Folder 401. SPP. WHMC.

"To the Women: Some Hints for Holiday Gift Shopping; Start Now and Buy Staples." *NYP*, Nov. 21, 1941.

"To the Women: Some Hints on Developing War Trends and the Policies to Adopt." *NYP*, Dec. 12, 1941.

"To the Women: You Can Get Jobs in the Financial Fields; Banks to Employ Thousands." *NYP*, July 6, 1942.

"To the Women: Your Buying on Time Plans Must be Cut or More Curbs Will Come." *NYP*, Dec. 26, 1941.

"To Tillie and Rosie." *NYP*, Nov. 17, 1950. Folder 358. SPP. WHMC.

"To Women Who Overbuy: You're Forcing Scarcities, Rigid Control, Rising Costs." *NYP*, Dec. 19, 1941.

"Treasury Ban on Free Riding Being Violated." *NYP*, June 2, 1936.

"Twelve Men against the Nation." *Reader's Digest*, Nov. 1942, 1–4.

"U.S. Fund to Freeze Gold en Route Here." *NYP*, March 21, 1938.

"U.S. to Trace Aniline Link." *NYP*, Nov. 27, 1941.

"We Are a Nation of Working Wives." *NYP*, May 2, 1950. Folder 355. SPP. WHMC.

"What Every Woman Should Know about Her Husband," *Good Housekeeping*, Aug. 9, 1944, 39.

"What's a Wife Worth?" *NYP*, July 13, 1966. Folder 452. SPP. WHMC.

"Who Gets Hurt?" *NYP*, Apr. 14, 1947. Folder 336. SPP. WHMC.

"Woman's Place in Future Will be Outside the Home, Experts at Forum Agree." *NYP*, Nov. 7, 1941.

"Women and U.S. Jobs." *NYP*, May 6, 1964. Folder 439. SPP. WHMC.

"Women Entering New Era of Financial Independence; Social Revolution Coming." *NYP*, Jan. 7, 1942.

"Women Find Job Equality in Big Machines That Need Little Strength to Operate." *NYP*, 9 Jan. 1942.

"Women in Finance . . . Ethel Mercereau, Partner in E. A. Pierce and Company, Rose from Stenographer to Dominant Place in Business." *NYP*, June 20, 1936.

"Women in Finance . . . Mina Bruere Left the Concert Stage for Banking Career; Don't Imitate Men, Be Original, Is Her Advice to Women." *NYP*, June 18, 1936.

"Women in Finance . . . Mrs. Foster, Who Writes Books and Plays the Market, Believes a Career and Marriage Simply Do Not Mix." *NYP*, July 2, 1936.

"Women in Finance . . . Mrs. Jacob Riis Finds Romance in the Ticker Tape; 'Being in Wall Street Keeps You Alive to World.'" *NYP*, June 23, 1936.

"Women in Finance . . . Louise Watson, Partner in Investment Firm, Finds Market Thrilling and Gives a Bit of Advice on Trading Risks." *NYP*, June 16, 1936.

"Women in Finance . . . Miss Andress Knows All the Answers, and Questions, Too: She's a Collector of 'Firsts' in Business and in Books." *NYP*, June 25, 1936.

"Women in Finance . . . Miss Cook Has Keen Appetite for Food and Selling, So the World Lost a Lawyer and Gained a Financier." *NYP*, June 27, 1936.

"Women in Finance . . . Miss Eggleston 'Needed the Money'; She Speculated and Won; So Another Woman Financier Began a Career in Wall Street." *NYP*, July 7, 1936.

"Women in Finance . . . Miss Fuchs Believes Good Housekeeper Makes Good Banker; Finds Greatest Human Interest in the Trust Department." *NYP*, July 9, 1936.

"Women in Finance . . . Miss Taylor, World's First Woman Investment Counsel, Is Changing the 'Men Only' Psychology of Wall Street." *NYP*, June 30, 1936.

"Women Workers Excel Men in Thousands of War Jobs; Good at Light, Detail Tasks." *NYP*, Jan. 12, 1942.

"Women's Wealth." *NYP*, Sept. 20, 1950. Folder 356. SPP. WHMC.

"Working Mothers." *NYP*, May 7, 1953. Folder 373. SPP. WHMC.

"Working Wives Open New Fields." *NYP*, May 10, 1950. Folder 355. SPP. WHMC.

"Your Money or Your Life: Here's How You Can Make Your Money Grow." *LHJ*, May 1947, 61. SPP. WHMC.

Speeches, Broadcast Recordings, Books, and Periodicals

"1929 Curb Market Dealings." *New York Times*, Jan. 1, 1930.

"55 Journalists Named to Pulitzer Jury." Associated Press [via LexisNexis], Jan. 5, 1981.

"Advising the Masses." *Mutual Fund Sourcebook* (spring 1985): 11–12, 20. Folder 113. SPP. WHMC.

"A Most Helpful Brunette." *Newsweek*, March 18, 1957, 82–83.

"AP Newsfeatures Going on Tape-Wire." *Editor & Publisher*, Feb. 13, 1971. Folder 137. SPP. WHMC.

"B&B Unit Creates WIN Campaign in Five Busy Days." *Advertising Age*, Oct. 21, 1974. Folder 169. SPP. WHMC.

"BPW Gives Top Hat Awards." *Washington Post and Times-Herald*, July 26, 1967, sec. C, 1.

"Business Editor Named to Head Writers' Group." *Washington Post and Times-Herald*, May 10, 1971, sec. D, 12.

"City Desk." *St. Petersburg Times*, Apr. 1948. Folder 122. SPP. WHMC.

"Columnist Asks Creation of Wage-Price Controls." *Miami Herald*, Aug. 16, 1971. Folder 137. SPP. WHMC.

"Few Losers (or Winners) in WIN Campaign." *New York Times*, March 23, 1975, 165.

"Guest List for Dinner Last Night to Emil Schram." *Wall Street Journal*, June 26, 1941.

"Housewife's View." *Time*, June 16, 1958, 61.

"Katharine Graham Named Most Influential." Associated Press [via LexisNexis], Nov. 11, 1979.

"Mr. and Mrs. Sylvia Porter: It's a Title He Doesn't Mind." *People*, Nov. 18, 1974. Folder 138. SPP. WHMC.

"Nominating Judges Are Chosen for Pulitzer Prizes in Journalism." *New York Times*, Jan. 5, 1981, sec. B, 5.

"Pantepec Raises Shorts Interest: Flurry Following Stock Tip Moves American Exchange Total Up 79,748 Shares." *New York Times*, Jan. 21, 1955, sec. A, 29.

"Pre-Script." *American*, July 1939. Folder 117. SPP. WHMC.

"Stock Market Trading for December." *New York Times*, Jan. 1, 1936.

"Sylvia & You." *Time*, Nov. 28, 1960, 46–52.

"Sylvia Porter 'Edits Every Word' in Her Magazine." *Advertising Age*, Feb. 6, 1984. Folder 113. SPP. WHMC.

"Sylvia Porter Has Golden Touch." *Advertising Age*, Oct. 18, 1984. Folder 113. SPP. WHMC.

"Sylvia Porter: One in 10,000." *Editor & Publisher*, Feb. 5, 1949. Folder 123. SPP. WHMC.

"Sylvia Porter; Widely Read Financial Columnist and Author." *Los Angeles Times*, June 7, 1991, sec. A, 24.

"The Business News Luminaries." TJFR Group, 1999. Available from http://www .newsbios.com/newslum/notables.htm, accessed Aug. 5, 2007.

"The Story of the Personality behind the By-Line." June 1, 1948. Folder 122. SPP. WHMC.

"The VIP Line: Columnist Asks Creation of Wage-Price Controls." *Miami Herald*, Aug. 16, 1971. Folder 137. SPP. WHMC.

"They Just Have More Money." *St. Petersburg Times*, May 25, 1987, sec. E, 2.

"Wall Street Whispers." *Finance*, Feb. 1972. Folder 137. SPP. WHMC.

"Wall Street's Black Monday Claims First Magazine Victim." *Media Industry Newsletter*, Jan. 11, 1989. Folder 115. SPP. WHMC.

"War Work Is Put Ahead of Politics." *New York Times*, Jan. 17, 1942, 20.

"WIN Motto Is Loser as Ford Committee Drops Theme." *Detroit Sunday News*, March 9, 1975, sec. E, 4.

"Women in Journalism Program Scores Success with Lectures, Luncheons." *50th Anniversary Times* 1, no. 11 (University of Missouri: Feb. 1959). Box 29. Folder 897. Sara Lockwood Williams Papers. WHMC.

"Women Will Get Headliners' Prizes." *New York Times*, May 28, 1943, 42.

Ade, Ginny. "Sylvia Porter, Successful Business Columnist, Invites Others to Cash In." *Progressive Woman* (Nov. 1971): 20–22.

Baer, Jean. *The Self-Chosen: "Our Crowd" Is Dead, Long Live Our Crowd*. New York: Arbor House, 1982.

Barnes, Fred. "The White House Campaign That Became a Wry Joke." *Washington Star-Times*, Feb. 12, 1975. Folder 179. SPP. WHMC.

Barnett, David. N.t. Sept. 28, 1974. Folder 166. SPP. WHMC.

Battelle, Phyllis. "Sylvia Porter: A Friend's View." *Seattle Post-Intelligencer*, Feb. 9, 1975, sec. D, 3.

Benjamin, Louise Paine. "Your Money or Your Life: Here's How You Can Make Yourself Grow." *LHJ*, May 1947, 65.

Bernstein, Jack. "PR Faves Include 'Time,' 'Journal.'" *Advertising Age*, Nov. 2, 1987, 59.

———. "PR Execs Pick Favored Media." *Advertising Age*, Oct. 31, 1988, 12.

Boroson, Warren. "A Worthy Showing from New Jersey." *(Morris County, NJ) Daily Record*, Oct. 1, 1996, sec. B, 1.

Carlson, Gene. Wire report. United Press International, Sept. 27, 1974. Folder 166. SPP. WHMC.

Chapman, William. "President's 'WIN' Program Faltering." Dec. 20, 1974. Folder 175. SPP. WHMC.

Charlton, Linda. "WIN, the Anti-Inflation Slogan, Scrapped after a Losing Season." *New York Times*, March 9, 1975, 32.

Cogil, Stephen. "Booksellers Bullish on Christmas Prospects." *Publisher's Weekly*, Nov. 10, 1975, 35–36.

Crane, Burton. "Winchell Scored for Market Tips at Senate Inquiry." *New York Times*, March 5, 1955, sec. A., 1.

Curtis, Olga. "Sylvia Porter, and How to Make Money Though Married." *Denver Sunday Post*, July 21, 1963. Empire Magazine, 16–17. Folder 129. SPP. WHMC.

Daugherty, Greg. "Where Were the Germans and the *Times* When Sylvia Porter's Needed Them Most?" *Business Journalism Review* (fall 1989): 28–29, 42. Folder 115. SPP. WHMC.

Davis, Melissa. "Personalities." *Washington Post*, Jan. 4, 1979, sec. B, 3.

Display Ad 23. *New York Times*, Nov. 17, 1947, sec. A, 25.

Display Ad 25. *Wall Street Journal*, Apr. 21, 1959, 19.

Display Ad 37. *New York Times*, Dec. 14, 1944, sec. A, 39.

Display Ad 125. *Wall Street Journal*, May 16, 1960, 28.

Display Ad 264. *New York Times,* Sept. 20, 1953, sec. BR, 14.

Dougherty, Philip H. "Sylvia Porter Magazine Off to Ambitious Start." *New York Times,* Nov. 15, 1983, sec. D, 34.

Eckman, Fern Marja. "Woman in the News: Inflation Tips for Ford." *New York Post Magazine,* Oct. 5, 1974. Folder 109. SPP. WHMC.

Eisenberg, Richard. "Matron of Money Markets Her Name." *USA Today,* Dec. 5, 1983, sec. B, 3. Folder 141. SPP. WHMC.

Fay, Ruth Hawthorne. "Women at the Top: Sylvia F. Porter." *Cue,* Nov. 19, 1949. Folder 126. SPP. WHMC.

Ford, Gerald (as President). "10/15/74—Future Farmers of America." Oct. 15, 1974. Box 2. President's Speeches and Statements. Gerald R. Ford Presidential Library. Available from http://www.fordlibrarymuseum.gov/library /document/0122/1252096.pdf, accessed June 16, 2013.

Fowler, Glenn. "Sylvia Porter, Financial Columnist, Is Dead at 77." *New York Times,* June 7, 1991, sec. B, 6.

Fury, Kathleen D. "Super-Sylvia." *LHJ,* Jan. 1976, 26.

Galeota, William. "Miss Porter's School: A Columnist's Advice Wields Wide Influence from Coast to Coast." *Wall Street Journal,* March 24, 1972, 1. Folder 137. SPP. WHMC.

Garcia, Bea. "Two S. Floridians Who Made Journalism History." *Miami Herald,* Dec. 28, 1999, sec. C, 1.

Germani, Clara. "Women and Money: Making It Means Managing It." *Christian Science Monitor,* March 15, 1982, 12.

Glenn, Marian. "Woman in Business." *Forbes,* Sept. 15, 1917, 30–34.

Goetze, Janet. "Journalist Pioneers Financial Column." *Oregonian,* May 11, 1971. Folder 137. SPP. WHMC.

Griswold, Denny. N.t. *Public Relations News,* Oct. 7, 1974. Folder 167. SPP. WHMC.

Hill, Katherine T. "Finance Editor Has Money Trouble Too: Like Other Women, Sylvia Porter Gets Balled Up over Paltry 10's and 20's." *Louisville (KY) Courier-Journal,* Oct. 13, 1949. Folder 125. SPP. WHMC.

Jarmusch, Betty. "The Summit, from the Valley." *New York Times,* Oct. 13, 1974, 251.

Jaycox, Betty. "Femininity and Wit Mask Sylvia's Money Expertise." *Akron (Ohio) Beacon Journal,* May 25, 1972. Folder 138. SPP. WHMC.

Kandel, Myron. N.t. *Review of the Financial Press* 2, no. 40 (Oct. 10, 1974). Folder 167. SPP. WHMC.

Kiplinger, Knight. "Chat with the Editor in Chief." *Changing Times: The Kiplinger Magazine,* July 1985, 5.

Lasser, J. K., and Sylvia F. Porter. *How to Live within Your Income*. New York: Simon & Schuster, 1948.

Lewis, Mildred, and Milton Lewis. *Famous Modern Newspaper Writers*. New York: Dodd, Mead, 1962.

Lockerman, Doris. "Women and the Dollar Sign." *Atlanta Constitution*, Sept. 27, 1950. Folder 127. SPP. WHMC.

Lyons, Leonard. "The Lyons Den." *Broadway Gazette*, 1943. Folder 119. SPP. WHMC.

———. "Broadway Gazette." *Washington Post*, May 1, 1946.

The Mary Margaret McBride Show. ABC, March 2, 1953. LWO 15577. Reel 231B. Audio recording kept at the Motion Picture, Broadcasting, and Recorded Sound Division, Library of Congress, Washington, DC.

Maxwell, Elsa. "Portias of the Press—One Is S. F. Porter." *NYP*, Dec. 22, 1942. Folder 119. SPP. WHMC.

McCardle, Dorothy. "Feminist 60s Urged by Saluted Sextet." *Washington Post and Times-Herald*, June 14, 1960, sec. B, 6.

McCluskey, Judy. "A Visit with Sylvia Porter." *Providence Sunday Journal*, Dec. 8, 1963. Folder 130. SPP. WHMC.

Meet the Press. NBC, Nov. 9, 1952. Accession no. T: 29909. Media no. 022401. Preserved television recording kept at the Museum of Television and Radio, New York City.

The Merv Griffin Show. NBC, Nov. 21, 1979. Accession no. B: 51266. Media no. 045159. Preserved television recording kept at the Museum of Television and Radio, New York City.

Millen, Cliff. "A Financial Editor Can Be Beautiful!" *Des Moines Tribune*, Oct. 18, 1949. Folder 125. SPP. WHMC.

Moore, Martha T. "Sylvia Porter: From Columnist to Publisher." Gannett Westchester Newspapers, Feb. 20, 1989. Folder 146. SPP. WHMC.

Olshin, Edith C. "Princess Charming of Wall Street." *Magazine Digest*, Nov. 1948, 113.

Poe, Randall. "How Porter Translates 'Bafflegab.'" *Across the Board*, July 1978. Folder 139. SPP. WHMC.

Porter, Sylvia. "The Brain Has No Sex." Folder 40. SPP. WHMC.

———. "A Charter of Economic Human Rights." Folder 51. SPP. WHMC.

———. "The Consumer's Stake in Distribution." Folder 45. SPP. WHMC.

———. "The Importance of Economics in Our World Today." Folder 43. SPP. WHMC.

———. "War—and Government Control of the Bond Markets." June 1940. Folder 38. SPP. WHMC.

———. "Women Are No Longer News." Folder 52. SPP. WHMC.

———. "How Far Can We Go Safely in Piling Up the War Debt?" *Executives' Club News*, Oct. 2, 1942. Folder 118. SPP. WHMC.

———. "Woman's Place in the Business World." March 1948. Folder 39. SPP. WHMC.

———. "The Automobile Dealer's Stake in the Consumer." 1954. Folder 48. SPP. WHMC.

———. Remarks Given at President Gerald Ford's Pre-Summit Conference on Inflation in Washington, DC. Sept. 20, 1974. Folder 72. SPP. WHMC.

———. Statement prepared for pre–summit conference on inflation in Washington, DC. Sept. 20, 1974. Folder 166. SPP. WHMC.

———. *Sylvia Porter's Money Book: How to Earn It, Spend It, Save It, Invest It, Borrow It—and Use It to Better Your Life*. Garden City, NY: Doubleday, 1975.

———. "The Inequitable Treatment of Women in Our Social Security System." 1977. Folder 78. SPP. WHMC.

Rosenthal, Benjamin [as U.S. Representative]. "30 Lawmakers Seek Halt to WIN Campaign's Partisan-Free Ad Blitz," press release issued Nov. 27, 1974. Folder 171. SPP. WHMC.

Rutberg, Sidney. "Sylvia Porter and the Will to WIN." W magazine, Nov. 29, 1974. Folder 110. SPP. WHMC.

Schneider, Walter E. "Wall Street 'Joan of Arc' Crusades in N.Y. Post." *Editor & Publisher Answers: "Who Is Sylvia?"* [pamphlet], Jan. 3, 1942. Folder 117. SPP. WHMC.

Shabecoff, Philip. "Ford Urges Steps to Curb Inflation." *New York Times*, Oct. 16, 1974. Folder 168. SPP. WHMC.

Sterba, James P. "New 'Advice' to Curb Inflation: Buy Now, Buy More—Spend!" *New York Times*, Nov. 17, 1974, 67. Folder 171. SPP. WHMC.

Talmey, Allene. "4 Unique Columnists." *Vogue*, Nov. 1, 1958, 112.

terHorst, Jerald. "WIN Program Creeping Back." *Chicago Tribune*, May 16, 1975. Folder 179, SPP. WHMC.

Today. NBC, Sept. 27, 1979. Videocassette. V.C.1. SPP. WHMC.

Town Meeting: Bulletin of America's Town Meeting of the Air. ABC, Nov. 7, 1950. Folder 128. SPP. WHMC.

Turner, Margaret. "From 'Mister' to Darling: People Stop to Look at Sylvia Porter, Then Stay to Listen." *Atlanta Journal and Constitution*, Oct. 1, 1950. Folder 128. SPP. WHMC.

Vanderpoel, Robert. "How High Can We Pile Up the Debt, Asks Glamour Girl." Oct. 3, 1942. Folder 118. SPP. WHMC.

Von Hoffman, Nicholas. "The Fumbling Feds: WIN with Anti-Saloon Tactics." *Washington Post*, Nov. 22, 1974, sec. B, 8.

Walker, Connecticut [Brooke Shearer]. "Columnist Sylvia Porter—She Cares about Your Money." *Parade*, Apr. 7, 1974. Folder 138. SPP. WHMC.

Watson, Douglas. "Win-Less Volunteer Program to Press Energy Conservation." *Washington Post*, March 12, 1975, 3. Folder 179. SPP. WHMC.

WDAU-TV Editorial No. 1257. Dec. 11, 1974. Folder 171. SPP. WHMC.

Whitney, Elizabeth. "Sylvia Porter: A Living Legend Becomes an Institution." *St. Petersburg Times*, Feb. 2, 1989, sec. I, 1.

Williams, Mack. "As the News-Tribune Sees It." *Tarrant County (TX) News-Tribune*, Sept. 13, 1974. Folder 166. SPP. WHMC.

Wilson, Ferman. "The Lady Squawks?" *Miami Herald*, Apr. 25, 1948. Folder 122. SPP. WHMC.

Woman Alive! PBS, Nov. 26, 1975. Accession no. T:15371. Media no. 022020. Preserved television recording kept at the Museum of Television and Radio, New York City.

Secondary Sources

Abrahamson, David. *Magazine-Made America: The Cultural Transformation of the Postwar Periodical*. Cresskill, NJ: Hampton Press, 1996.

Ashley, Laura, and Beth Olson. "Constructing Reality: Print Media's Framing of the Women's Movement, 1966 to 1986." *Journalism and Mass Communication Quarterly* 75, no. 2 (summer 1998): 263–77.

Beasley, Maurine H. "Eleanor Roosevelt's Press Conferences: Case Study in Class, Gender, and Race." *Social Science Journal* 37, no. 4 (2000): 517–28.

———. "Recent Directions for the Study of Women's History in American Journalism." *Journalism Studies* 2, no. 2 (2001): 207–20.

———. "The Emergence of Modern Media, 1900–1945." In *The Media in America: A History*, 5th ed., ed. Wm. David Sloan, 283–302. Northport, AL: Vision Press, 2002.

Beasley, Maurine H., and Sheila J. Gibbons. *Taking Their Place: A Documentary History of Women and Journalism*. 2nd ed. State College, PA: Strata, 2003.

Becker, Lee, and Tudor Vlad, Jisu Huh, and Nancy Mace. "Annual Enrollment Report: Graduate and Undergraduate Enrollments Increase Sharply." *Journalism and Mass Communication Educator* 58, no. 3 (fall 2003): 273–90.

Belford, Barbara. *Brilliant Bylines: A Biographical Anthology of Notable Newspaperwomen in America*. New York: Columbia University Press, 1986.

Blumler, Jay G., and Michael Gurevitch. "Rethinking the Study of Political Communication." In *Mass Media and Society*, ed. James Curran and Michael Gurevitch, 155–72. 3rd ed. London: Arnold, 2000.

Braden, Maria. *She Said What? Interviews with Women Newspaper Columnists*. Lexington: University Press of Kentucky, 1993.

Braverman, Jordan. *To Hasten the Homecoming: How Americans Fought World War II through the Media*. Lanham, MD: Madison Books, 1996.

Chafe, William. *The American Woman: Her Changing Social, Economic, and Political Roles, 1920–1970*. New York: Oxford University Press, 1972.

Clark, Mary Marshall. Oral history interview with Eileen Shanahan. May 30, 1992. Washington Press Club Foundation. Washington, DC. Available from http://beta.wpcf.org/oralhistory/shan1.html, accessed Jan. 16, 2013.

Cott, Nancy F. *The Grounding of Modern Feminism*. New Haven, CT: Yale University Press, 1987.

Cramer, Judith, and Pamela Creedon, eds. *Women in Mass Communication*. 3rd ed. Thousand Oaks, CA: Sage, 2007.

Denzin, Norman K., and Yvonna S. Lincoln, eds. *The Landscape of Qualitative Research: Theories and Issues*. Thousand Oaks, CA: Sage, 1998.

Douglas, Susan J. *Where the Girls Are: Growing Up Female with the Mass Media*. New York: Random House, 1994.

Emery, Michael, and Edwin Emery, with Nancy L. Roberts. *The Press and America: An Interpretive History of the Mass Media*. 8th ed. Needham Heights, MA: Allyn & Bacon, 1996.

Evans, Sara M. *Born for Liberty: A History of Women in America*. New York: Simon & Schuster, 1989; Free Press Paperbacks, 1997.

Feldstein, Mark. "The Journalistic Biography: Methodology, Analysis and Writing." *Journalism Studies* 7, no. 3 (June 2006): 469–78.

Francis, David R. "A 'Life-Cycle' View of Financial Planning." *Christian Science Monitor*, Feb. 17, 1984, sec. B, 12.

Friedan, Betty. *The Feminine Mystique*. New York: W. W. Norton, 1963, 2001.

Galbraith, John Kenneth. *The Great Crash*. 3rd ed. Boston: Houghton Mifflin, 1972.

Geertz, Clifford. *The Interpretation of Cultures*. New York: Basic Books, 1973, 2000.

Gilbert, James. *Another Chance: Postwar America, 1945–1968*. Philadelphia: Temple University Press, 1981.

Goldin, Claudia D. "The Role of World War II in the Rise of Women's Employment." *American Economic Review* 81, no. 4 (Sept. 1991): 741–56.

Greenwald, Marilyn. *A Woman of the Times: Journalism, Feminism, and the Career of Charlotte Curtis.* Athens: University of Ohio Press, 1999.

Halberstam, David. *The Best and the Brightest.* Twentieth Anniversary ed. New York: Random House, 1972; Reprint, Ballantine Books, 1992.

Halberstam, David. *The Fifties.* New York: Fawcett Columbine, 1993.

Harrison, Cynthia. *On Account of Sex: The Politics of Women's Issues, 1945–1968.* Berkeley and Los Angeles: University of California Press, 1988.

Hartmann, Susan M. "Women's Employment and the Domestic Ideal in the Early Cold War Years." In *Not June Cleaver: Women and Gender in Postwar America: 1945–1960,* ed. Joanne Meyerowitz, 84–100. Philadelphia: Temple University Press, 1994.

Henry, Susan. "Changing Media History through Women's History." In *Women in Mass Communication: Challenging Gender Values,* ed. Pamela J. Creedon. Newbury Park, CA: Sage, 1989.

Horowitz, Daniel. *Betty Friedan and the Making of the Feminine Mystique: The American Left, the Cold War, and Modern Feminism.* Amherst: University of Massachusetts Press, 1998.

Howell, Thomas. "The Writers' War Board: U.S. Domestic Propaganda in World War II." *Historian* 59, no. 4 (1997): 795–812.

Hummer, Patricia M. *The Decade of Elusive Promise: Professional Women in the United States, 1920–1930.* Ann Arbor: UMI Research Press, 1979.

Kammen, Michael. *American Culture, American Tastes: Social Change and the 20th Century.* New York: Alfred A. Knopf, 1999; Reprint, Basic Books, 1999.

Kessler-Harris, Alice. *Out to Work: A History of Wage-Earning Women in the United States.* New York: Oxford University Press, 1982.

Kitch, Carolyn. *The Girl on the Magazine Cover: The Origins of Visual Stereotypes in American Mass Media.* Chapel Hill: University of North Carolina Press, 2001.

Kobler, John. *Luce: His Time, Life, and Fortune.* Garden City, NY: Doubleday, 1968.

Leff, Mark H. "The Politics of Sacrifice on the American Home Front in World War II." *Journal of American History* 77, no. 4 (March 1991): 1296–318.

Lerner, Gerda. "Placing Women in History: Definitions and Challenges." *Feminist Studies* 3, nos. 1–2 (fall 1975): 5–14; reprinted in *Major Problems in Women's History,* ed. Mary Beth Norton and Ruth M. Alexander, 1–8. 3rd ed. Boston: Houghton Mifflin, 2003.

Lieberman, Trudy. "What Ever Happened to Consumer Reporting?" *Columbia Journalism Review* (Sept.–Oct. 1994): 34.

Lind, Rebecca Ann, and Colleen Sabo. "The Framing of Feminists and Feminism in News and Public Affairs Programs in U.S. Electronic Media." *Journal of Communication* 52, no. 1 (March 2002): 211–28.

Marshall, Catherine, and Gretchen B. Rossman. *Designing Qualitative Research*. 3rd ed. Thousand Oaks, CA: Sage, 1999.

Matthaei, Julie A. *An Economic History of Women in America: Women's Work, the Sexual Division of Labor, and the Development of Capitalism*. New York: Schocken Books, 1982.

May, Elaine Tyler. *Homeward Bound: American Families in the Cold War Era*. New York: Basic Books, 1988.

McQuail, Denis. *Mass Communication Theory: An Introduction*. 3rd ed. Thousand Oaks, CA: Sage, 1994.

Meyerowitz, Joanne, ed. *Not June Cleaver: Women and Gender in Postwar America, 1945–1960*. Philadelphia: Temple University Press, 1994.

Mieczkowski, Yanek. *Gerald Ford and the Challenges of the 1970s*. Lexington: University Press of Kentucky, 2005.

Mills, Kay. *A Place in the News: From the Women's Pages to the Front Page*. New York: Dodd, Mead, 1988.

Mitchell, Catherine C. "The Place of Biography in the History of News Women." *American Journalism* 7, no. 1 (1990): 23–32.

Mott, Frank Luther. *American Journalism: A History, 1690–1960*. 3rd ed. New York: Macmillan, 1962.

Muncy, Robyn. *Creating a Female Dominion in American Reform: 1890–1935*. New York: Oxford University Press, 1991.

Murray, Michael D. "The Contemporary Media: 1974–Present." In *The Media in America: A History*, ed. Wm. David Sloan, 465–86. 5th ed. Northport, AL: Vision Press, 2002.

Nelson, Edward. "The Great Inflation of the Seventies: What Really Happened?" *Advances in Macroeconomics* 5, no. 1 (2005). Available at http://www.bepress.com/bejm/advances/vol5/iss1/art3, accessed Dec. 5, 2010.

Nerone, John. "The Future of Communication History." *Critical Studies in Media Communication* 23, no. 3 (Aug. 2006): 254–62.

Parsons, Wayne. *The Power of the Financial Press: Journalism and Economic Opinion in Britain and America*. New Brunswick, NJ: Rutgers University Press, 1990.

Potter, Jeffrey. *Men, Money and Magic: The Story of Dorothy Schiff*. New York: Coward, McCann & Geoghegan, 1976.

Quirt, John. *The Press and the World of Money*. Byron, CA: Anton and California Courier, 1993.

Robertson, Nan. *The Girls in the Balcony: Women, Men, and the* New York Times. New York: Random House, 1992; Lincoln, NE: iUniverse, 2000.

Rosen, Ruth. *The World Split Open: How the Modern Women's Movement Changed America*. New York: Penguin Books, 2000.

Rosenberg, Jerry R. *Inside the* Wall Street Journal. New York: Macmillan, 1982.

Ross, Ishbel. *Ladies of the Press: The Story of Women in Journalism by an Insider*. New York: Harper & Bros., 1936.

Rothman, Sheila M. *Woman's Proper Place: A History of Changing Ideals and Practices, 1870 to the Present*. New York: Basic Books, 1978.

Roush, Chris. *Show Me the Money: Writing Business and Economics Stories for Mass Communication*. Mahwah, NJ: Lawrence Erlbaum, 2004.

Rowen, Hobart. "The Past and Future of Financial Reporting." *Washington Post*, Sept. 12, 1993, sec. H, 1.

Saporito, Bill. "How the Economy Became Hot News in the Last 100 Years." *Columbia Journalism Review* (March–Apr. 1999): 47.

Schilpp, Madelon Golden, and Sharon M. Murphy. *Great Women of the Press*. Carbondale: Southern Illinois University Press, 1983.

Schudson, Michael. *Discovering the News: A Social History of American Newspapers*. New York: Basic Books, 1978.

———. "Historical Approaches to Communication Studies." In *A Handbook of Qualitative Methodologies for Mass Communication Research*, ed. Klaus Bruhn Jensen and Nicholas W. Jankowski, 175–89. New York: Routledge, 1991.

Startt, James, and Wm. David Sloan. *Historical Methods in Mass Communication*. Hillsdale, NJ: Lawrence Erlbaum, 1989.

Stelzner, Hermann G. "Ford's War on Inflation: A Metaphor That Did Not Cross." *Communication Monographs* 44 (Nov. 1977): 284–97.

Tarbell, Ida. *All in the Day's Work: An Autobiography*. New York: Macmillan, 1939; Reprint, Urbana and Chicago: University of Illinois Press, 2003.

Walker, Nancy A. *Shaping Our Mothers' World: American Women's Magazines*. Jackson: University Press of Mississippi, 2000.

Ware, Susan. *It's One o'Clock and Here Is Mary Margaret McBride: A Radio Biography*. New York: New York University, 2005.

Yang, Mei-ling. "Creating the Kitchen Patriot: Media Promotion of Food Rationing and Nutrition Campaigns on the American Home Front during World War II." *American Journalism* 22, no. 3 (summer 2005): 55–75.

Index